WRITER: JONATHAN HICKMAN

ARTISTS: MIRKO COLAK [#20-21], ALESSANDRO VITTI [#21-24] & DAVID MARQUEZ [#24]

COLOR ARTIST: IMAGINARY FRIENDS' STUDIO WITH ANDRES MOSSA [#21]

LETTERER: ARTMONKEYS' DAVE LANPHEAR

COVER ARTISTS: JIM CHEUNG, MARK MORALES & JUSTIN PONSOR [#20-22] AND PAUL RENAUD [#23-24]

ASSISTANT EDITOR: RACHEL PINNELAS

EDITORS: BILL ROSEMANN & LAUREN SANKOVITCH

COLLECTION EDITOR: **JENNIFER GRÜNWALD**
EDITORIAL ASSISTANTS: **JAMES EMMETT & JOE HOCHSTEIN**
ASSISTANT EDITORS: **ALEX STARBUCK & NELSON RIBEIRO**
EDITOR, SPECIAL PROJECTS: **MARK D. BEAZLEY**
SENIOR EDITOR, SPECIAL PROJECTS: **JEFF YOUNGQUIST**
SENIOR VICE PRESIDENT OF SALES: **DAVID GABRIEL**
SVP OF BRAND PLANNING & COMMUNICATIONS: **MICHAEL PASCIULLO**

EDITOR IN CHIEF: **AXEL ALONSO**
CHIEF CREATIVE OFFICER: **JOE QUESADA**
PUBLISHER: **DAN BUCKLEY**
EXECUTIVE PRODUCER: **ALAN FINE**

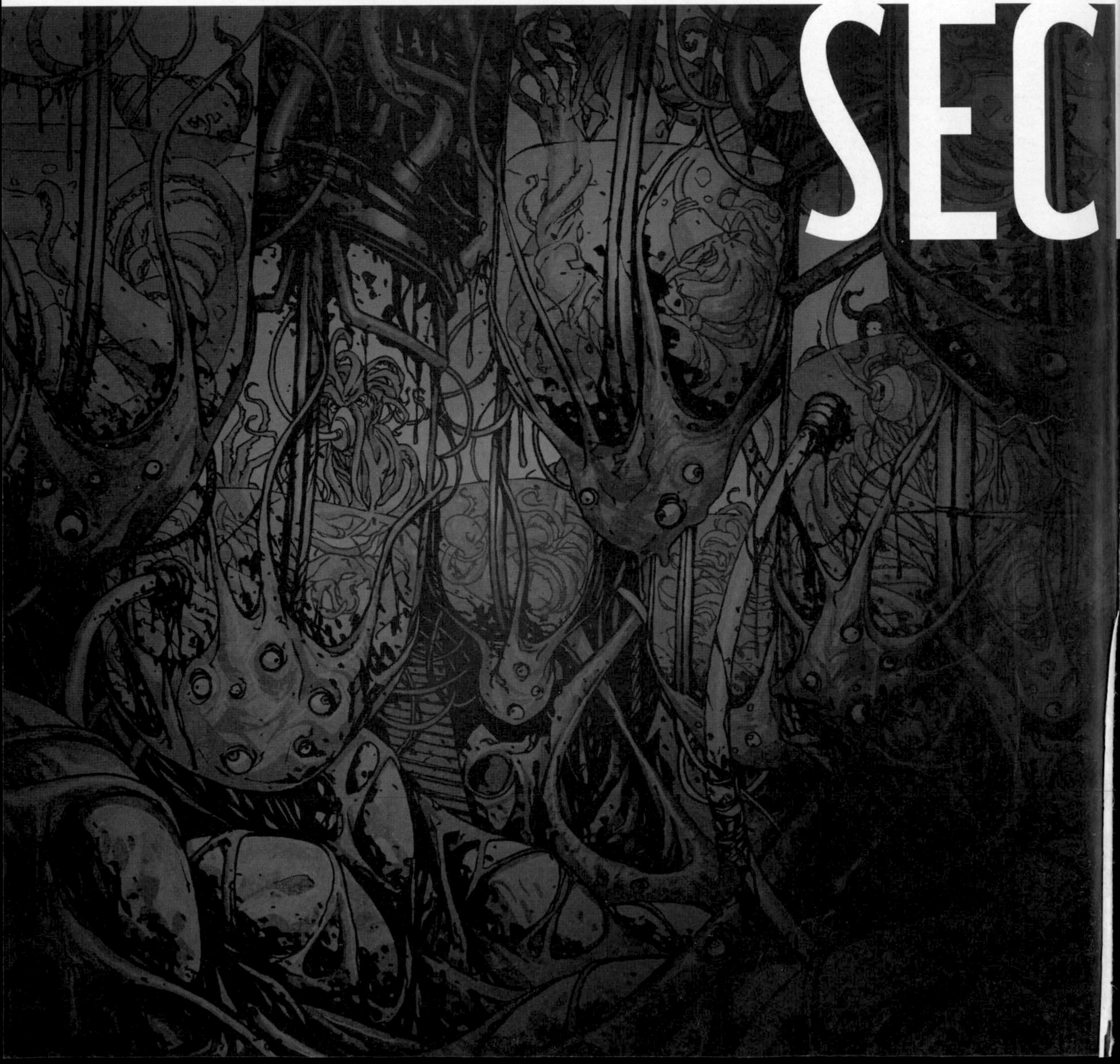
SEC

# RET WARRIORS

CREATED BY: **BRIAN MICHAEL BENDIS & ALEX MALEEV**

**SECRET WARRIORS VOL. 5: NIGHT.** Contains material originally published in magazine form as SECRET WARRIORS #20-24. First printing 2011. Hardcover ISBN# 978-0-7851-4802-9. Softcover ISBN# 978-0-7851-4803-6. Published by MARVEL WORLDWIDE, INC., a subsidiary of MARVEL ENTERTAINMENT, LLC. OFFICE OF PUBLICATION: 135 West 50th Street, New York, NY 10020. Copyright © 2010 and 2011 Marvel Characters, Inc. All rights reserved. Hardcover: $19.99 per copy in the U.S. and $21.99 in Canada (GST #R127032852). Softcover: $14.99 per copy in the U.S. and $16.50 in Canada (GST #R127032852). Canadian Agreement #40668537. All characters featured in this issue and the distinctive names and likenesses thereof, and all related indicia are trademarks of Marvel Characters, Inc. No similarity between any of the names, characters, persons, and/or institutions in this magazine with those of any living or dead person or institution is intended, and any such similarity which may exist is purely coincidental. Printed **in the U.S.A.** ALAN FINE, EVP - Office of the President, Marvel Worldwide, Inc. and EVP & CMO Marvel Characters B.V.; DAN BUCKLEY, Publisher & President - Print, Animation & Digital Divisions; JOE QUESADA, Chief Creative Officer; JIM SOKOLOWSKI, Chief Operating Officer; DAVID BOGART, SVP of Business Affairs & Talent Management; TOM BREVOORT, SVP of Publishing; C.B. CEBULSKI, SVP of Creator & Content Development; DAVID GABRIEL, SVP of Publishing Sales & Circulation; MICHAEL PASCIULLO, SVP of Brand Planning & Communications; JIM O'KEEFE, VP of Operations & Logistics; DAN CARR, Executive Director of Publishing Technology; JUSTIN F. GABRIE, Director of Publishing & Editorial Operations; SUSAN CRESPI, Editorial Operations Manager; ALEX MORALES, Publishing Operations Manager; STAN LEE, Chairman Emeritus. Marvel.com, please contact John Dokes, SVP Integrated Sales and Marketing, at jdokes@marvel.com. For Marvel subscription inquiries, please call 800-217-9158. **Manufactured between 4/25/2011**

SECRET W

# WARRIORS

## VOL FIVE NIGHT

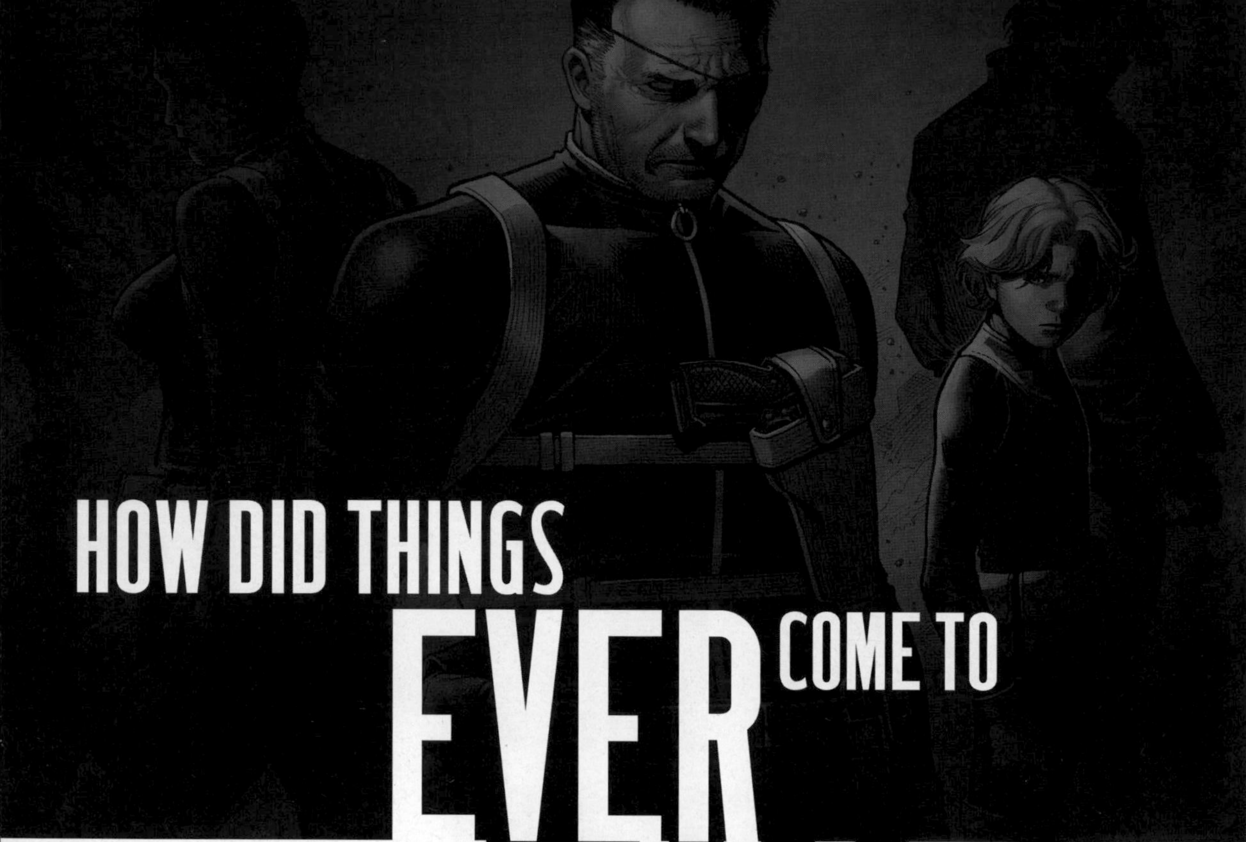

# HOW DID THINGS EVER COME TO THIS

# SIX MONTHS LATER

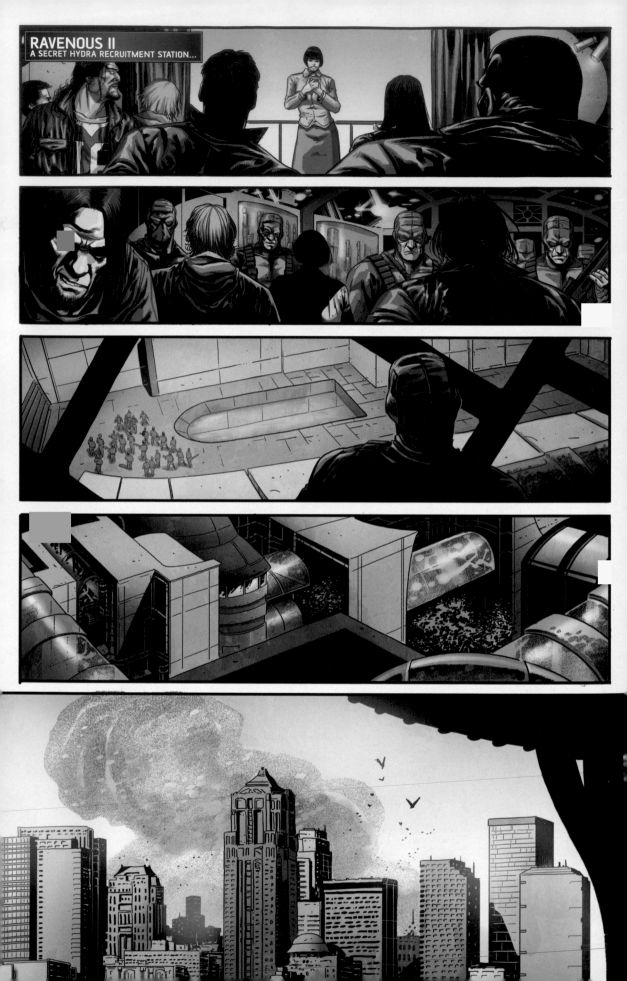

RAVENOUS II
A SECRET HYDRA RECRUITMENT STATION...

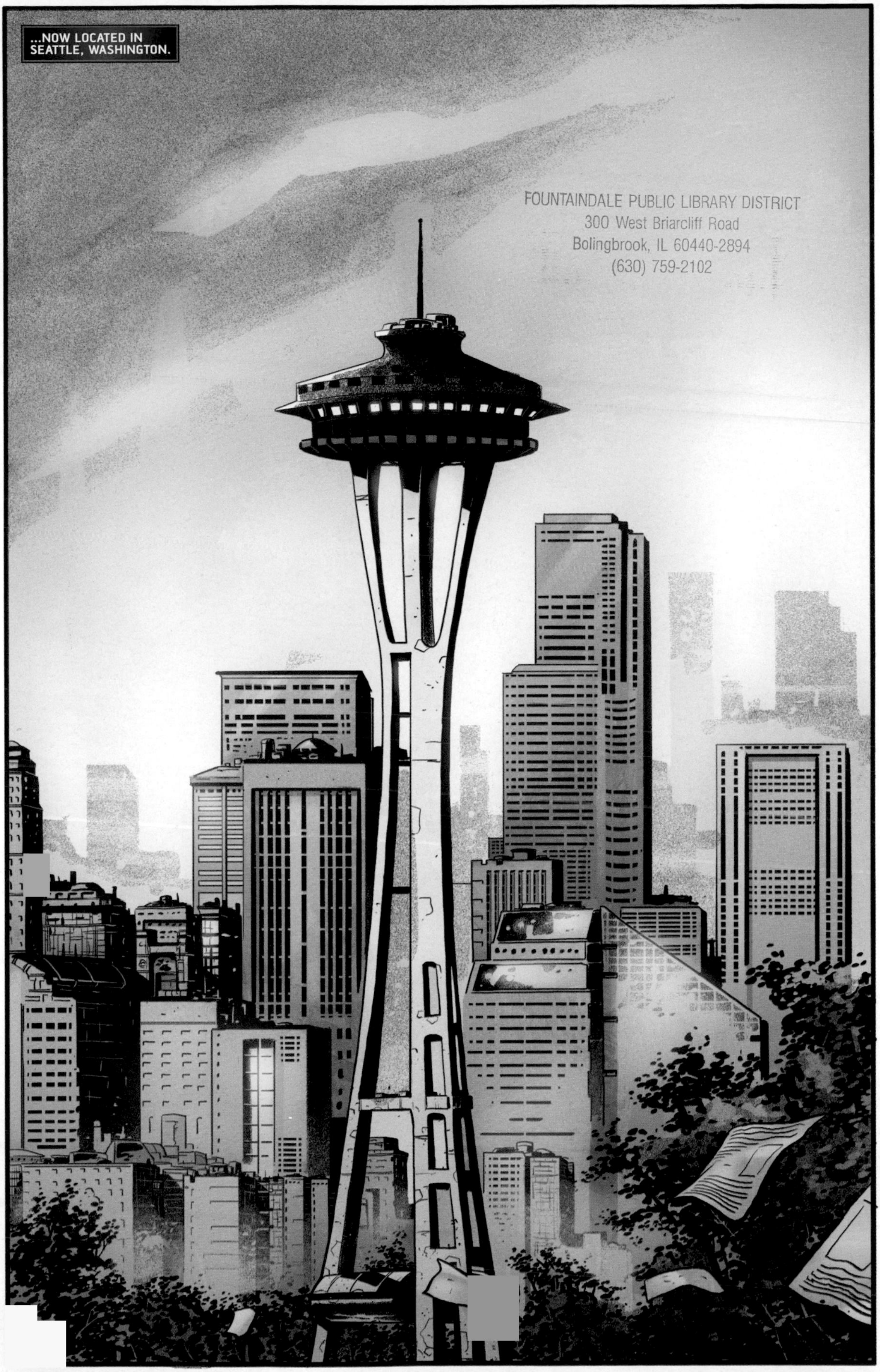
...NOW LOCATED IN SEATTLE, WASHINGTON.

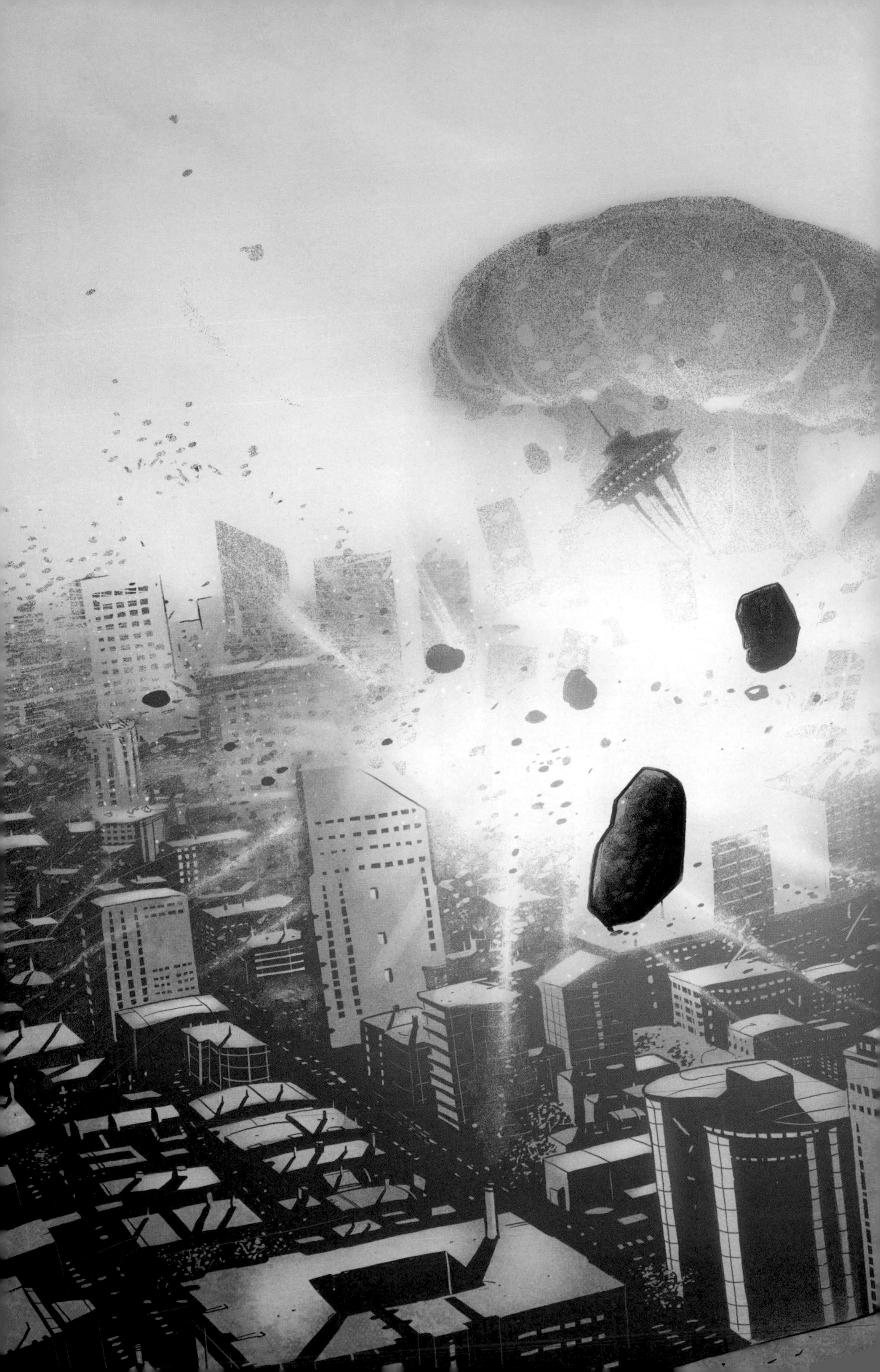

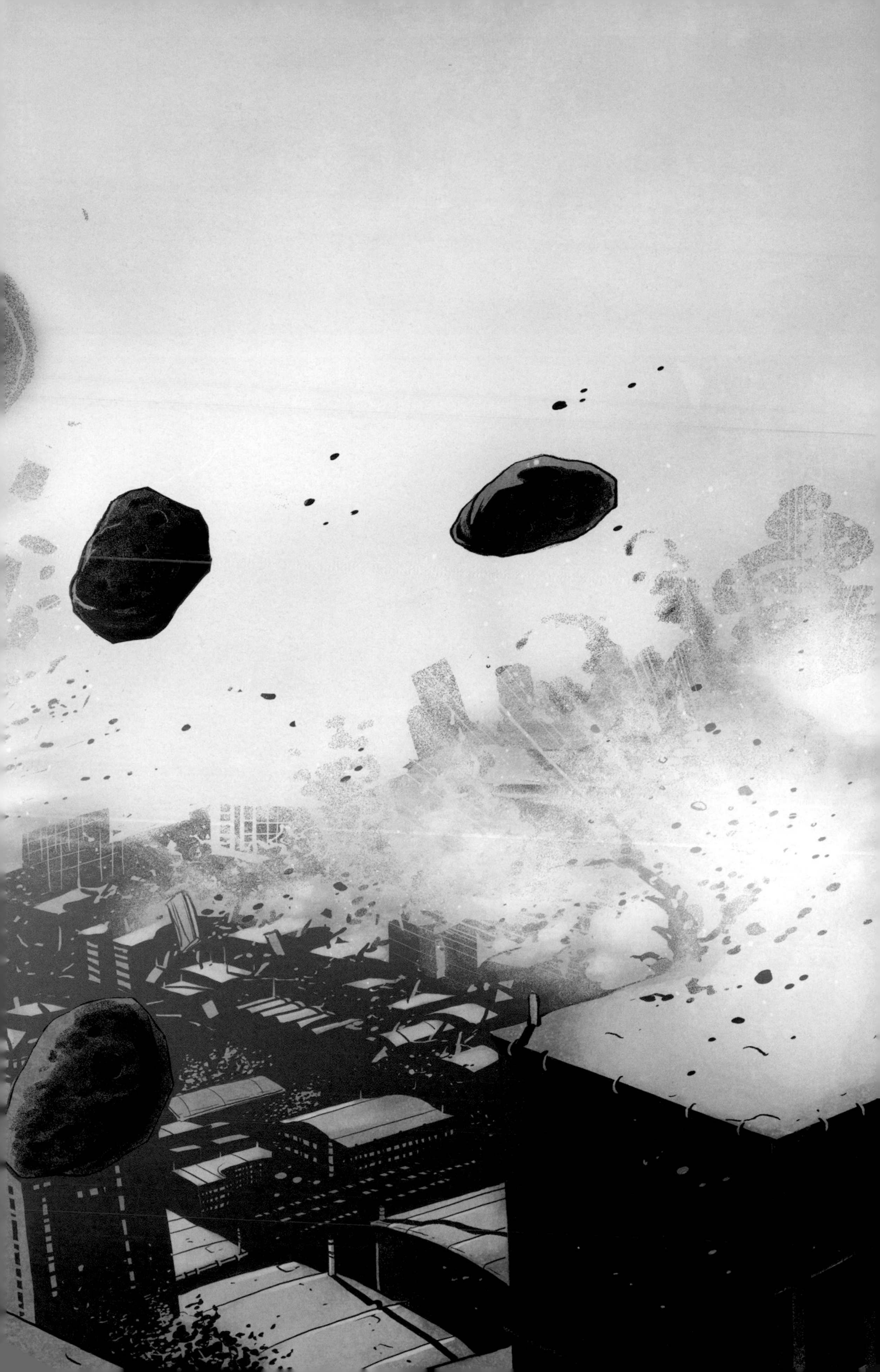

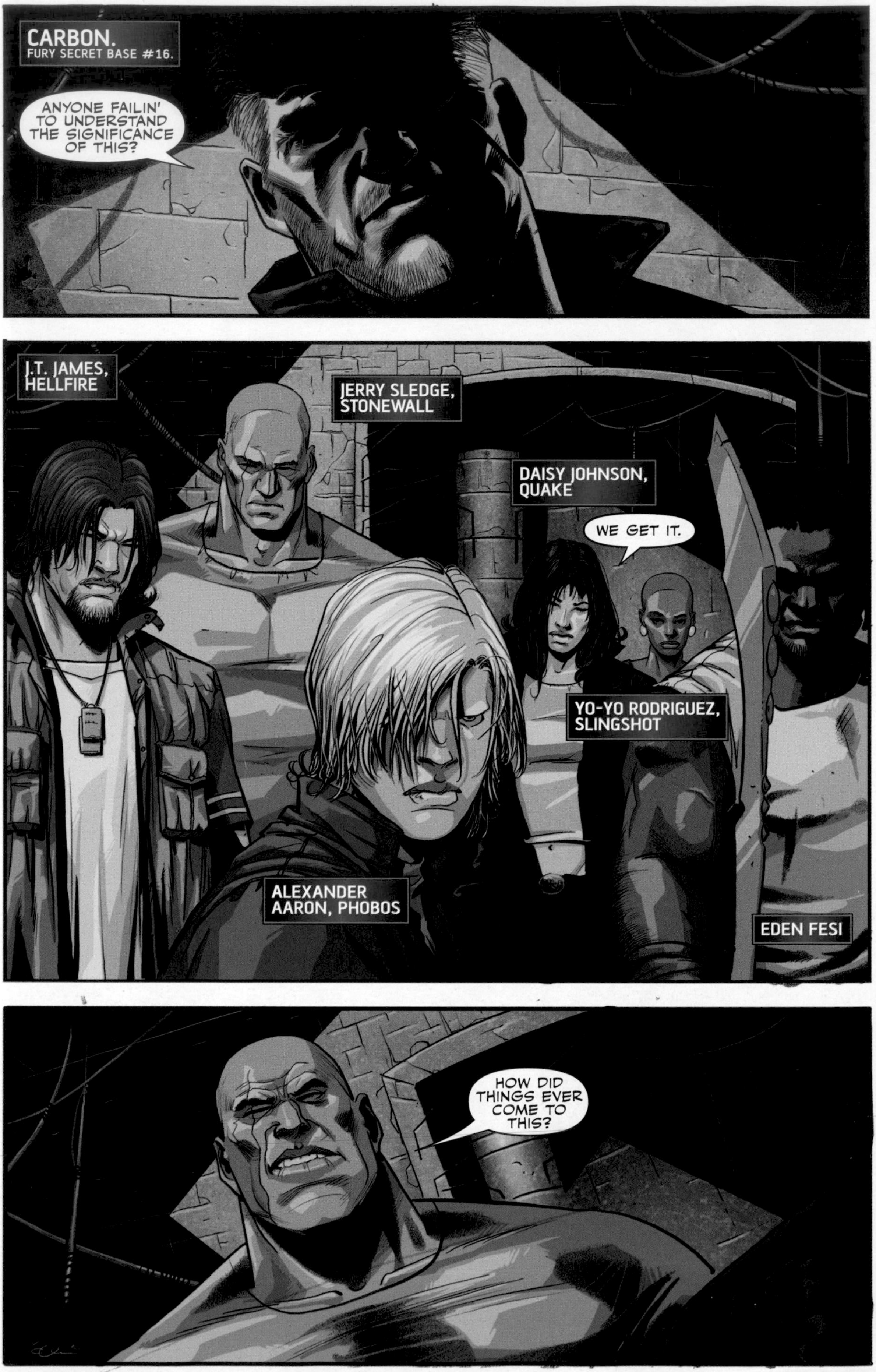
CARBON.
FURY SECRET BASE #16.
ANYONE FAILIN' TO UNDERSTAND THE SIGNIFICANCE OF THIS?
J.T. JAMES, HELLFIRE
JERRY SLEDGE, STONEWALL
DAISY JOHNSON, QUAKE
WE GET IT.
YO-YO RODRIGUEZ, SLINGSHOT
ALEXANDER AARON, PHOBOS
EDEN FESI
HOW DID THINGS EVER COME TO THIS?

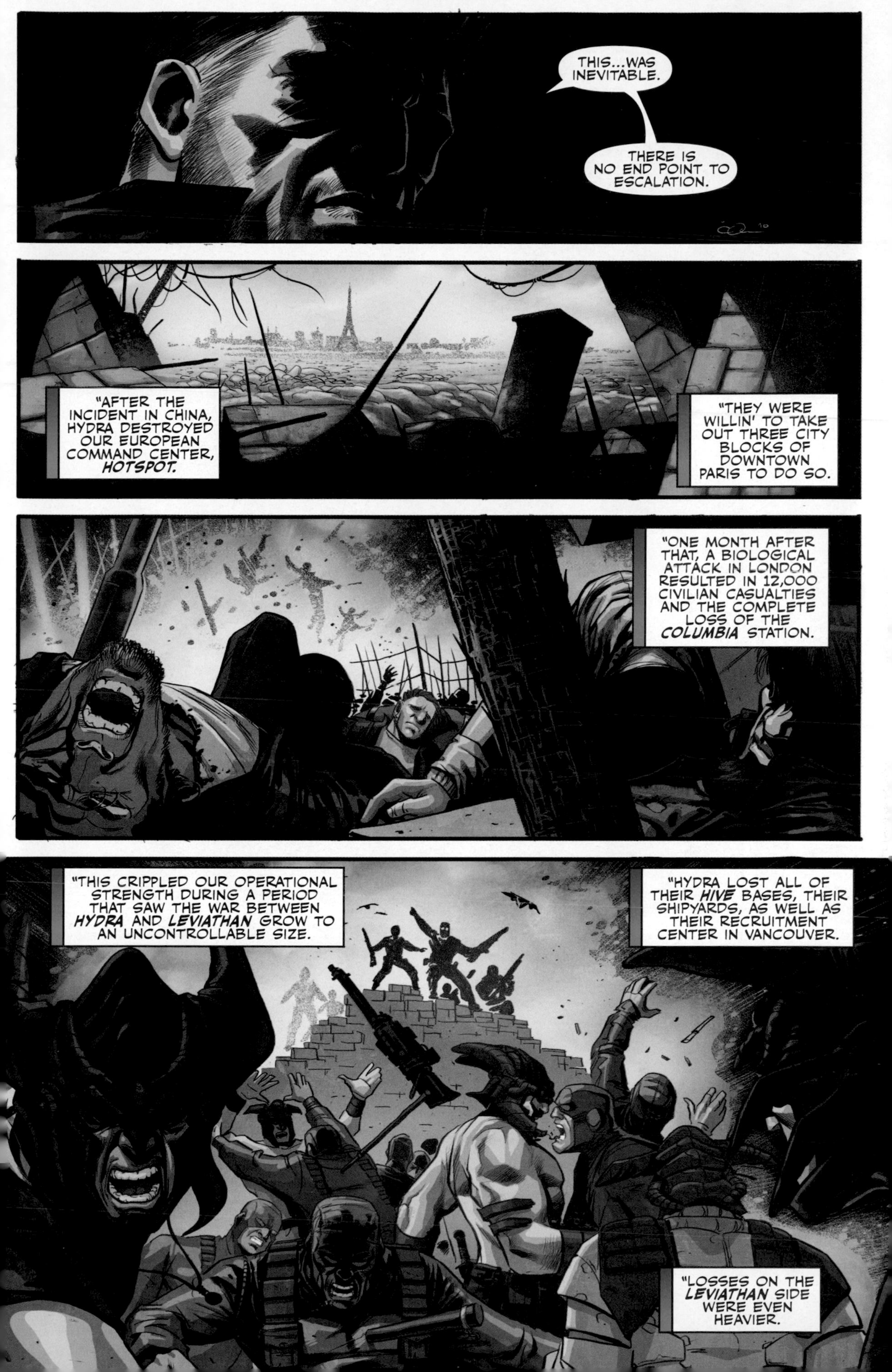

THIS...WAS INEVITABLE.
THERE IS NO END POINT TO ESCALATION.
"AFTER THE INCIDENT IN CHINA, HYDRA DESTROYED OUR EUROPEAN COMMAND CENTER, HOTSPOT.
"THEY WERE WILLIN' TO TAKE OUT THREE CITY BLOCKS OF DOWNTOWN PARIS TO DO SO.
"ONE MONTH AFTER THAT, A BIOLOGICAL ATTACK IN LONDON RESULTED IN 12,000 CIVILIAN CASUALTIES AND THE COMPLETE LOSS OF THE COLUMBIA STATION.
"THIS CRIPPLED OUR OPERATIONAL STRENGTH DURING A PERIOD THAT SAW THE WAR BETWEEN HYDRA AND LEVIATHAN GROW TO AN UNCONTROLLABLE SIZE.
"HYDRA LOST ALL OF THEIR HIVE BASES, THEIR SHIPYARDS, AS WELL AS THEIR RECRUITMENT CENTER IN VANCOUVER.
"LOSSES ON THE LEVIATHAN SIDE WERE EVEN HEAVIER.

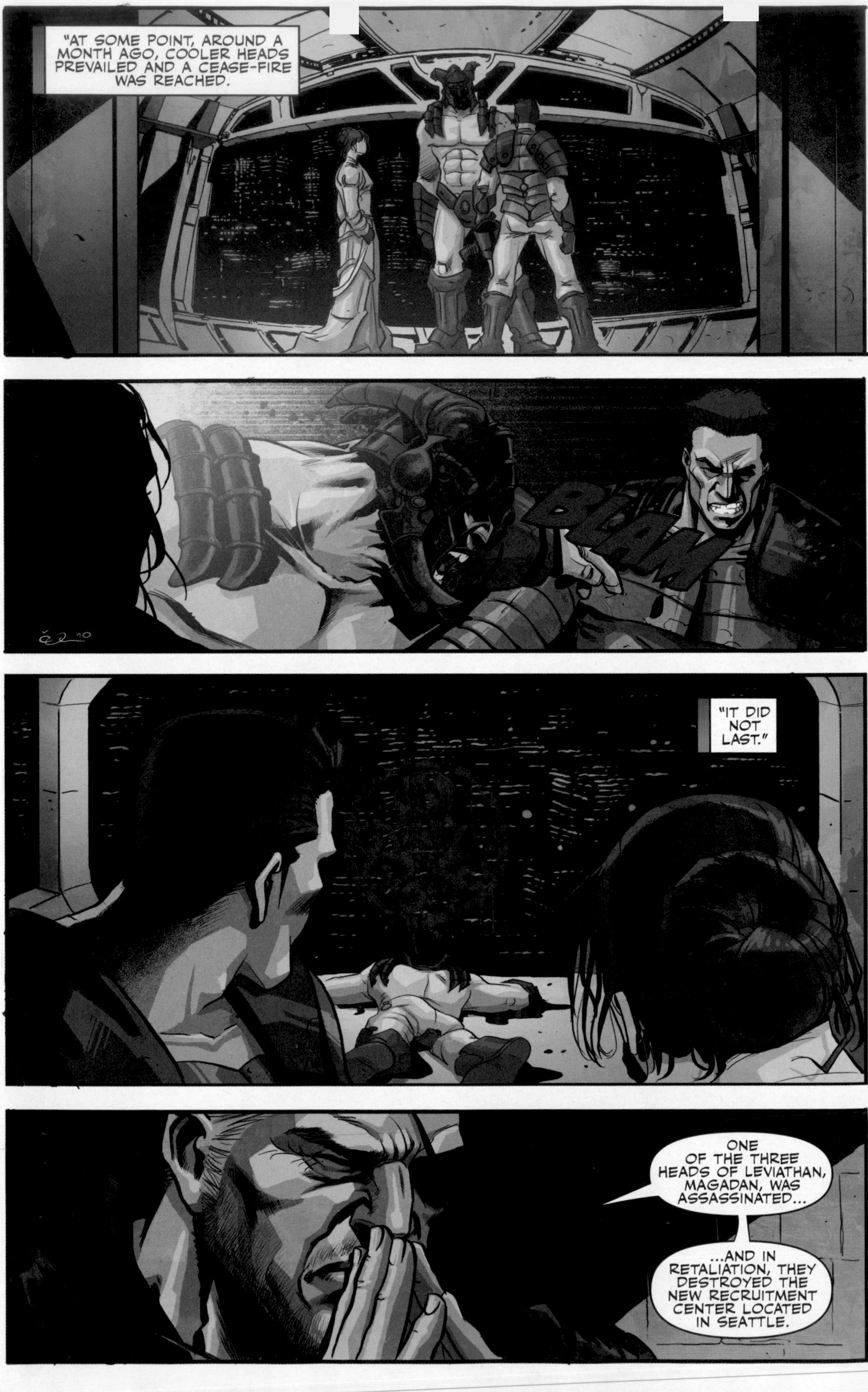
"AT SOME POINT, AROUND A MONTH AGO, COOLER HEADS PREVAILED AND A CEASE-FIRE WAS REACHED.
BLAM
"IT DID NOT LAST."
ONE OF THE THREE HEADS OF LEVIATHAN, MAGADAN, WAS ASSASSINATED...
...AND IN RETALIATION, THEY DESTROYED THE NEW RECRUITMENT CENTER LOCATED IN SEATTLE.

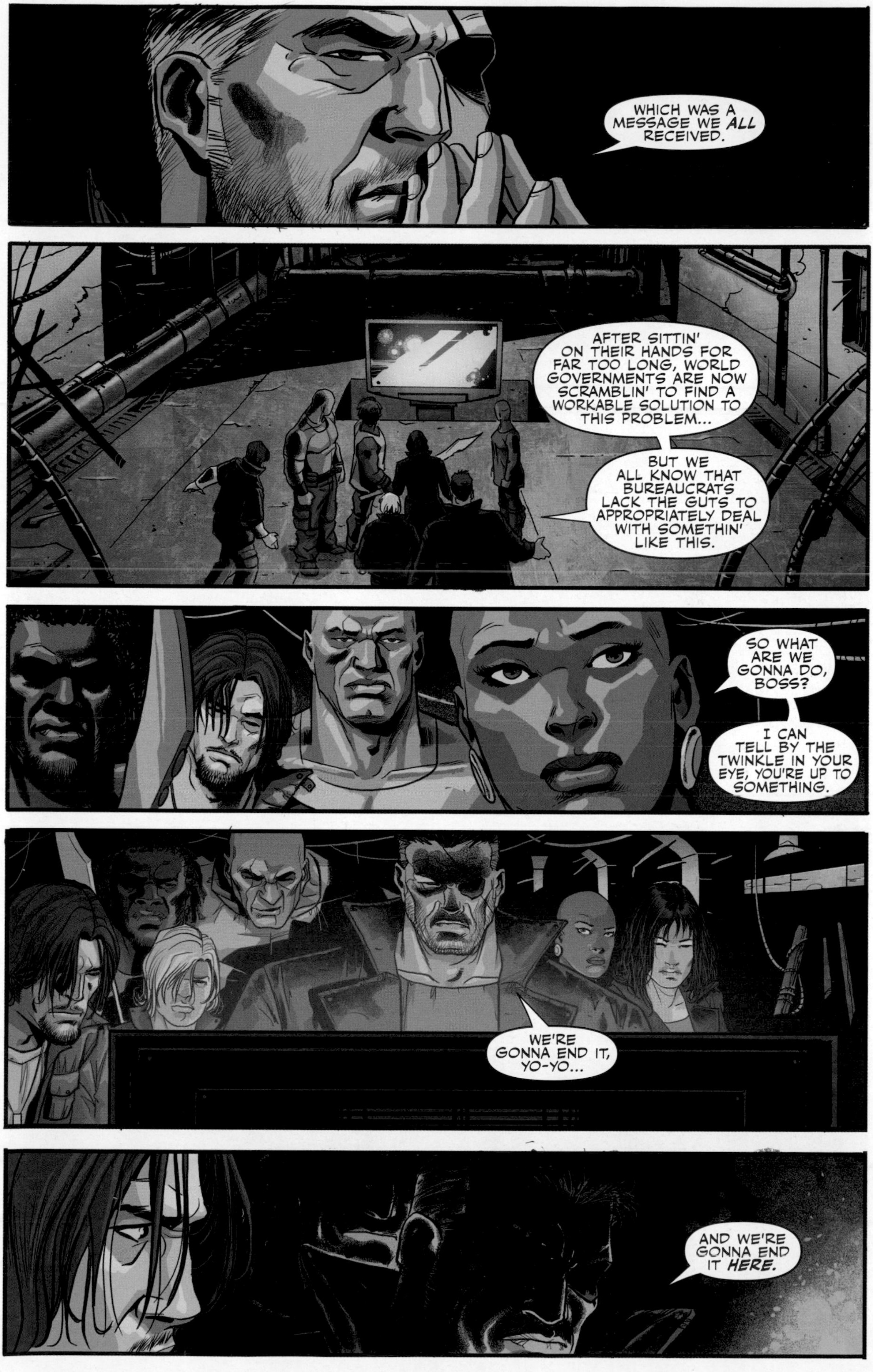
WHICH WAS A MESSAGE WE ALL RECEIVED.
AFTER SITTIN' ON THEIR HANDS FOR FAR TOO LONG, WORLD GOVERNMENTS ARE NOW SCRAMBLIN' TO FIND A WORKABLE SOLUTION TO THIS PROBLEM...
BUT WE ALL KNOW THAT BUREAUCRATS LACK THE GUTS TO APPROPRIATELY DEAL WITH SOMETHIN' LIKE THIS.
SO WHAT ARE WE GONNA DO, BOSS?
I CAN TELL BY THE TWINKLE IN YOUR EYE, YOU'RE UP TO SOMETHING.
WE'RE GONNA END IT, YO-YO...
AND WE'RE GONNA END IT HERE.

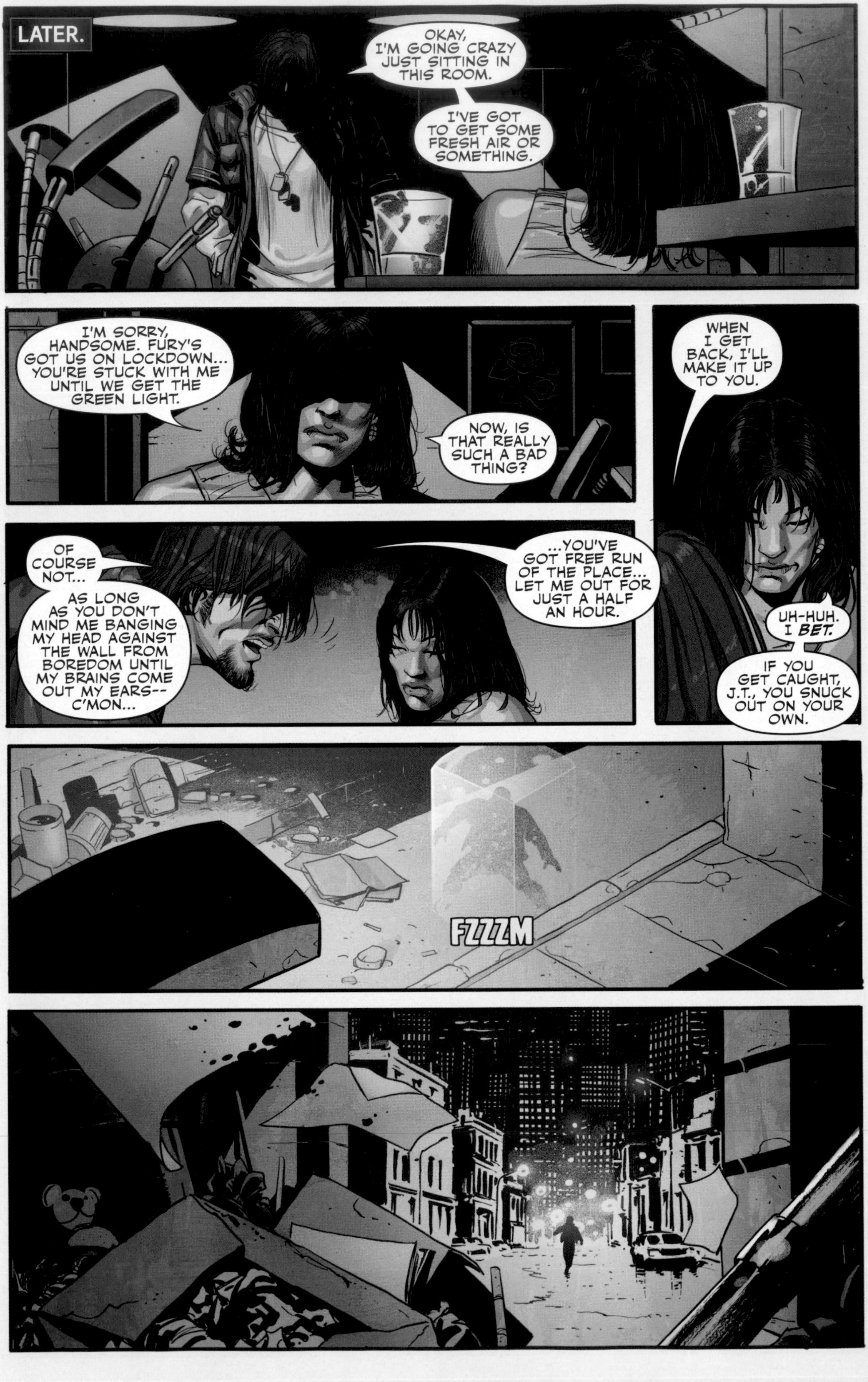
LATER.
OKAY, I'M GOING CRAZY JUST SITTING IN THIS ROOM.
I'VE GOT TO GET SOME FRESH AIR OR SOMETHING.
I'M SORRY, HANDSOME. FURY'S GOT US ON LOCKDOWN... YOU'RE STUCK WITH ME UNTIL WE GET THE GREEN LIGHT.
NOW, IS THAT REALLY SUCH A BAD THING?
OF COURSE NOT...
AS LONG AS YOU DON'T MIND ME BANGING MY HEAD AGAINST THE WALL FROM BOREDOM UNTIL MY BRAINS COME OUT MY EARS-- C'MON...
...YOU'VE GOT FREE RUN OF THE PLACE... LET ME OUT FOR JUST A HALF AN HOUR.
WHEN I GET BACK, I'LL MAKE IT UP TO YOU.
UH-HUH. I BET.
IF YOU GET CAUGHT, J.T., YOU SNUCK OUT ON YOUR OWN.
FZZZM

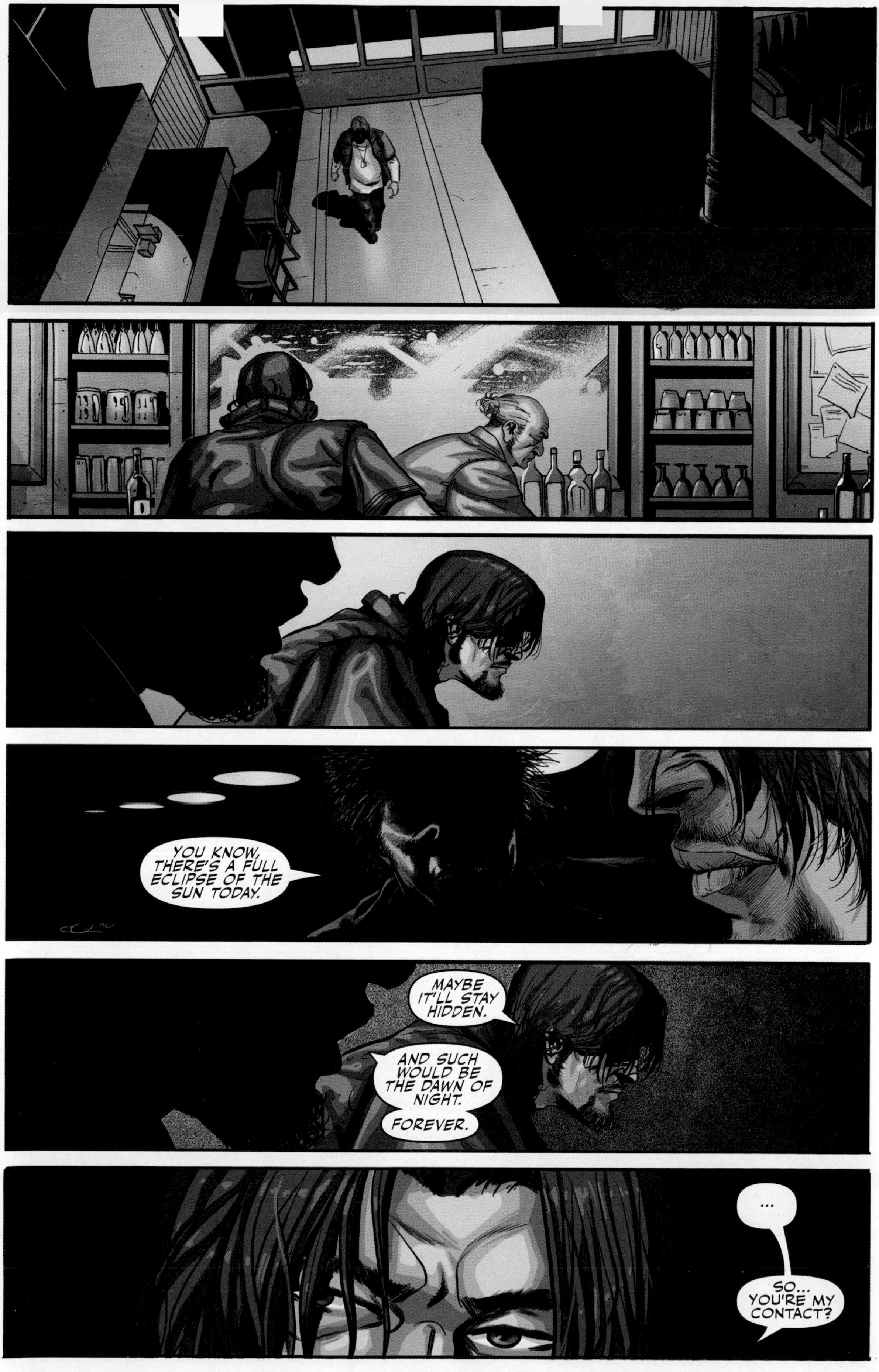
YOU KNOW, THERE'S A FULL ECLIPSE OF THE SUN TODAY.
MAYBE IT'LL STAY HIDDEN.
AND SUCH WOULD BE THE DAWN OF NIGHT.
FOREVER.
...
SO... YOU'RE MY CONTACT?

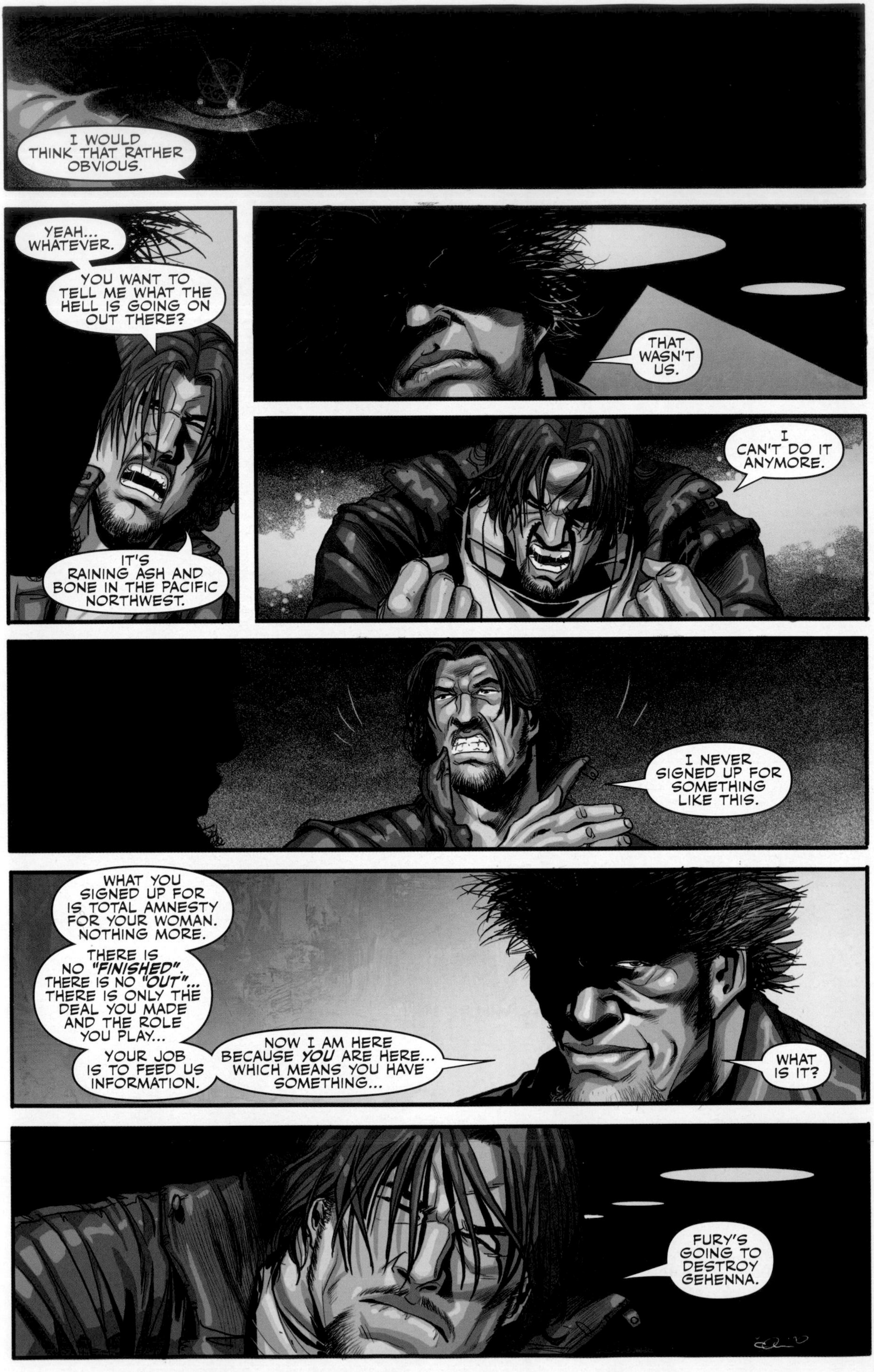
I WOULD THINK THAT RATHER OBVIOUS.
YEAH... WHATEVER.
YOU WANT TO TELL ME WHAT THE HELL IS GOING ON OUT THERE?
THAT WASN'T US.
IT'S RAINING ASH AND BONE IN THE PACIFIC NORTHWEST.
I CAN'T DO IT ANYMORE.
I NEVER SIGNED UP FOR SOMETHING LIKE THIS.
WHAT YOU SIGNED UP FOR IS TOTAL AMNESTY FOR YOUR WOMAN. NOTHING MORE.
THERE IS NO "FINISHED". THERE IS NO "OUT"... THERE IS ONLY THE DEAL YOU MADE AND THE ROLE YOU PLAY...
YOUR JOB IS TO FEED US INFORMATION.
NOW I AM HERE BECAUSE YOU ARE HERE... WHICH MEANS YOU HAVE SOMETHING...
WHAT IS IT?
FURY'S GOING TO DESTROY GEHENNA.

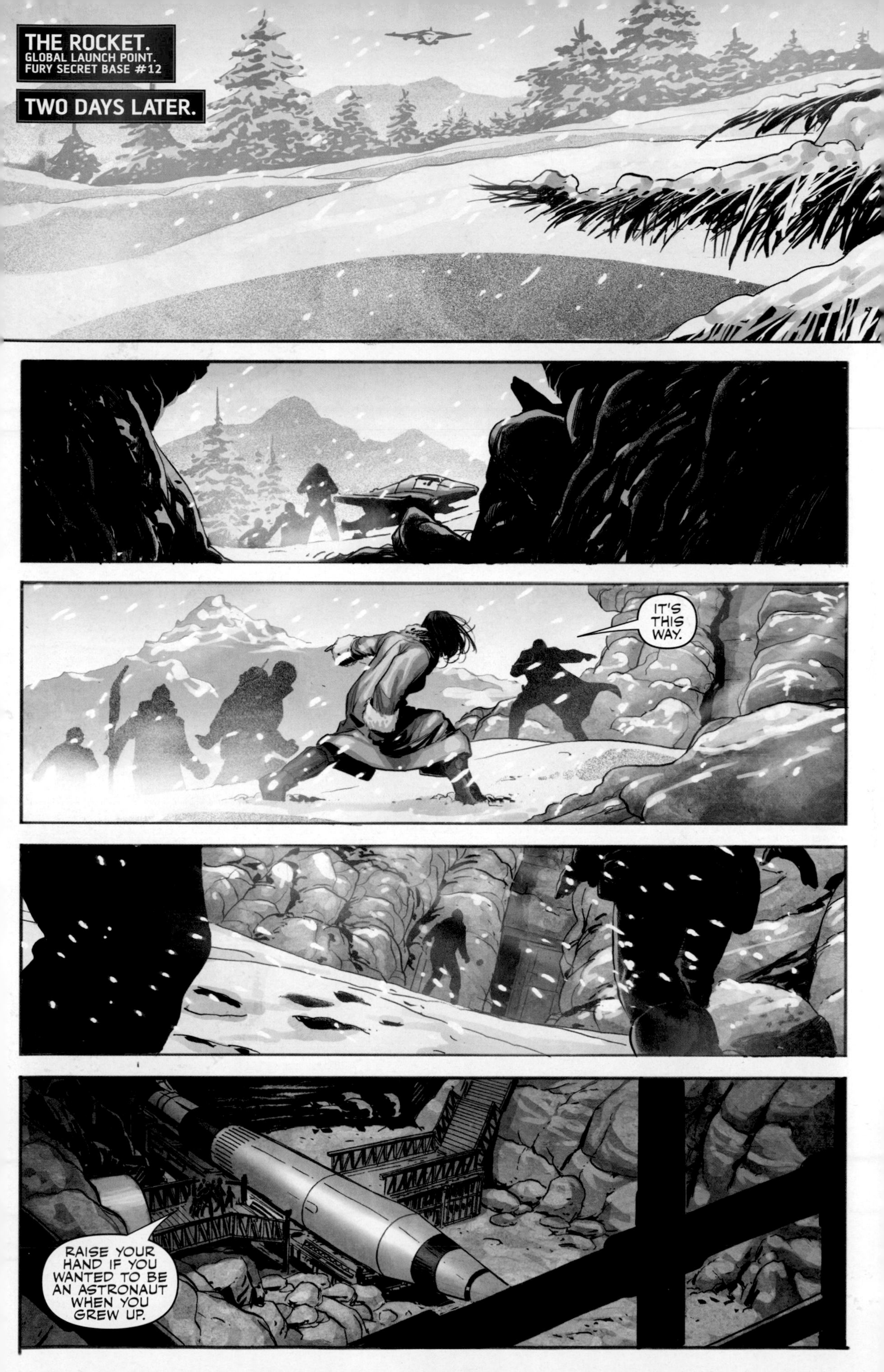
THE ROCKET.
GLOBAL LAUNCH POINT.
FURY SECRET BASE #12
TWO DAYS LATER.
IT'S THIS WAY.
RAISE YOUR HAND IF YOU WANTED TO BE AN ASTRONAUT WHEN YOU GREW UP.

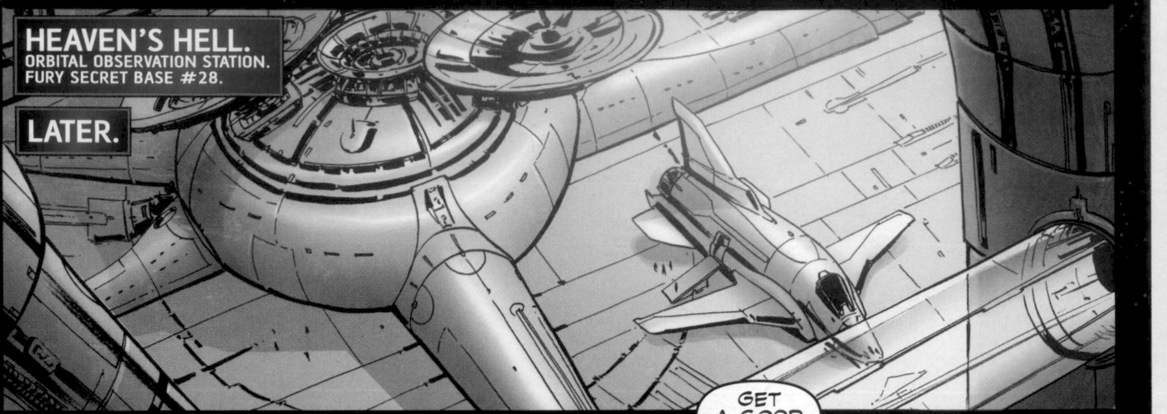
HEAVEN'S HELL.
ORBITAL OBSERVATION STATION.
FURY SECRET BASE #28.
LATER.

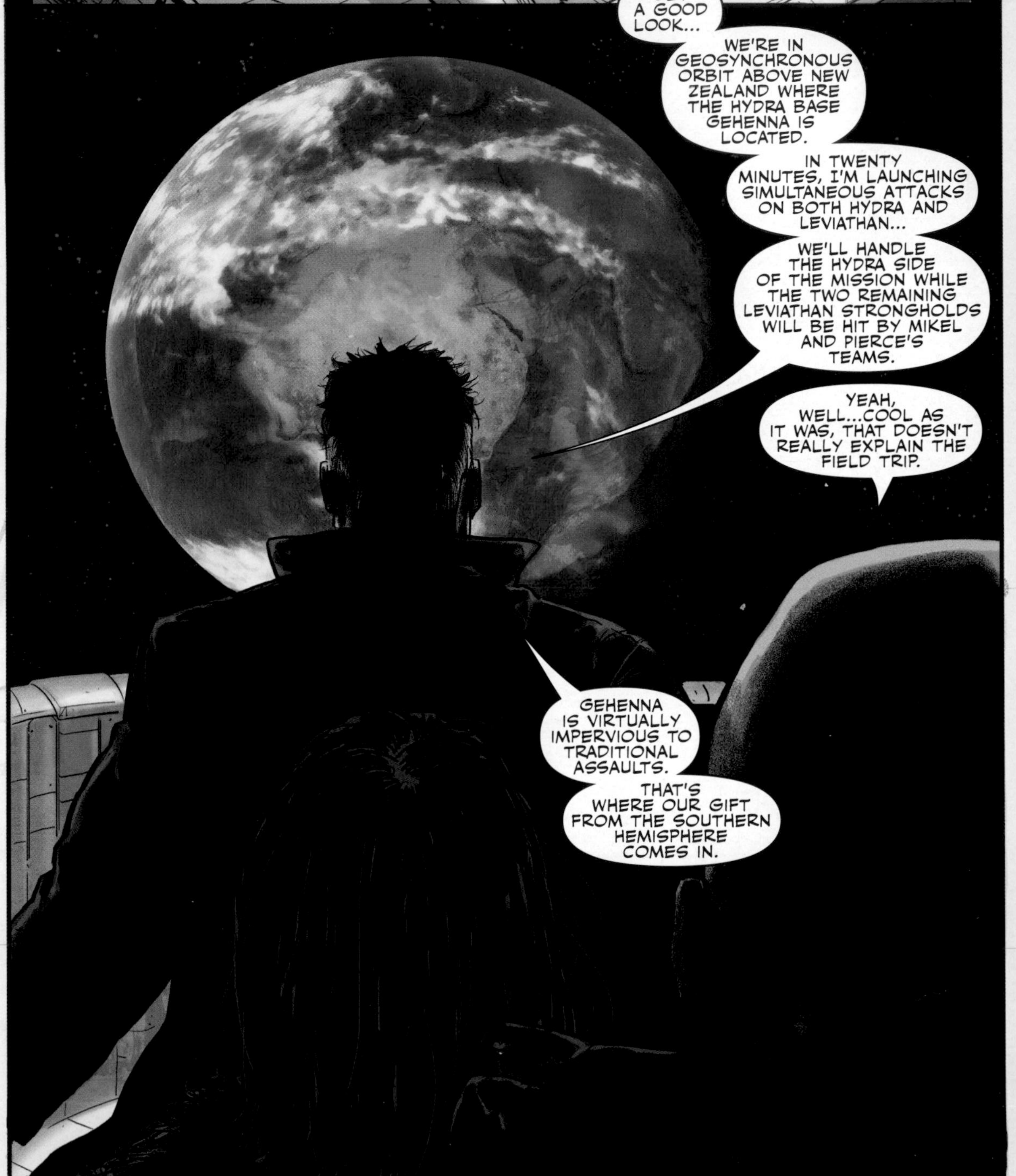
GET A GOOD LOOK...
WE'RE IN GEOSYNCHRONOUS ORBIT ABOVE NEW ZEALAND WHERE THE HYDRA BASE GEHENNA IS LOCATED.
IN TWENTY MINUTES, I'M LAUNCHING SIMULTANEOUS ATTACKS ON BOTH HYDRA AND LEVIATHAN...
WE'LL HANDLE THE HYDRA SIDE OF THE MISSION WHILE THE TWO REMAINING LEVIATHAN STRONGHOLDS WILL BE HIT BY MIKEL AND PIERCE'S TEAMS.
YEAH, WELL...COOL AS IT WAS, THAT DOESN'T REALLY EXPLAIN THE FIELD TRIP.
GEHENNA IS VIRTUALLY IMPERVIOUS TO TRADITIONAL ASSAULTS.
THAT'S WHERE OUR GIFT FROM THE SOUTHERN HEMISPHERE COMES IN.

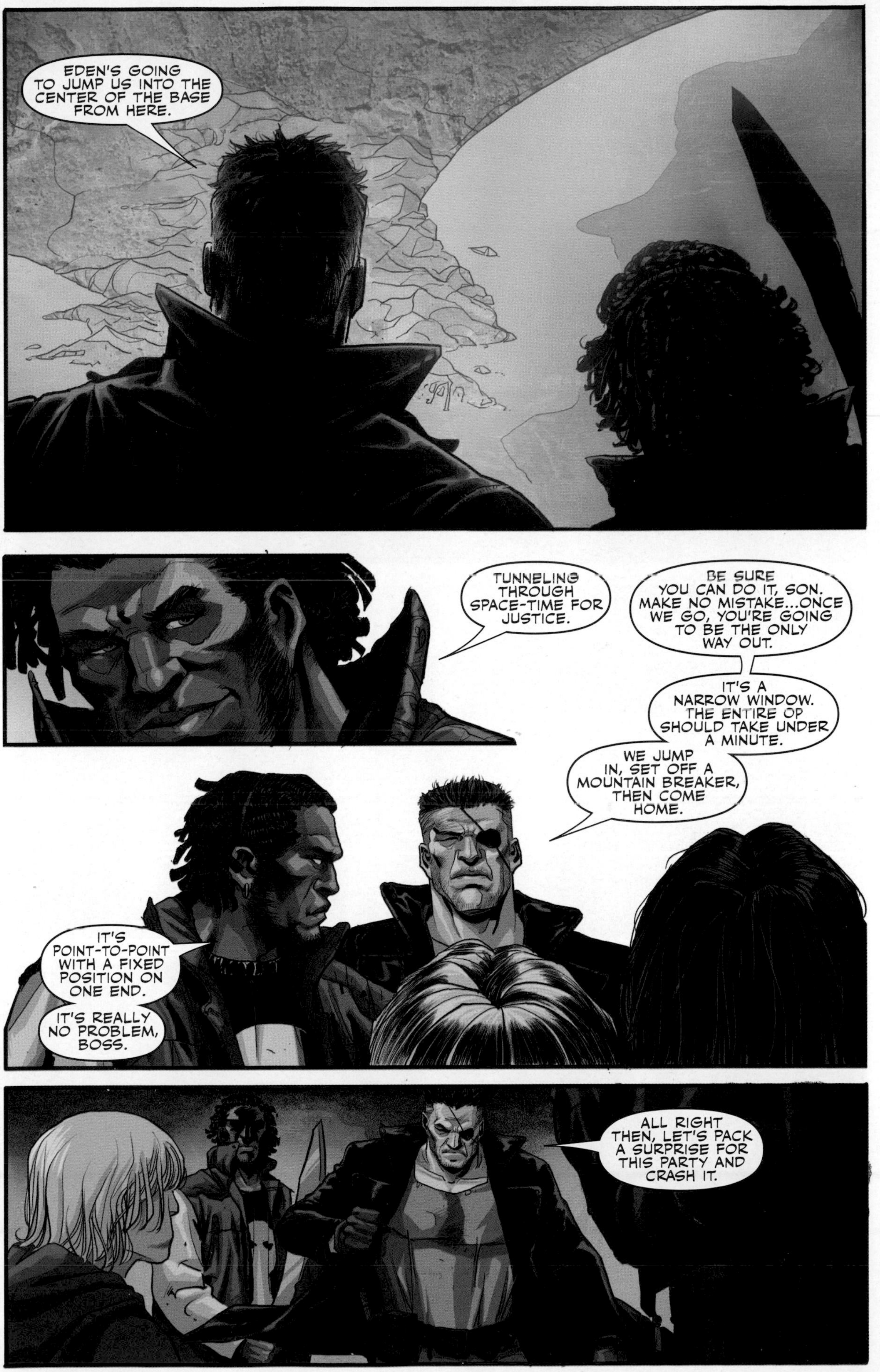
EDEN'S GOING TO JUMP US INTO THE CENTER OF THE BASE FROM HERE.
TUNNELING THROUGH SPACE-TIME FOR JUSTICE.
BE SURE YOU CAN DO IT, SON. MAKE NO MISTAKE...ONCE WE GO, YOU'RE GOING TO BE THE ONLY WAY OUT.
IT'S A NARROW WINDOW. THE ENTIRE OP SHOULD TAKE UNDER A MINUTE.
WE JUMP IN, SET OFF A MOUNTAIN BREAKER, THEN COME HOME.
IT'S POINT-TO-POINT WITH A FIXED POSITION ON ONE END.
IT'S REALLY NO PROBLEM, BOSS.
ALL RIGHT THEN, LET'S PACK A SURPRISE FOR THIS PARTY AND CRASH IT.

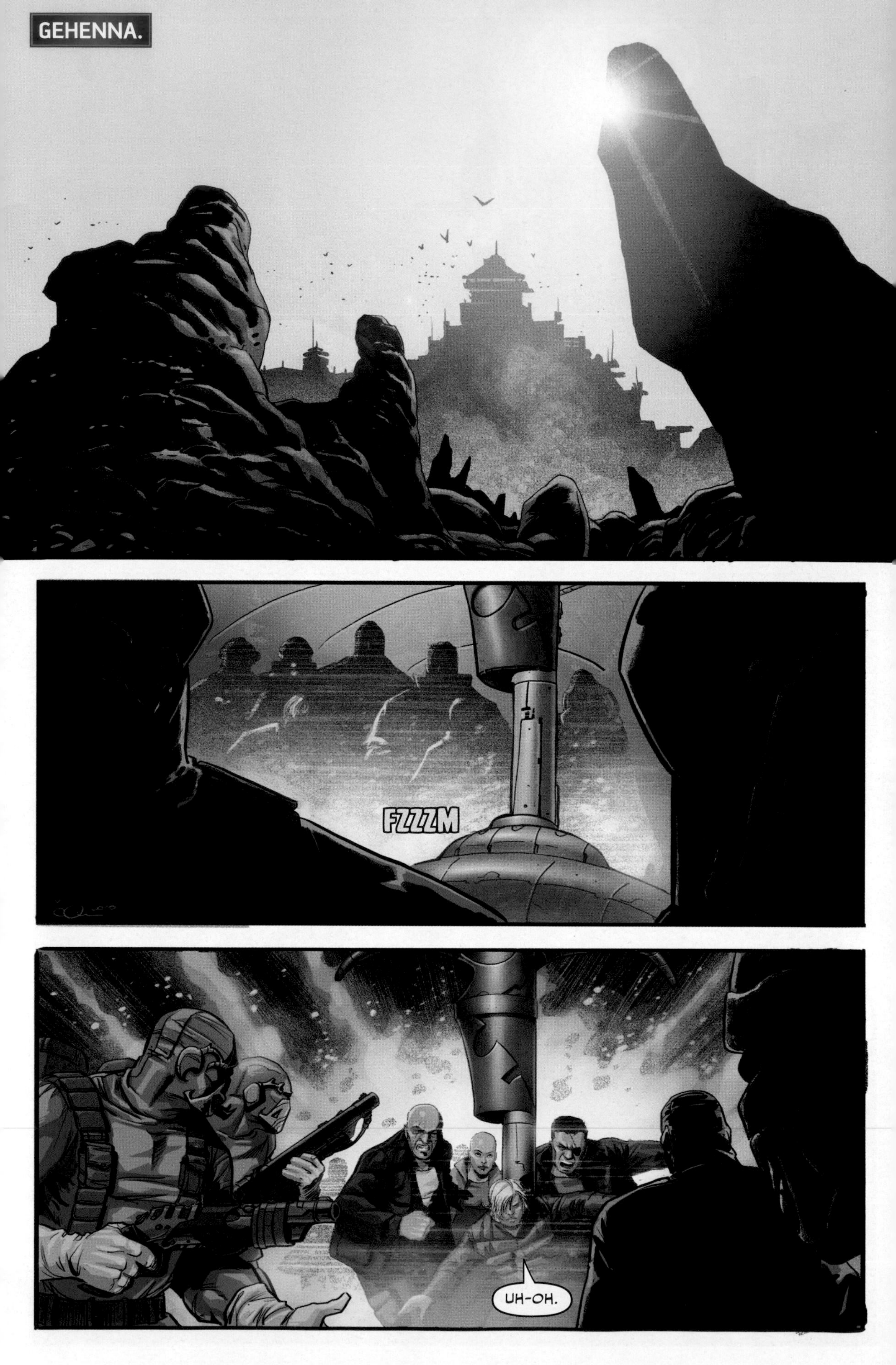
GEHENNA.
FZZZM
UH-OH.

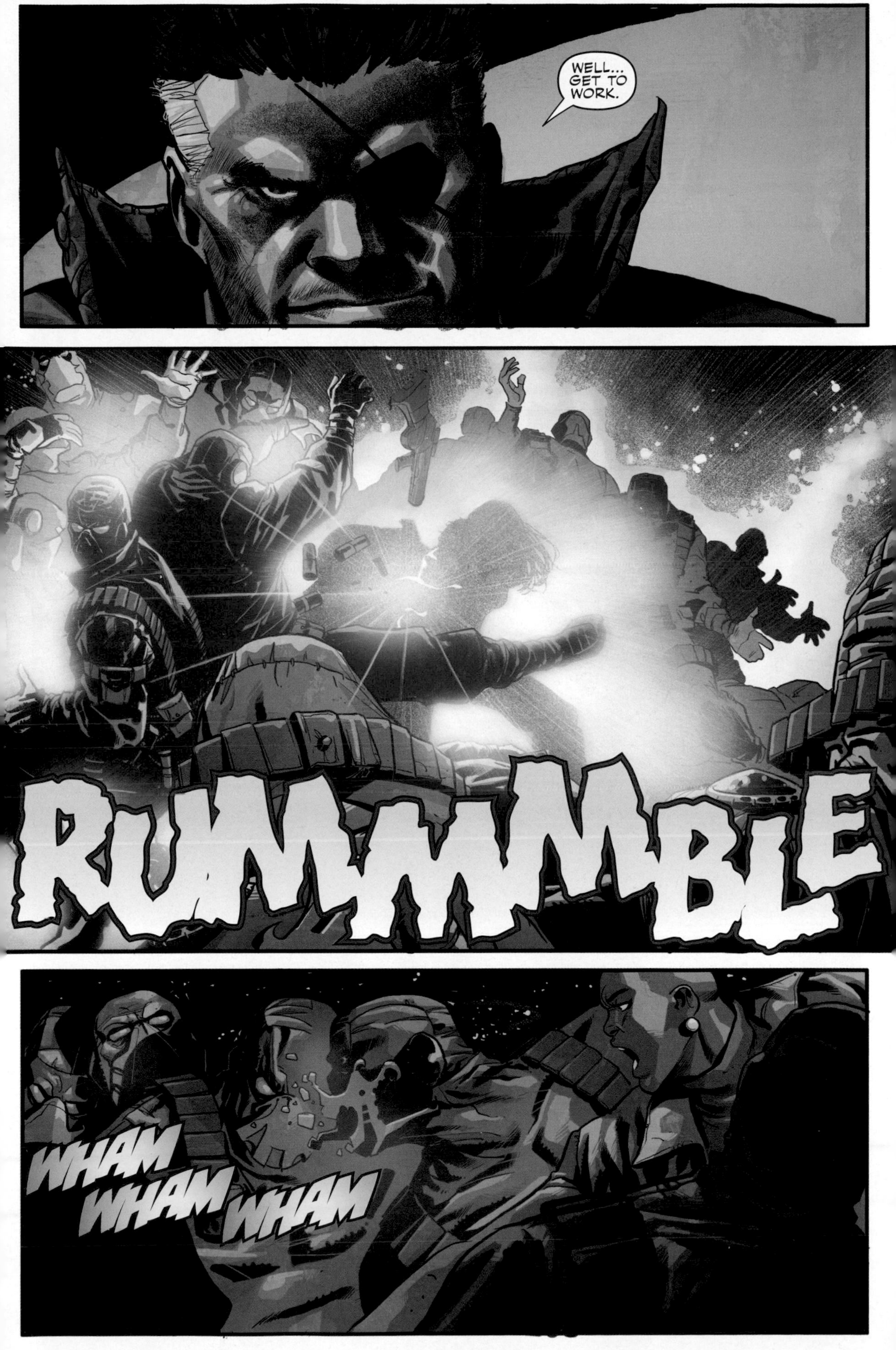
WELL... GET TO WORK.
RUMMMBLE
WHAM
WHAM
WHAM

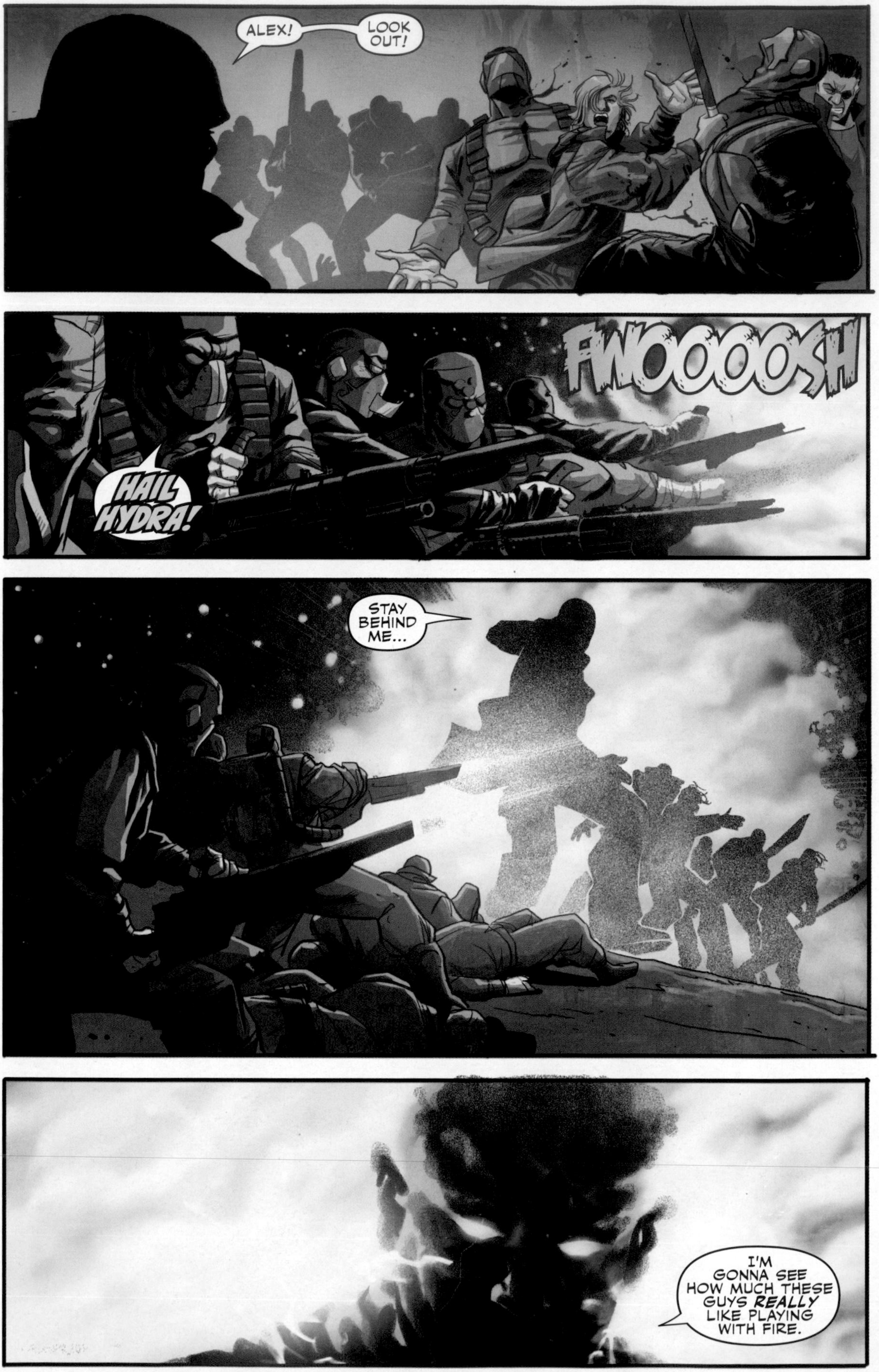
ALEX!
LOOK OUT!
FWOOOOSH
HAIL HYDRA!
STAY BEHIND ME...
I'M GONNA SEE HOW MUCH THESE GUYS REALLY LIKE PLAYING WITH FIRE.

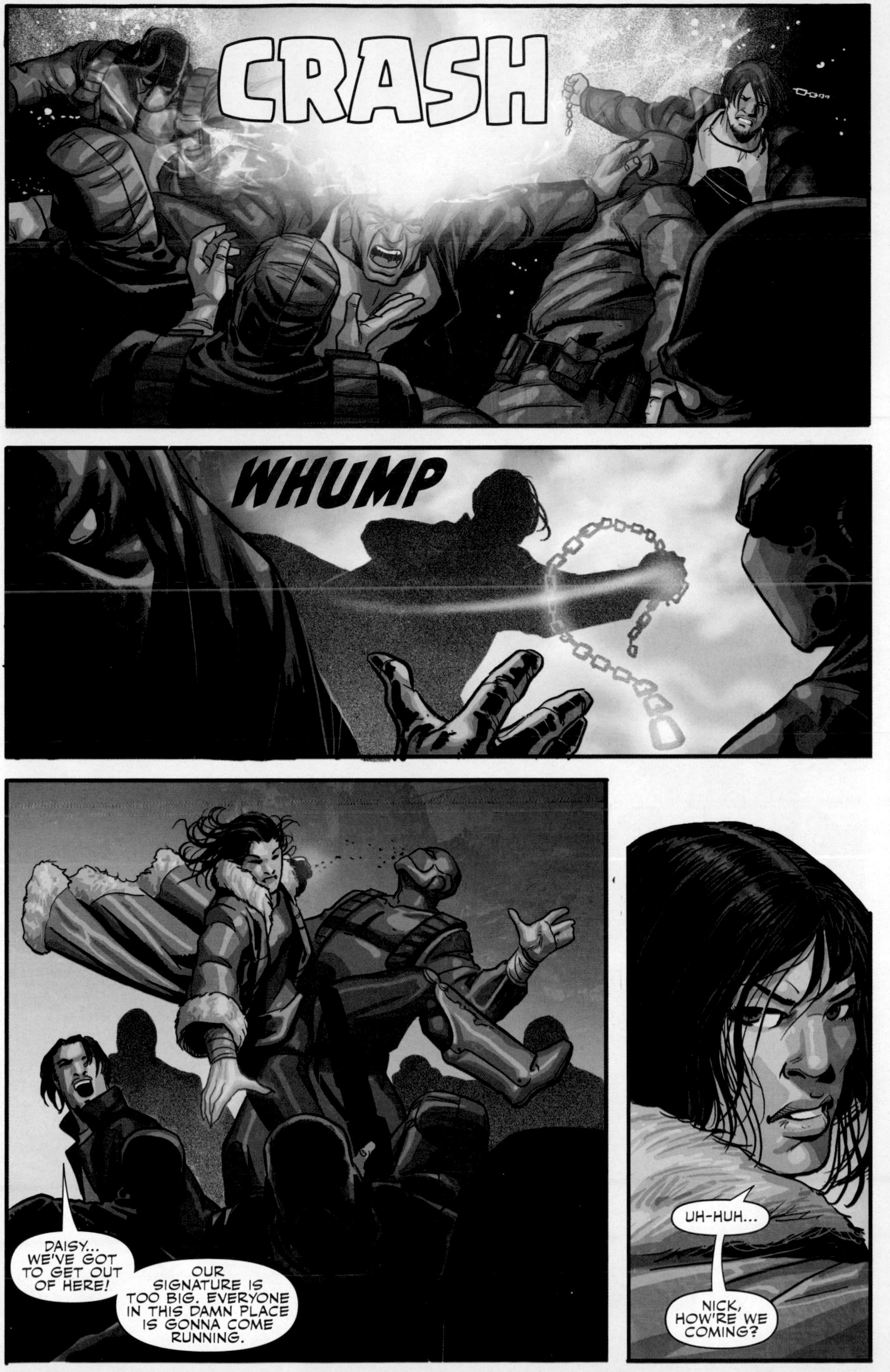
CRASH
WHUMP
DAISY... WE'VE GOT TO GET OUT OF HERE!
OUR SIGNATURE IS TOO BIG. EVERYONE IN THIS DAMN PLACE IS GONNA COME RUNNING.
UH-HUH...
NICK, HOW'RE WE COMING?

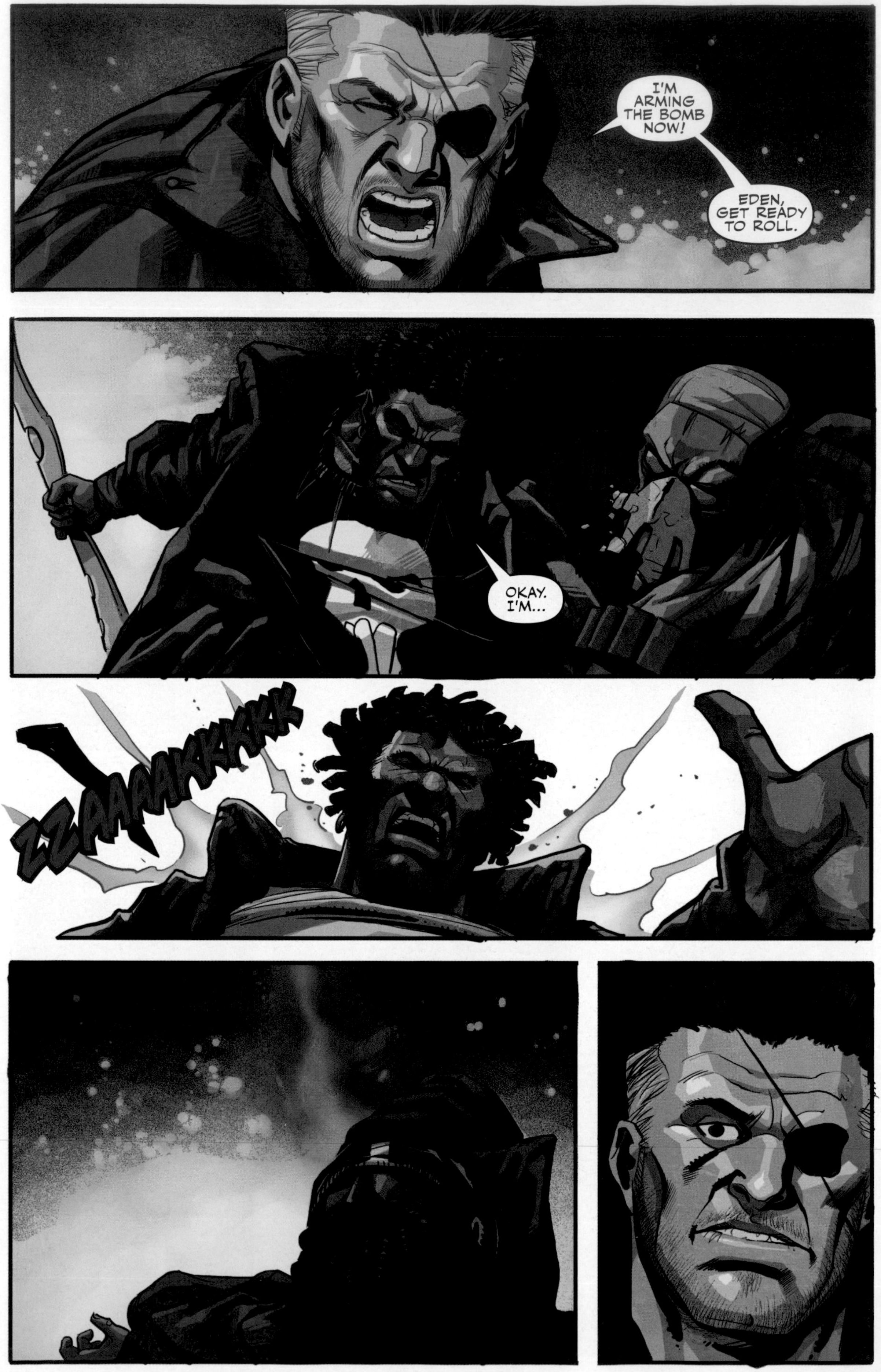
I'M ARMING THE BOMB NOW!
EDEN, GET READY TO ROLL.
OKAY. I'M...
ZZAAAAKKKKK

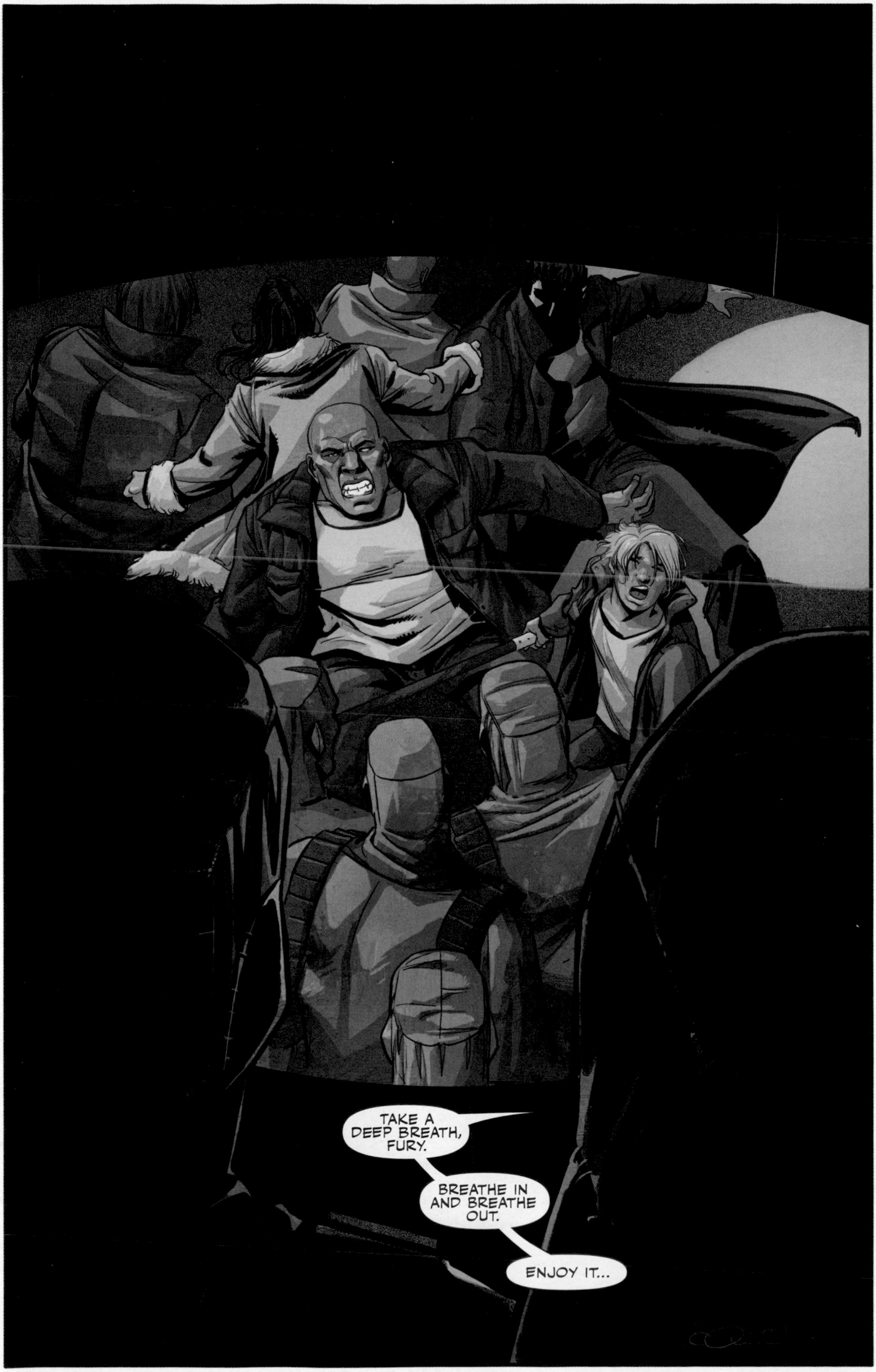
TAKE A DEEP BREATH, FURY.
BREATHE IN AND BREATHE OUT.
ENJOY IT...

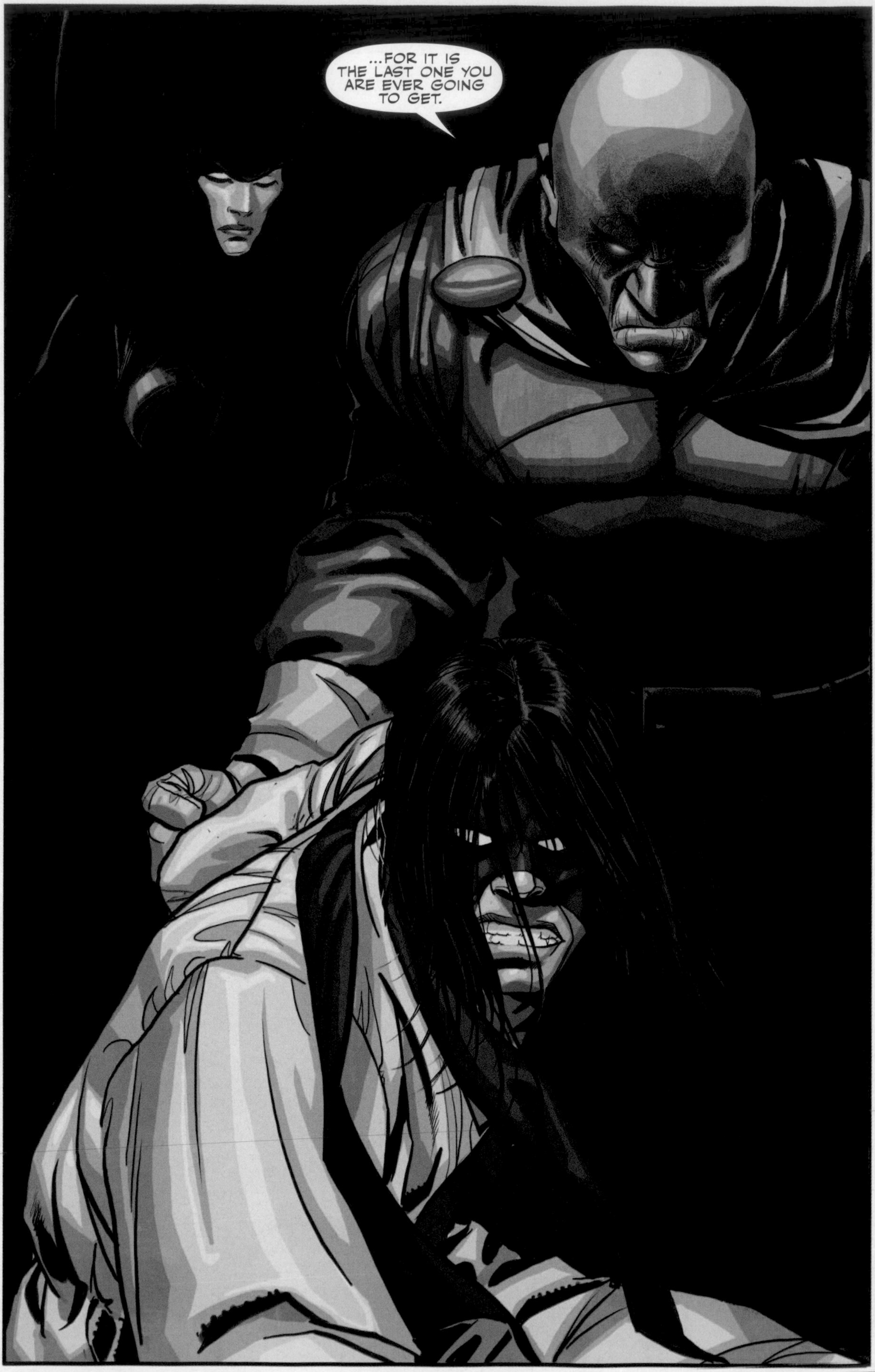
...FOR IT IS THE LAST ONE YOU ARE EVER GOING TO GET.

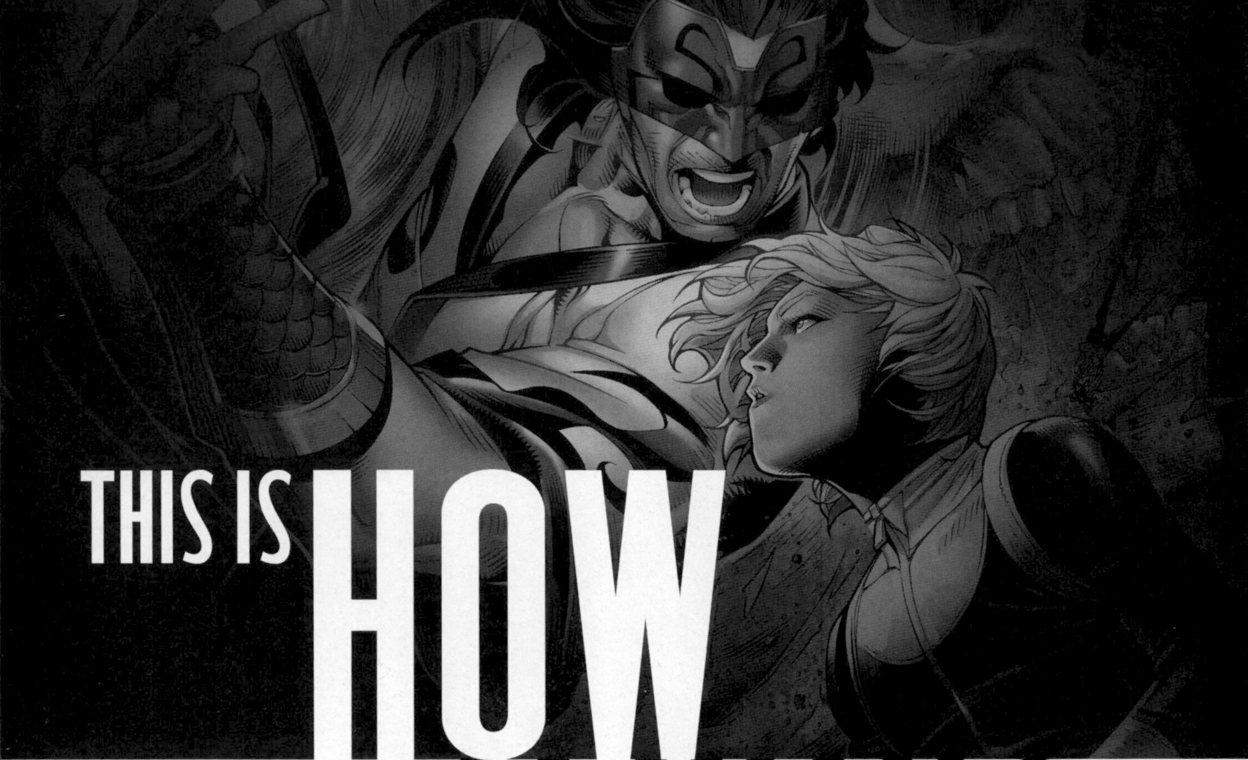

THIS IS HOW
IT WAS ALWAYS
GOING TO BE

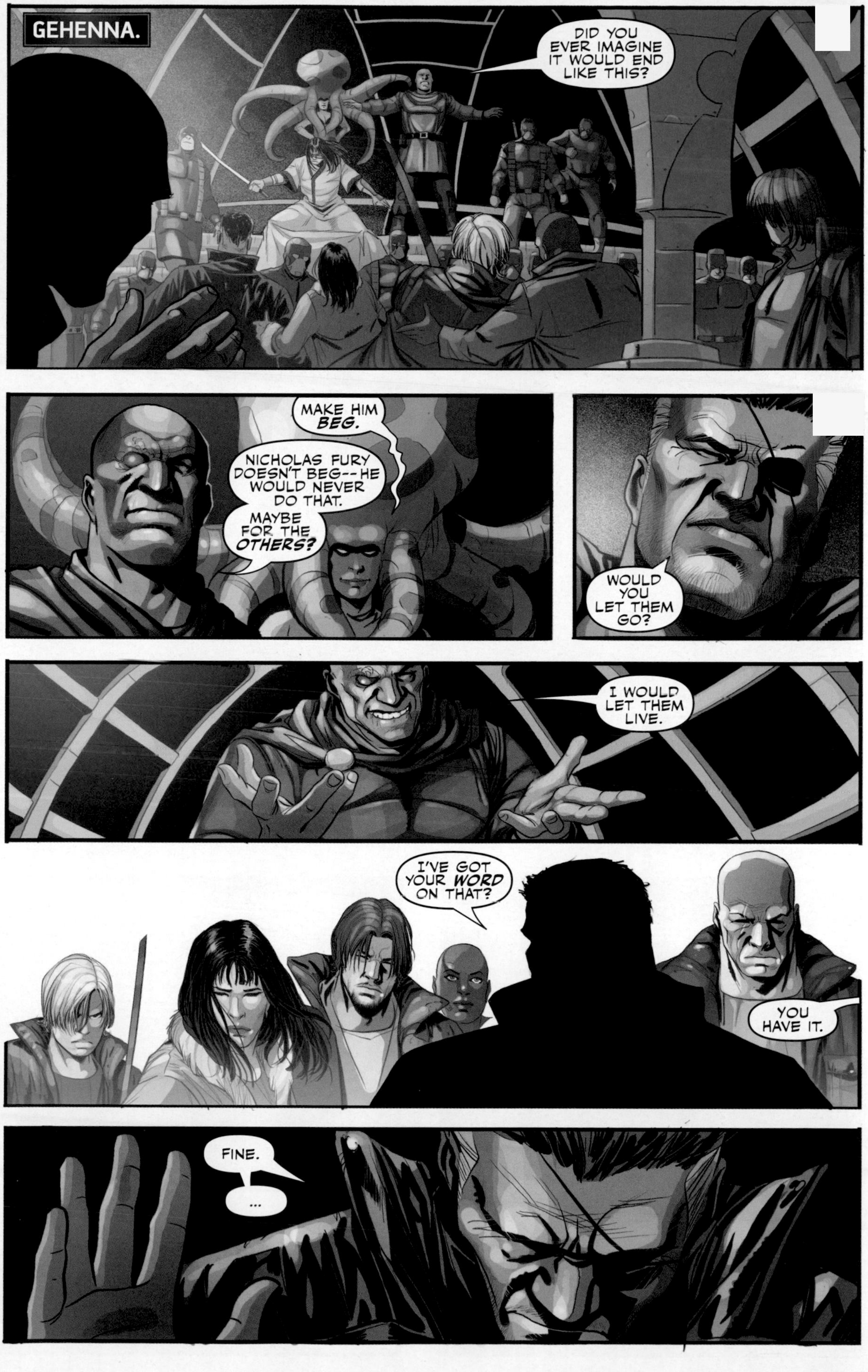
GEHENNA.
DID YOU EVER IMAGINE IT WOULD END LIKE THIS?
MAKE HIM BEG.
NICHOLAS FURY DOESN'T BEG--HE WOULD NEVER DO THAT.
MAYBE FOR THE OTHERS?
WOULD YOU LET THEM GO?
I WOULD LET THEM LIVE.
I'VE GOT YOUR WORD ON THAT?
YOU HAVE IT.
FINE.
...

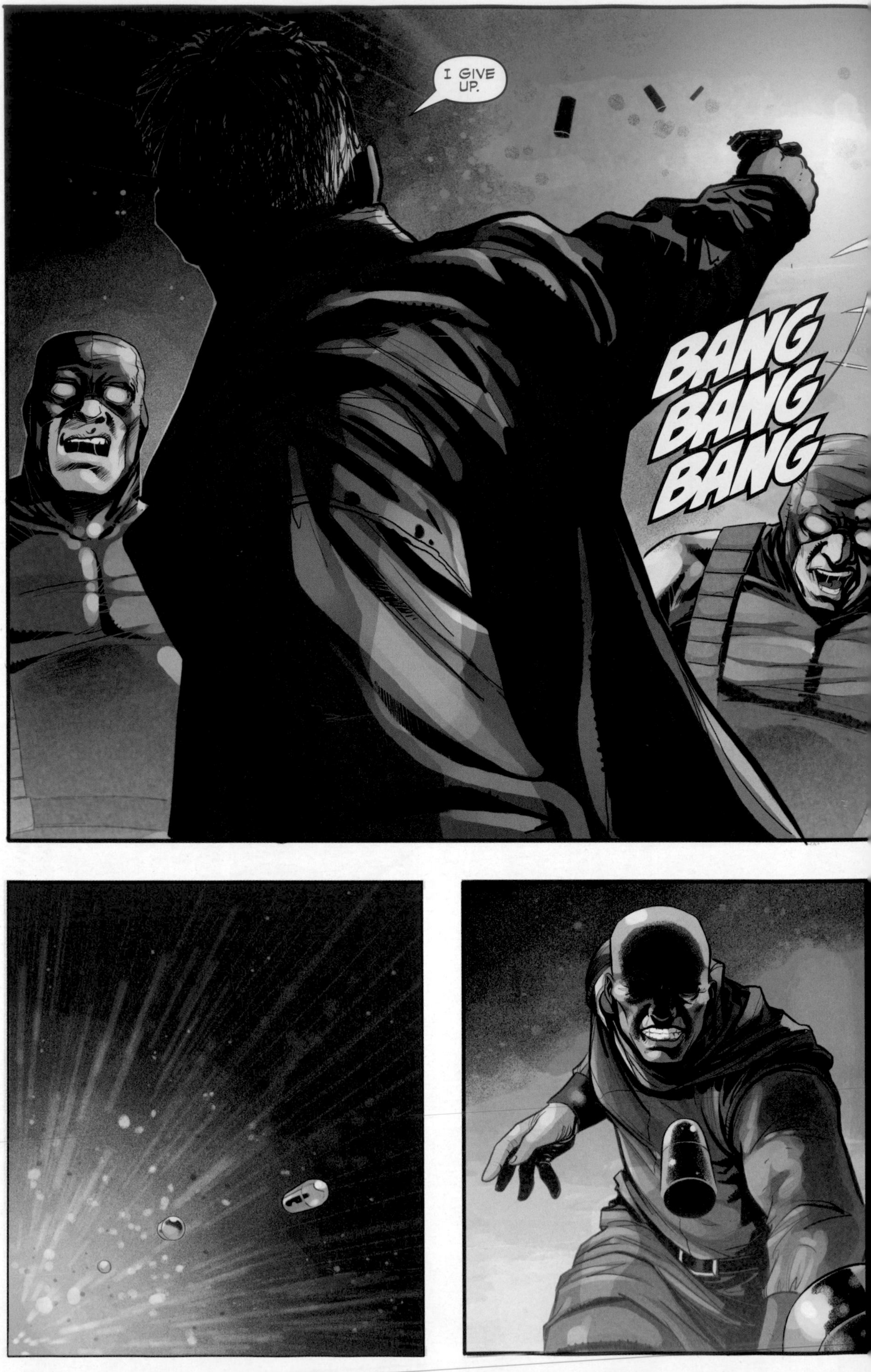
I GIVE UP.
BANG BANG BANG

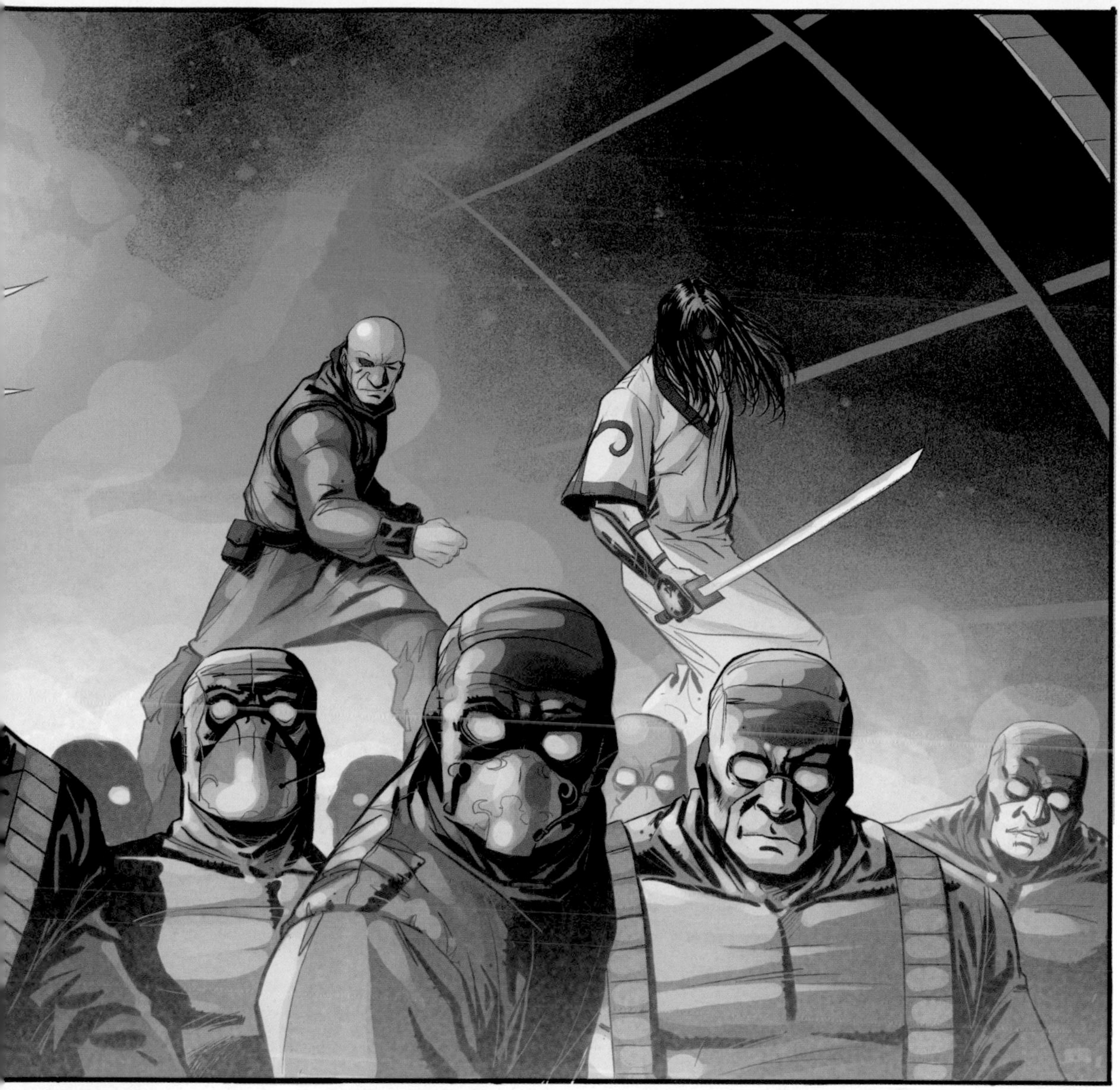
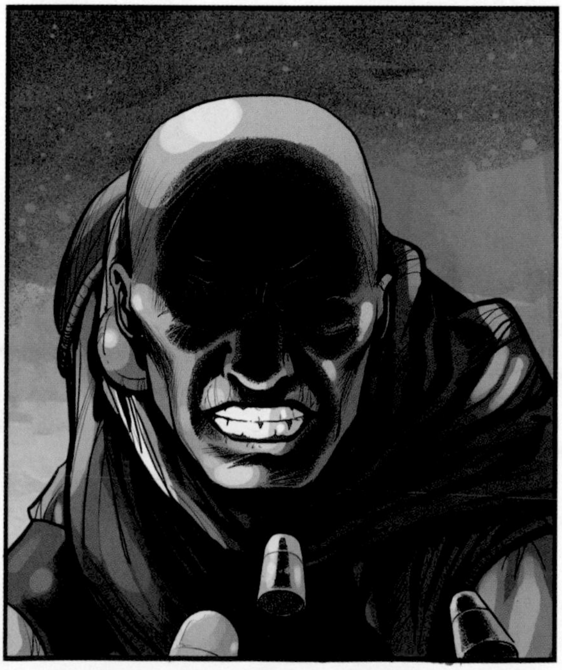
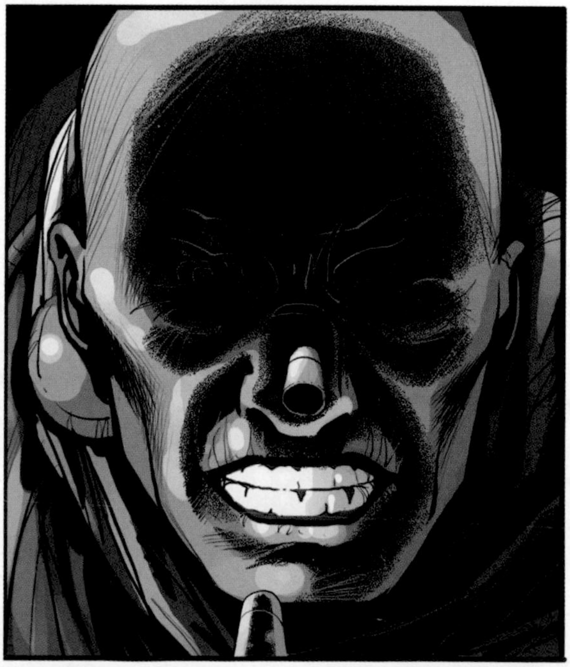

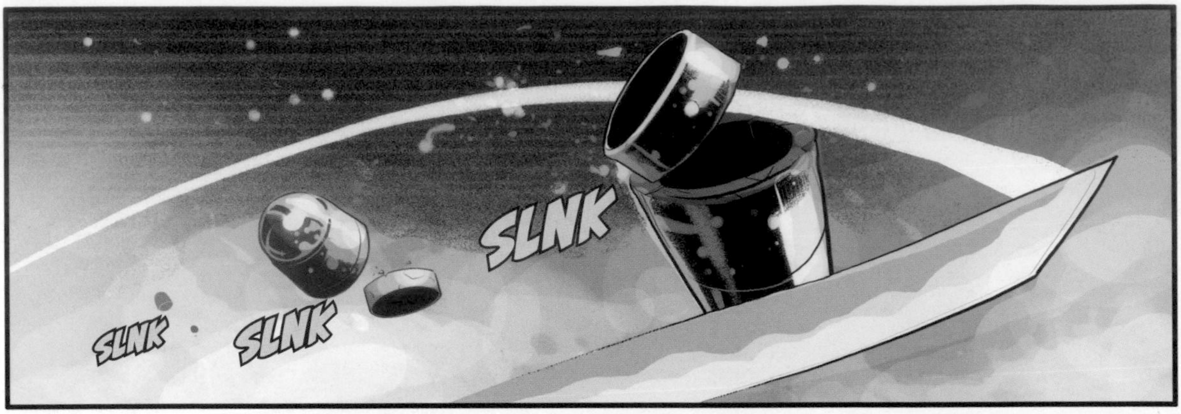
SLNK
SLNK
SLNK

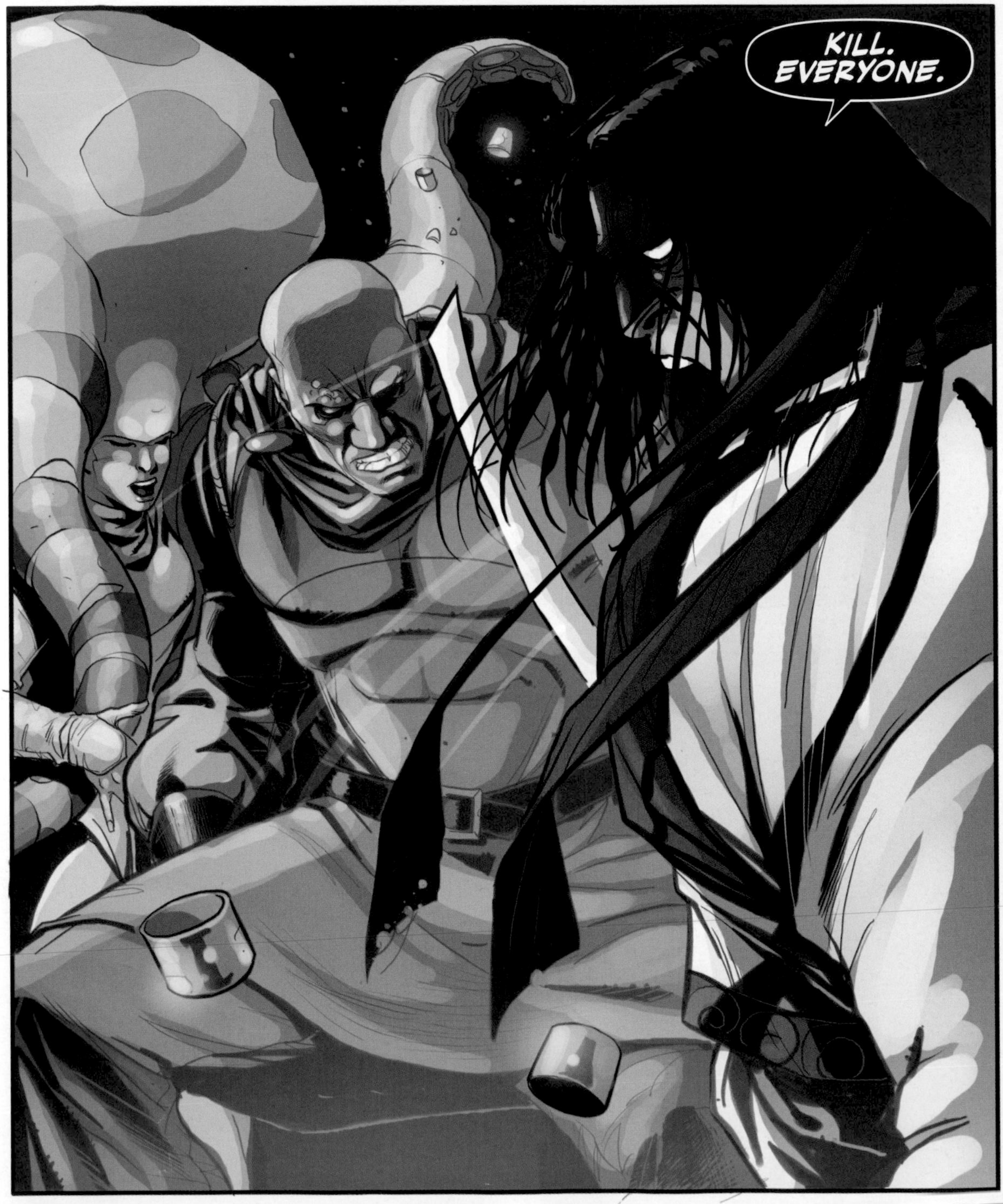
KILL. EVERYONE.

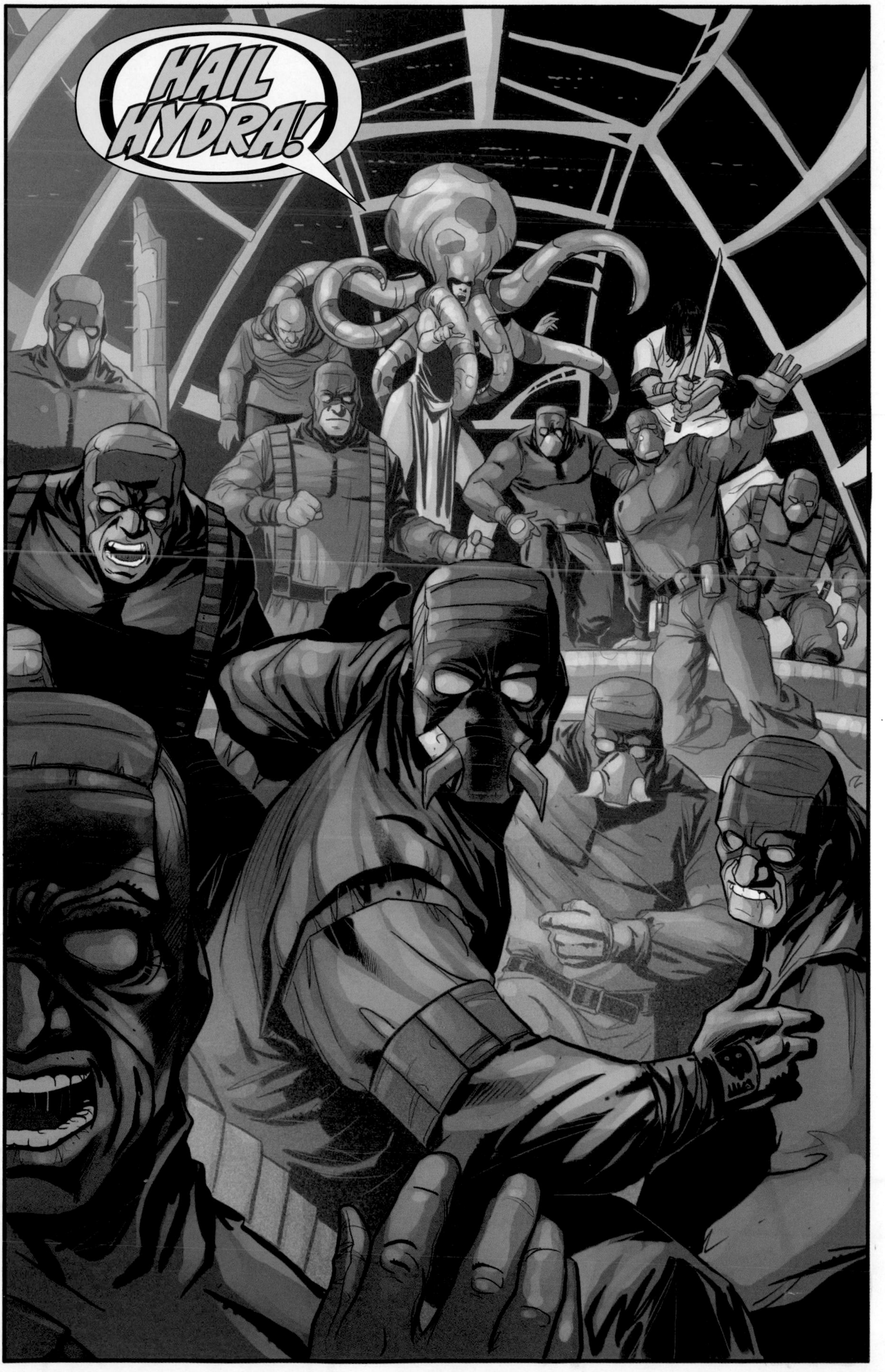
HAIL HYDRA!

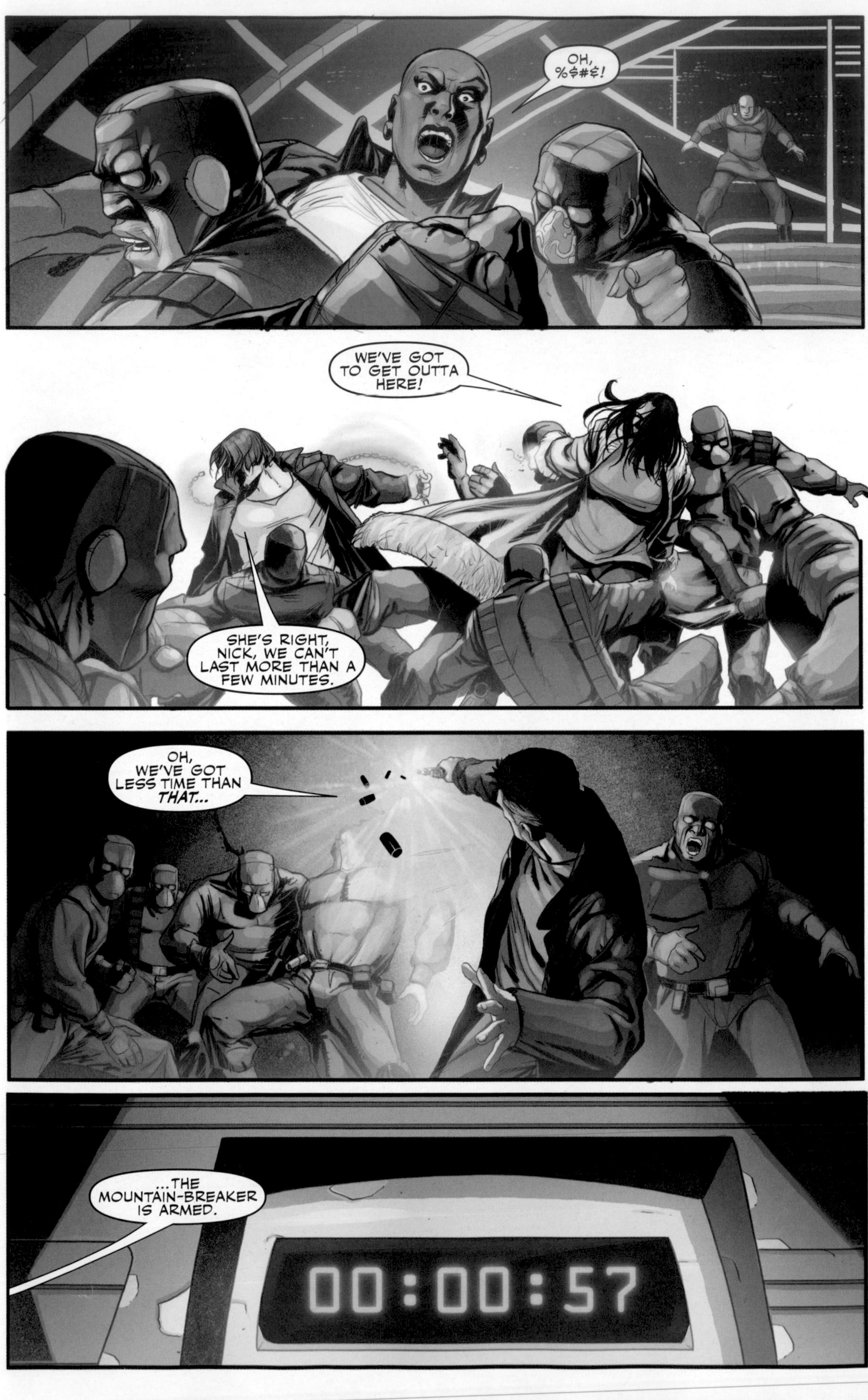
OH, %$#¢!
WE'VE GOT TO GET OUTTA HERE!
SHE'S RIGHT, NICK, WE CAN'T LAST MORE THAN A FEW MINUTES.
OH, WE'VE GOT LESS TIME THAN THAT...
...THE MOUNTAIN-BREAKER IS ARMED.
00:00:57

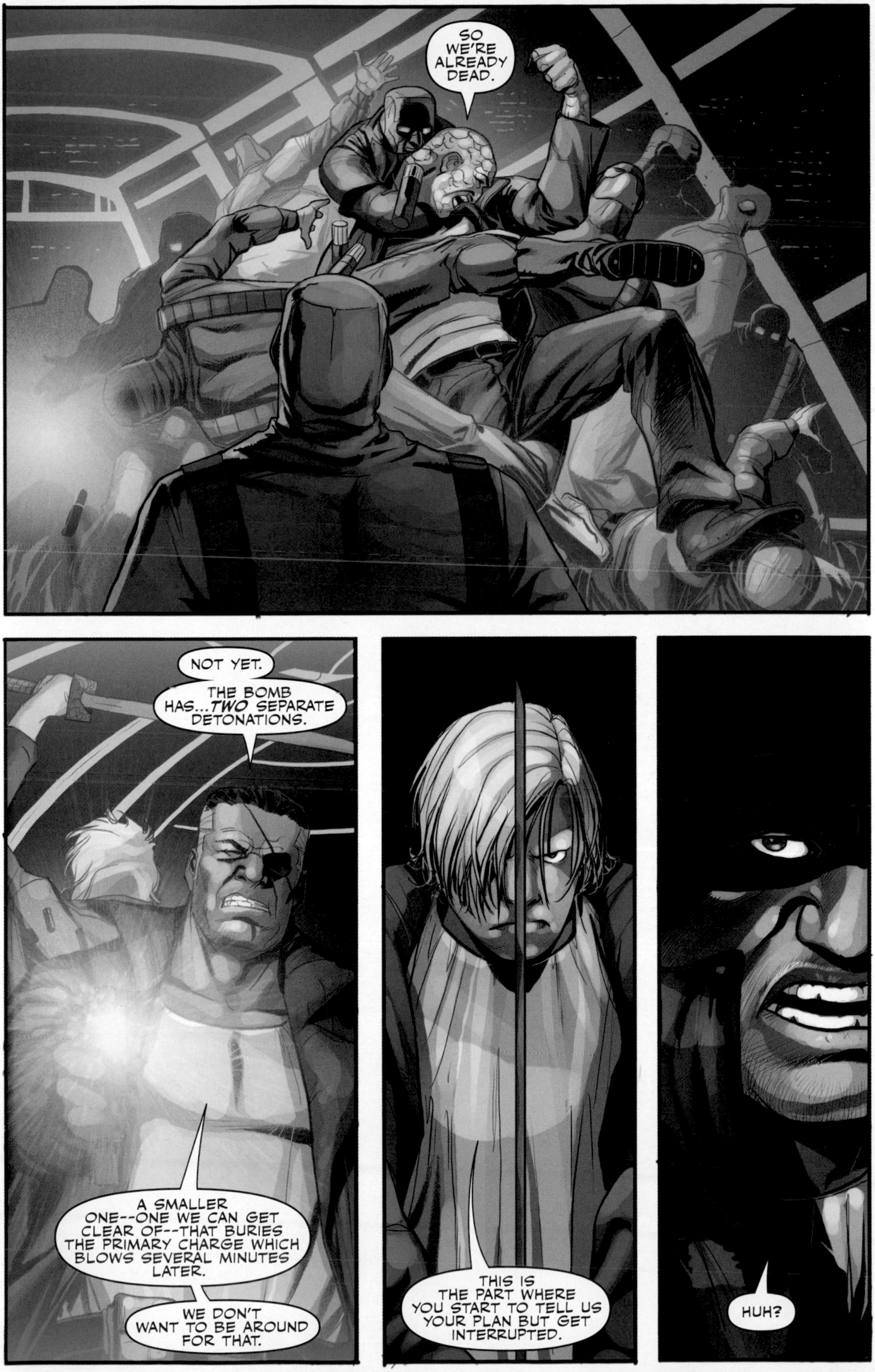
SO WE'RE ALREADY DEAD.
NOT YET.
THE BOMB HAS...TWO SEPARATE DETONATIONS.
A SMALLER ONE--ONE WE CAN GET CLEAR OF--THAT BURIES THE PRIMARY CHARGE WHICH BLOWS SEVERAL MINUTES LATER.
WE DON'T WANT TO BE AROUND FOR THAT.
THIS IS THE PART WHERE YOU START TO TELL US YOUR PLAN BUT GET INTERRUPTED.
HUH?

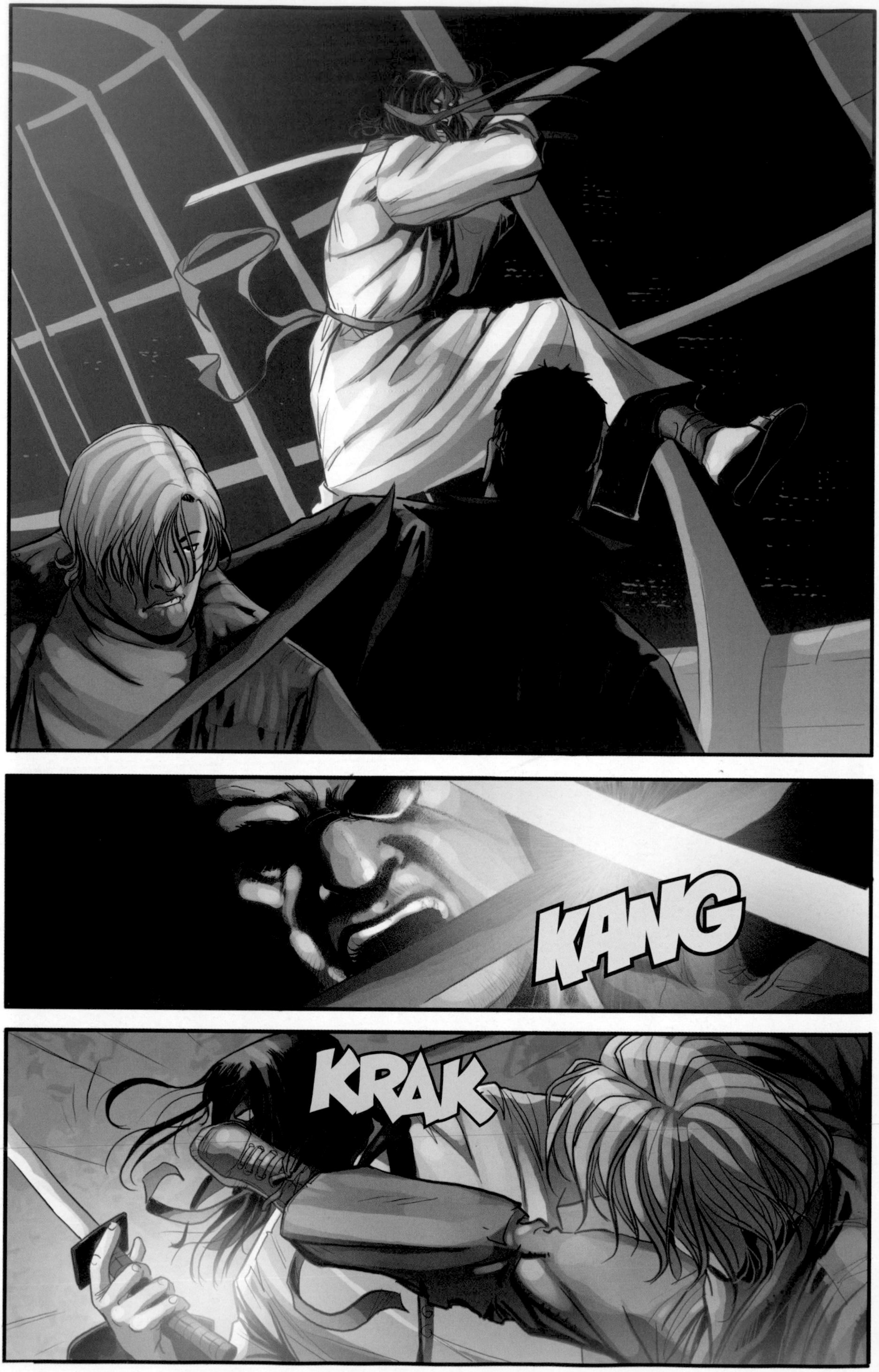
KANG
KRAK

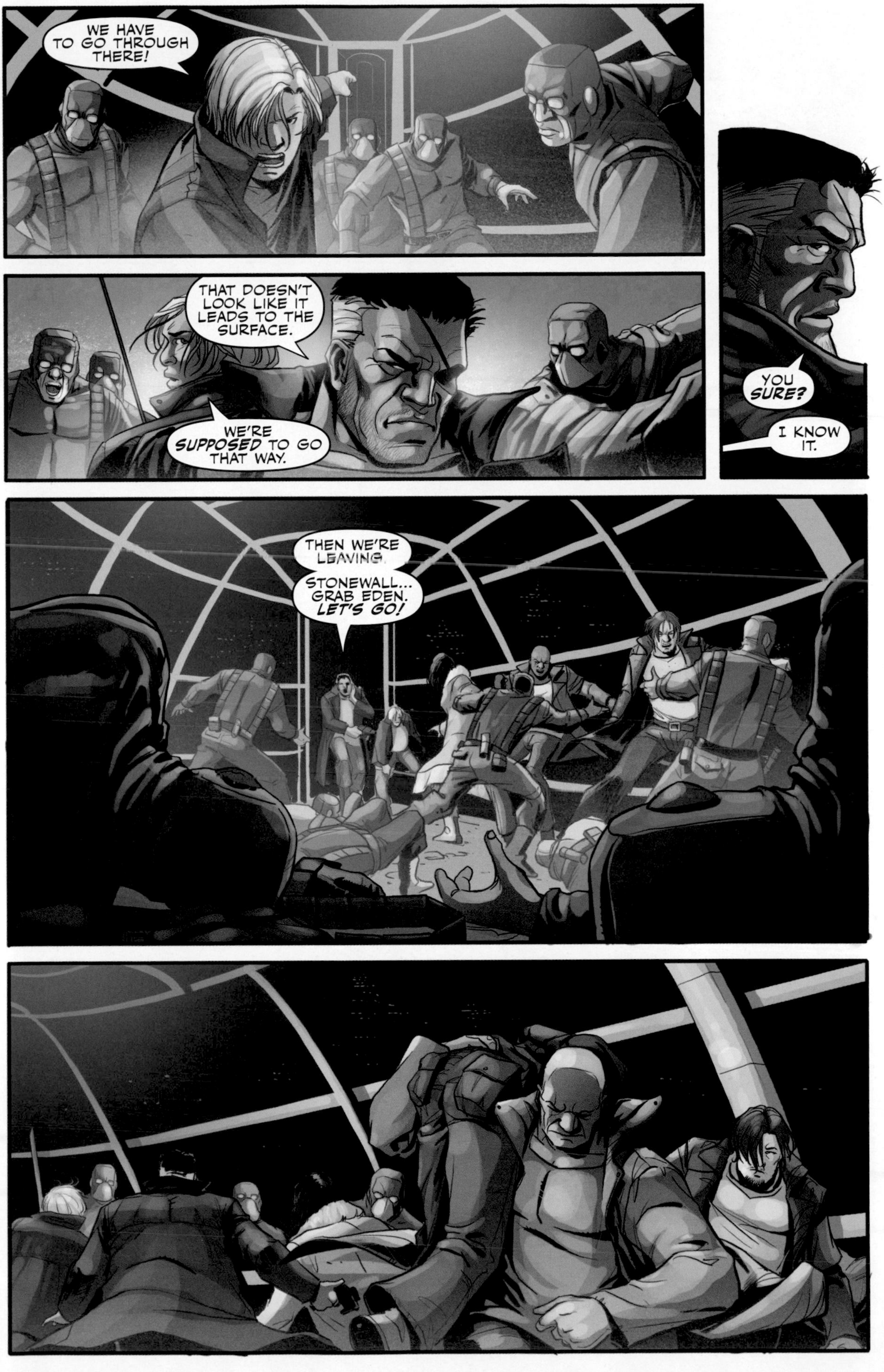
WE HAVE TO GO THROUGH THERE!
THAT DOESN'T LOOK LIKE IT LEADS TO THE SURFACE.
WE'RE *SUPPOSED* TO GO THAT WAY.
YOU *SURE?*
I KNOW IT.
THEN WE'RE LEAVING.
STONEWALL... GRAB EDEN. *LET'S GO!*

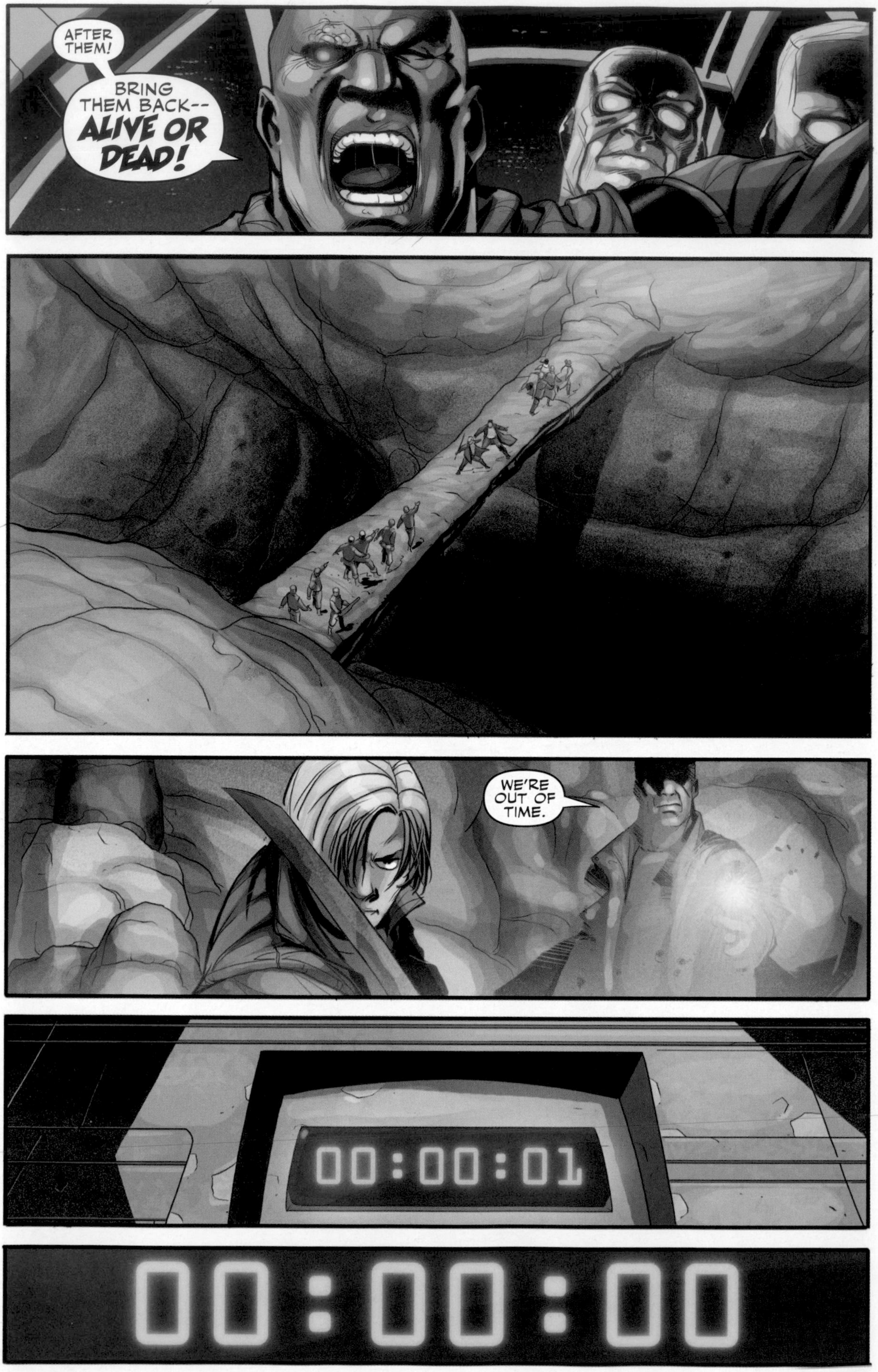
AFTER THEM!
BRING THEM BACK-- ALIVE OR DEAD!
WE'RE OUT OF TIME.
00:00:01
00:00:00

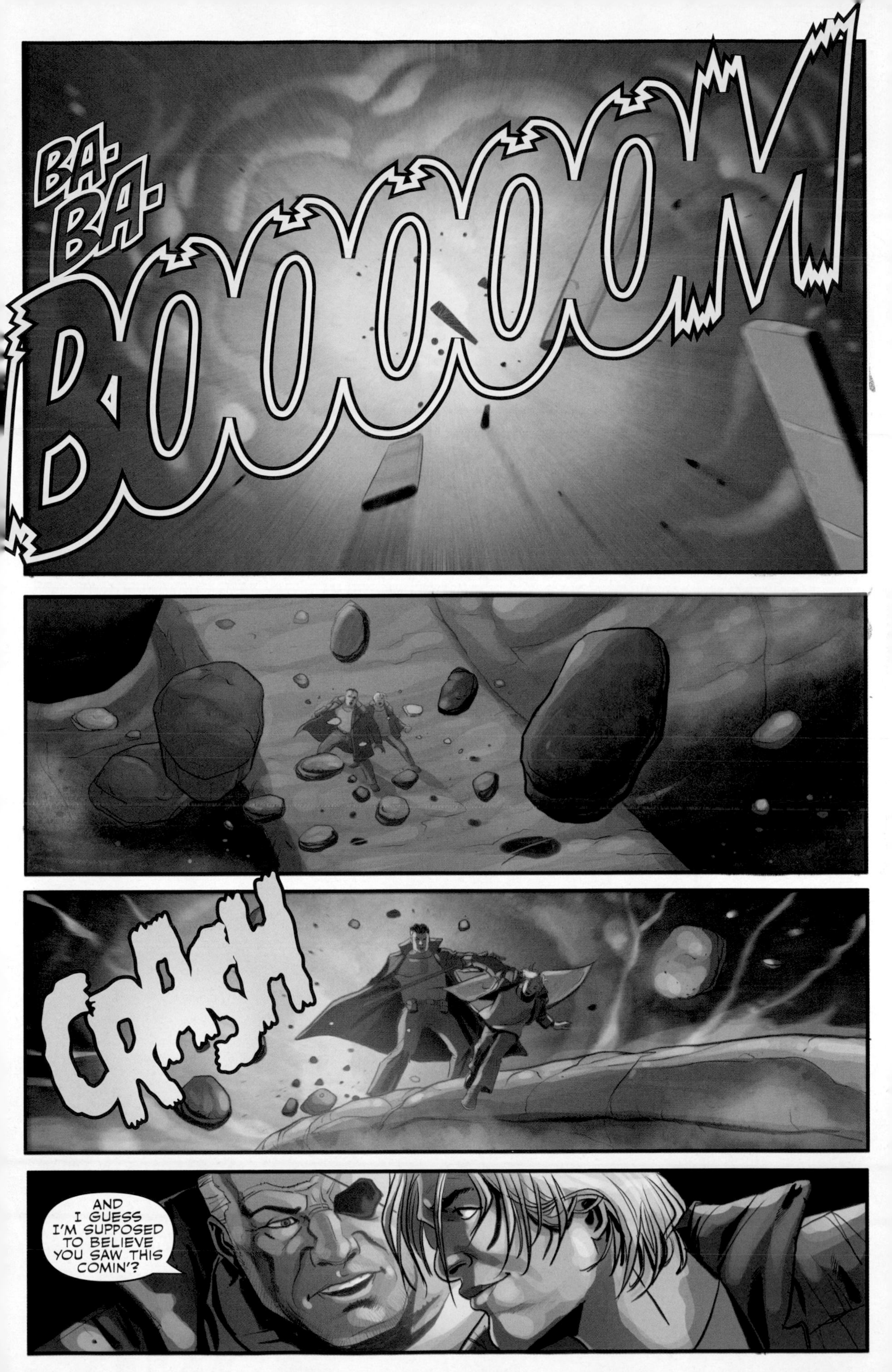
BA-BA-BOOOOOOM
CRASH
AND I GUESS I'M SUPPOSED TO BELIEVE YOU SAW THIS COMIN'?

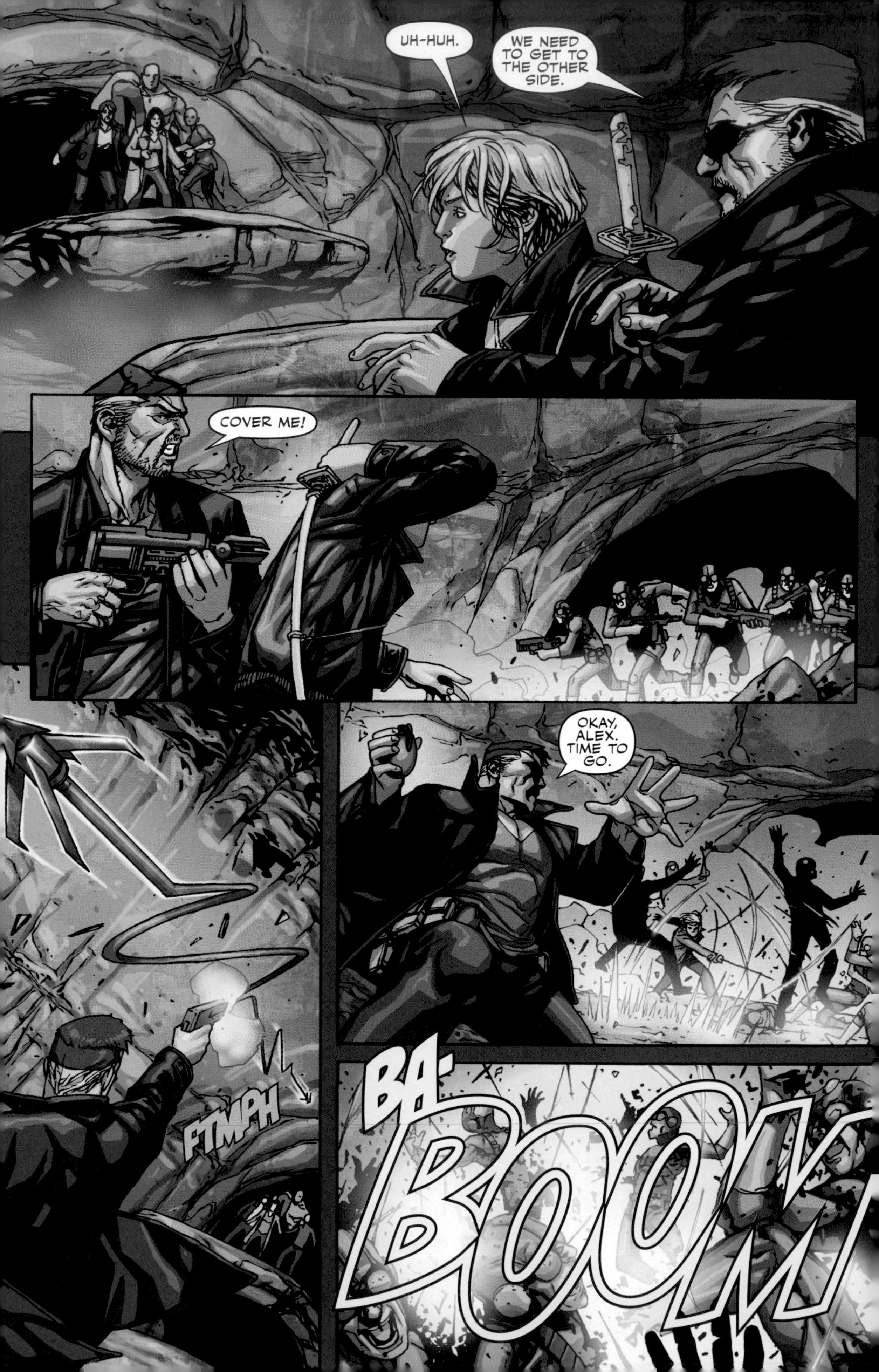
UH-HUH.
WE NEED TO GET TO THE OTHER SIDE.
COVER ME!
PTMPH
OKAY, ALEX. TIME TO GO.
BA-BOOM

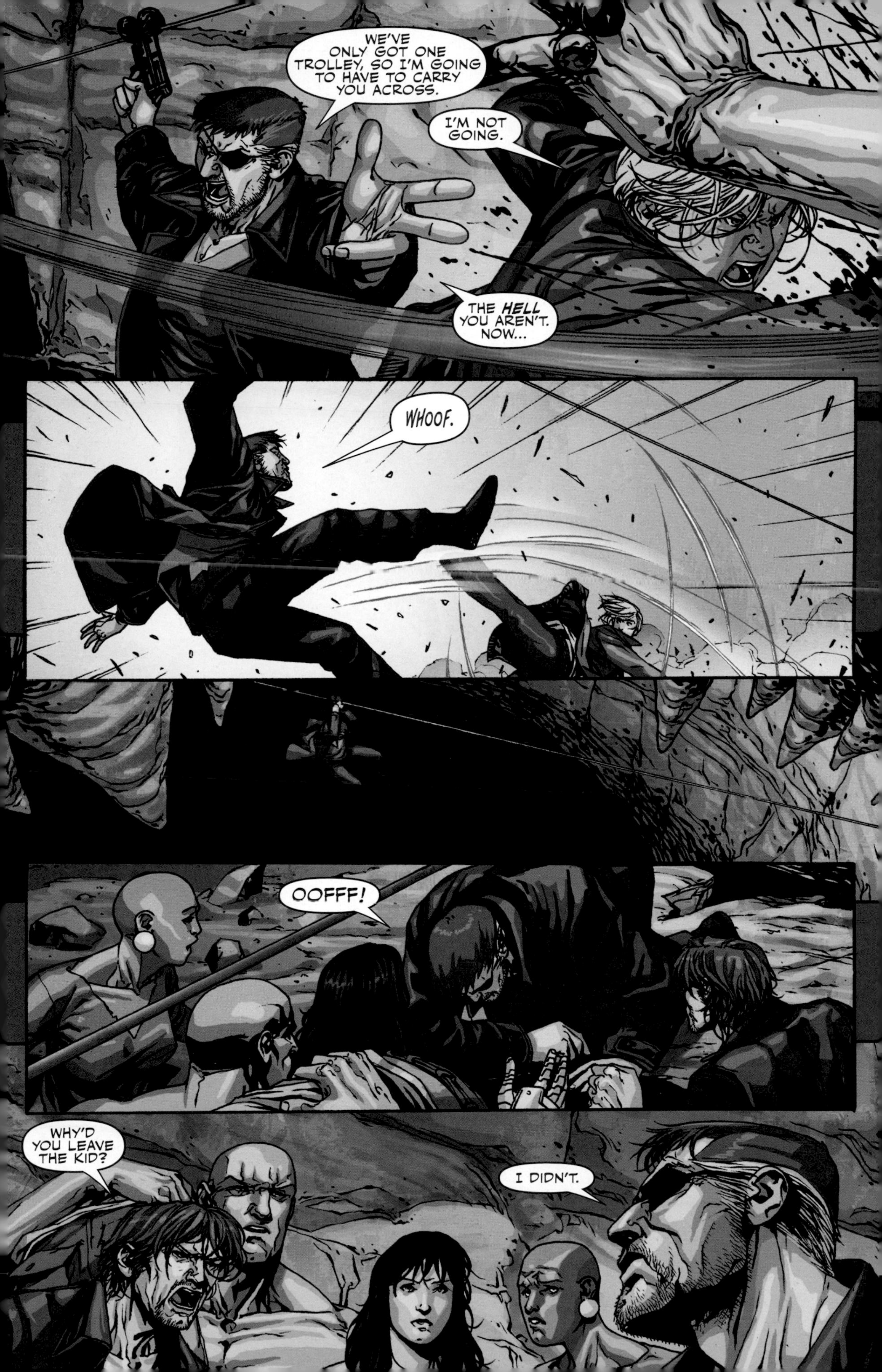
WE'VE ONLY GOT ONE TROLLEY, SO I'M GOING TO HAVE TO CARRY YOU ACROSS.
I'M NOT GOING.
THE *HELL* YOU AREN'T. NOW...
WHOOF.
OOFFF!
WHY'D YOU LEAVE THE KID?
I DIDN'T.

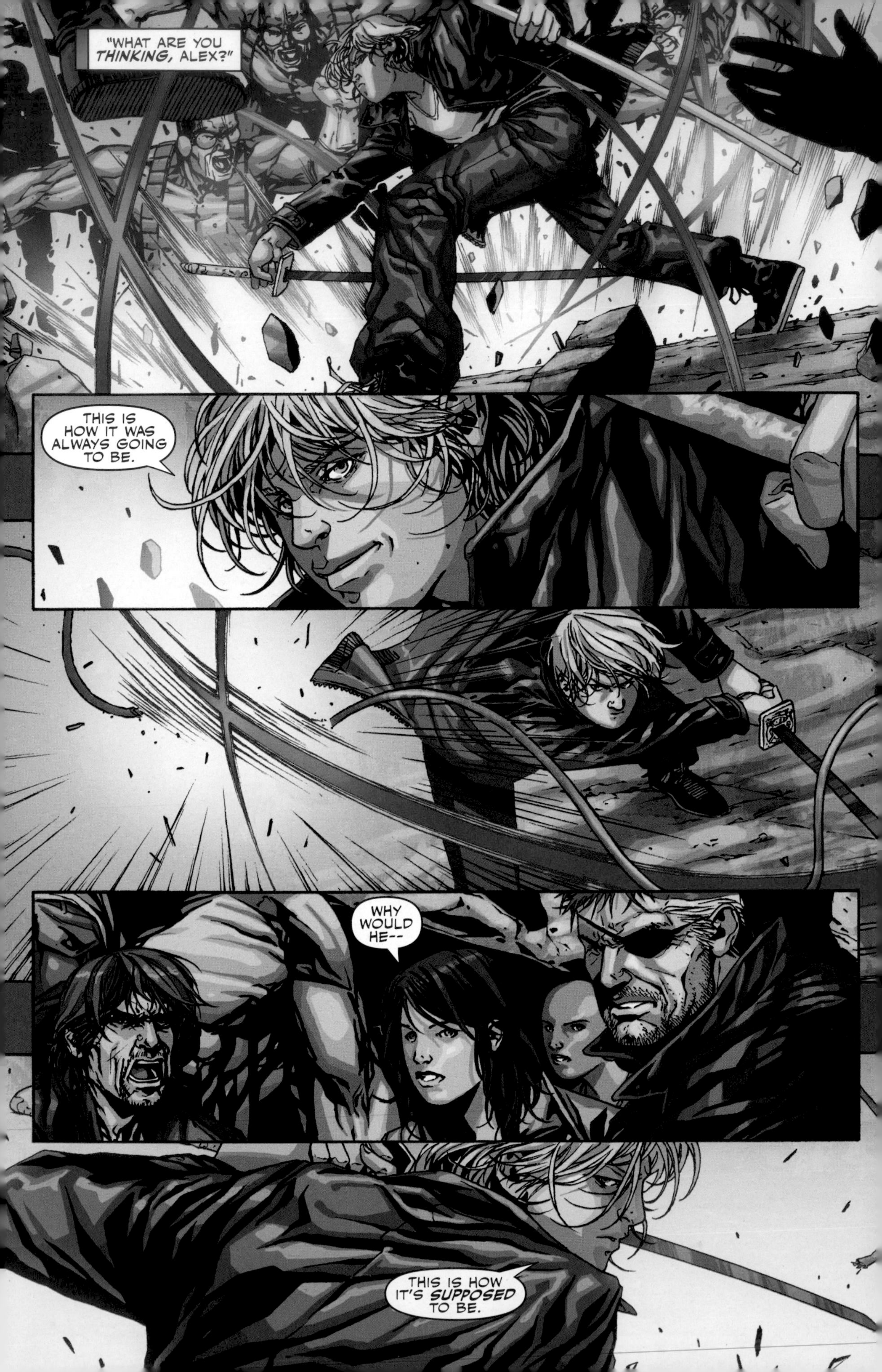
"WHAT ARE YOU THINKING, ALEX?"
THIS IS HOW IT WAS ALWAYS GOING TO BE.
WHY WOULD HE--
THIS IS HOW IT'S SUPPOSED TO BE.

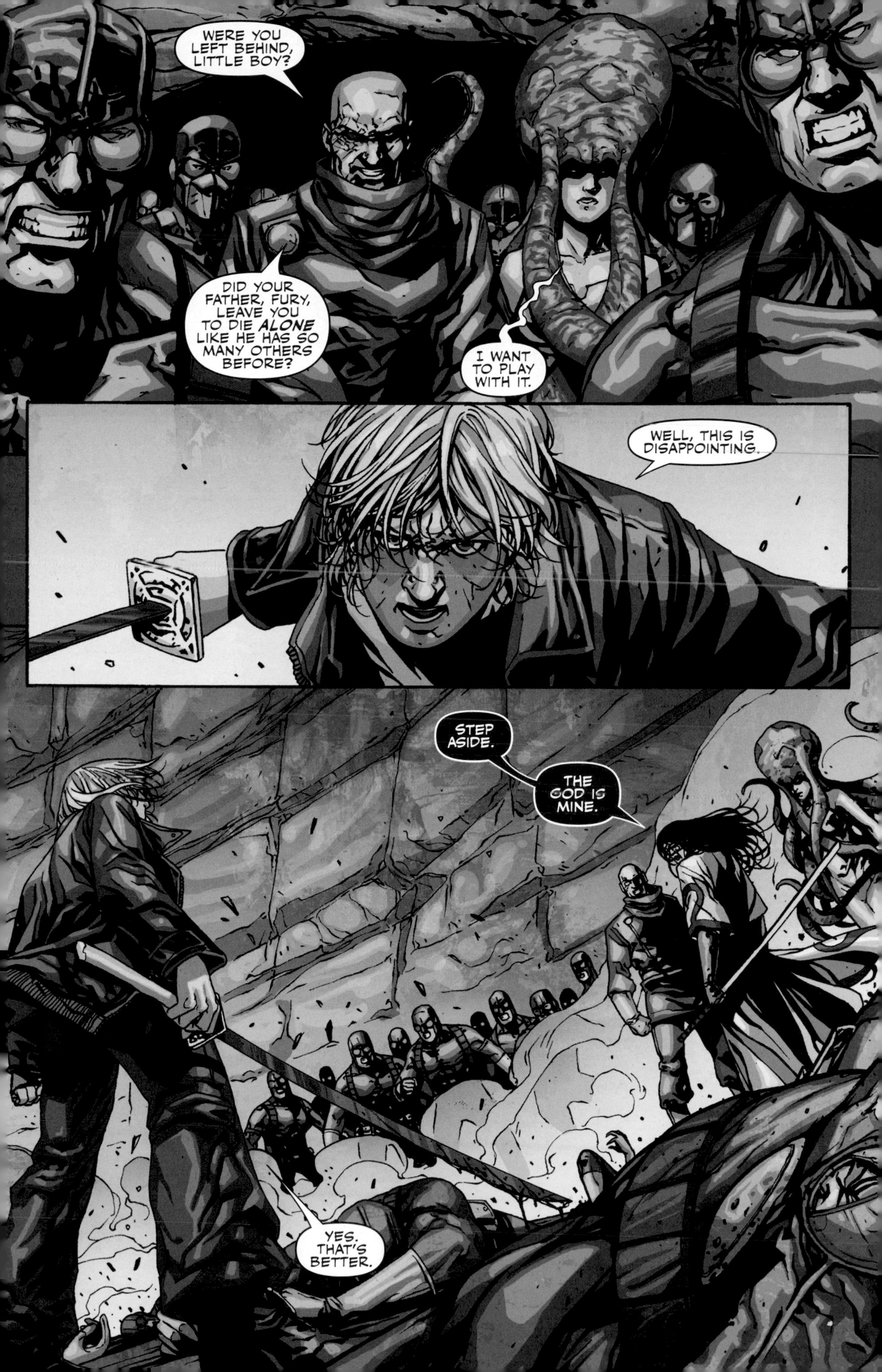

WERE YOU LEFT BEHIND, LITTLE BOY?
DID YOUR FATHER, FURY, LEAVE YOU TO DIE ALONE LIKE HE HAS SO MANY OTHERS BEFORE?
I WANT TO PLAY WITH IT.
WELL, THIS IS DISAPPOINTING.
STEP ASIDE.
THE GOD IS MINE.
YES. THAT'S BETTER.

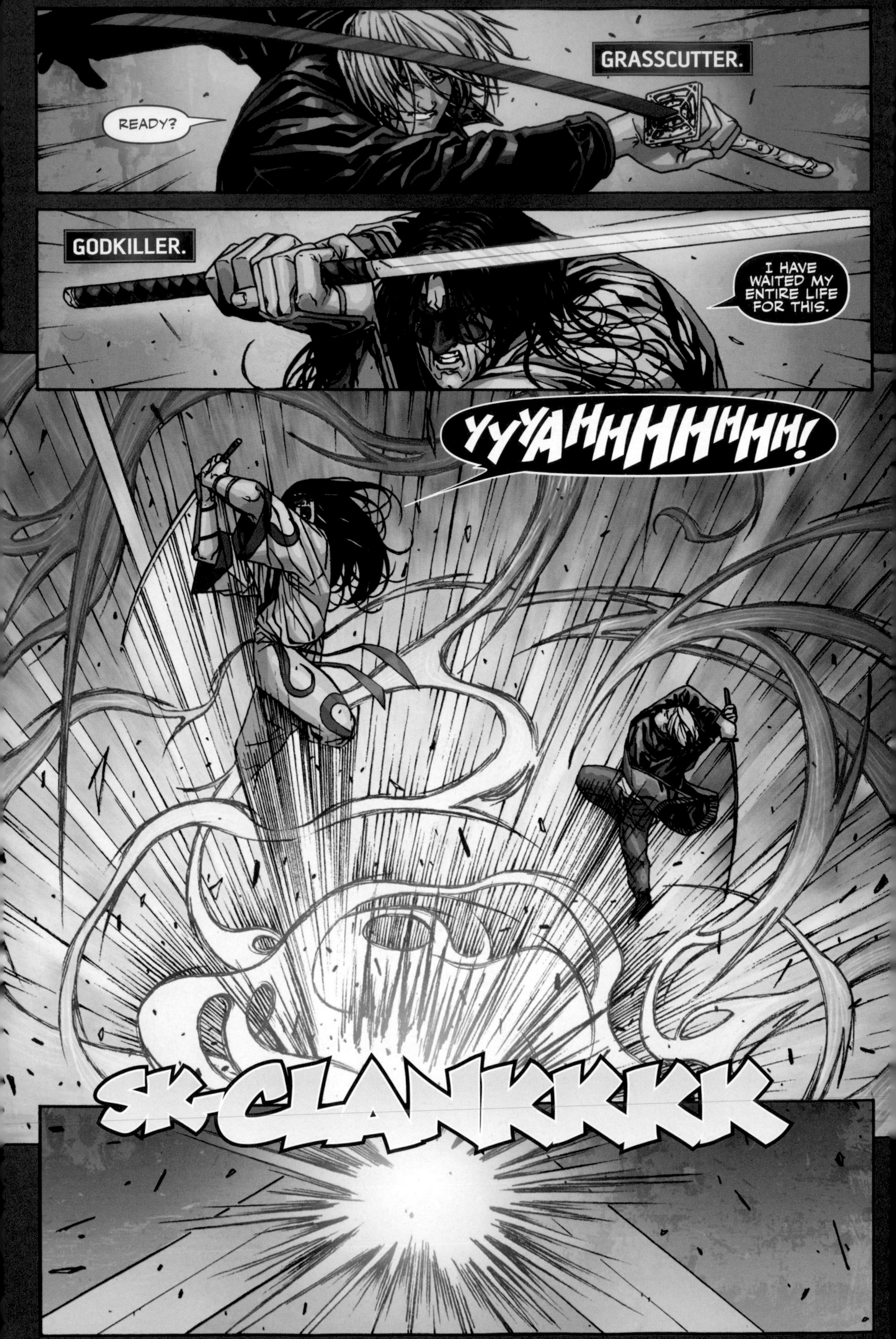
GRASSCUTTER.
READY?
GODKILLER.
I HAVE WAITED MY ENTIRE LIFE FOR THIS.
YYYAHHHHHHHHH!
SK-CLANKKKK

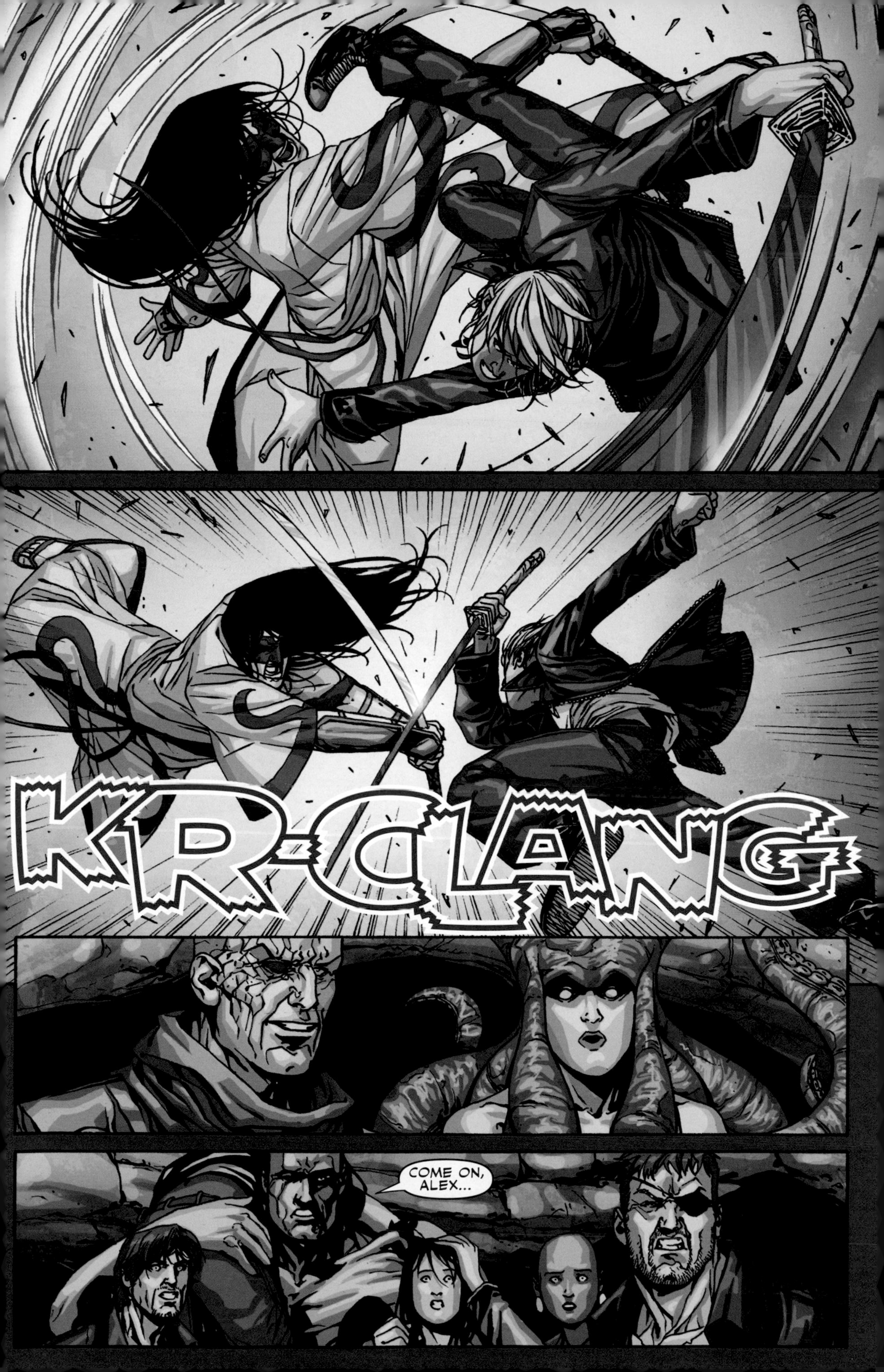
KR-CLANG
COME ON, ALEX...

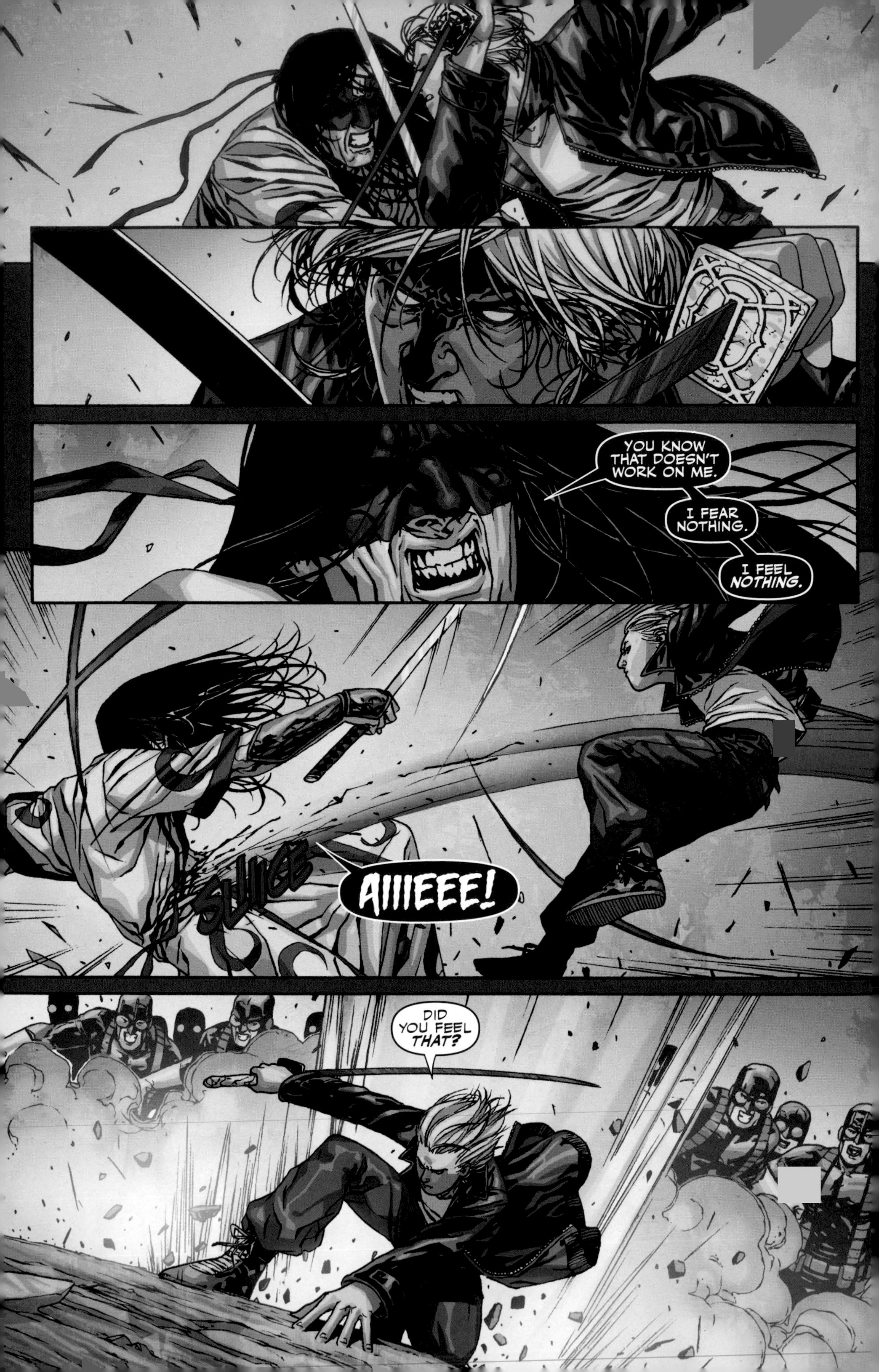
YOU KNOW THAT DOESN'T WORK ON ME.
I FEAR NOTHING.
I FEEL *NOTHING.*
SLIICE
AIIIEEE!
DID YOU FEEL *THAT?*

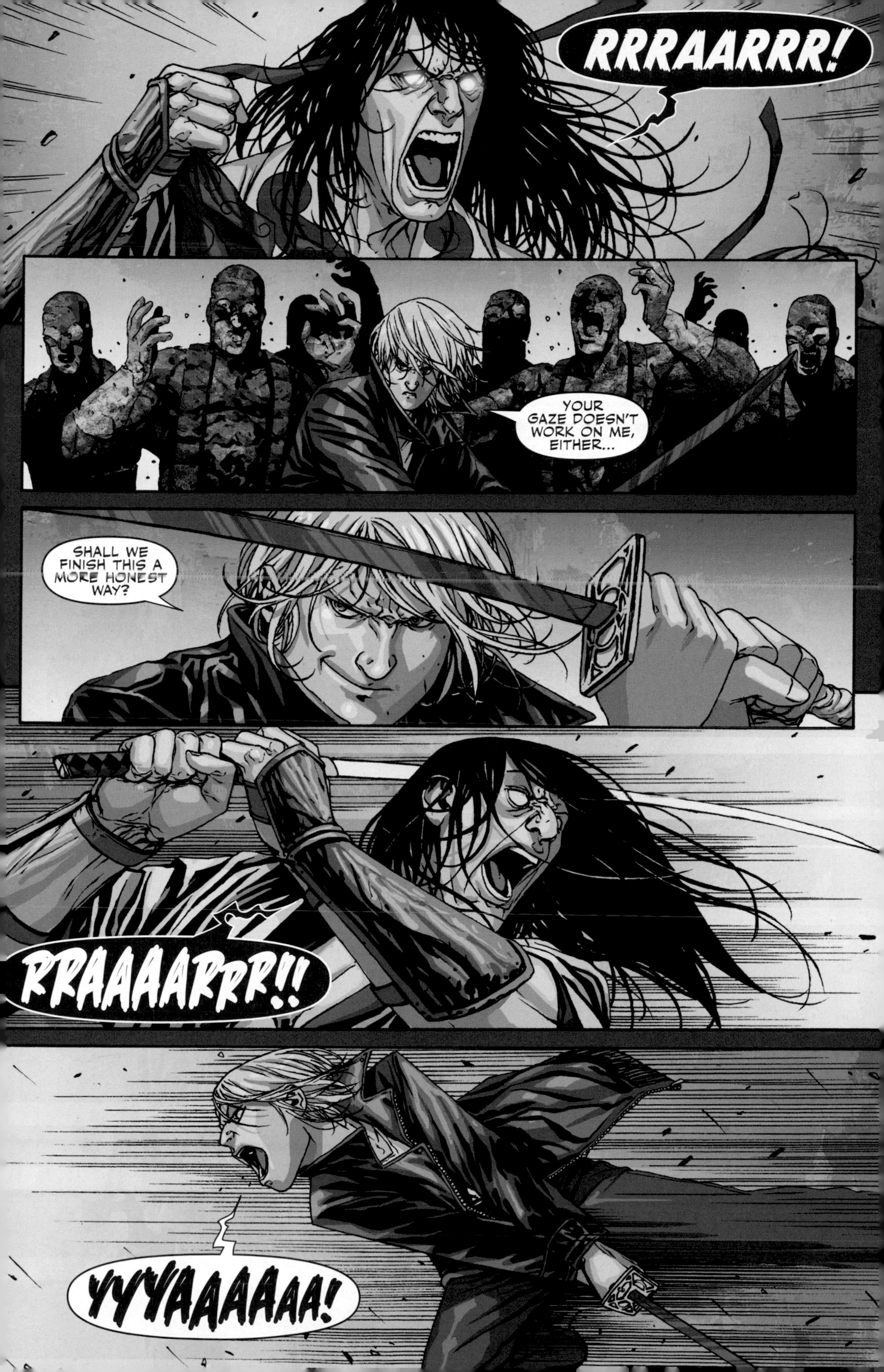
RRRAARRR!
YOUR GAZE DOESN'T WORK ON ME, EITHER...
SHALL WE FINISH THIS A MORE HONEST WAY?
RRAAAARRR!!
YYYAAAAAA!

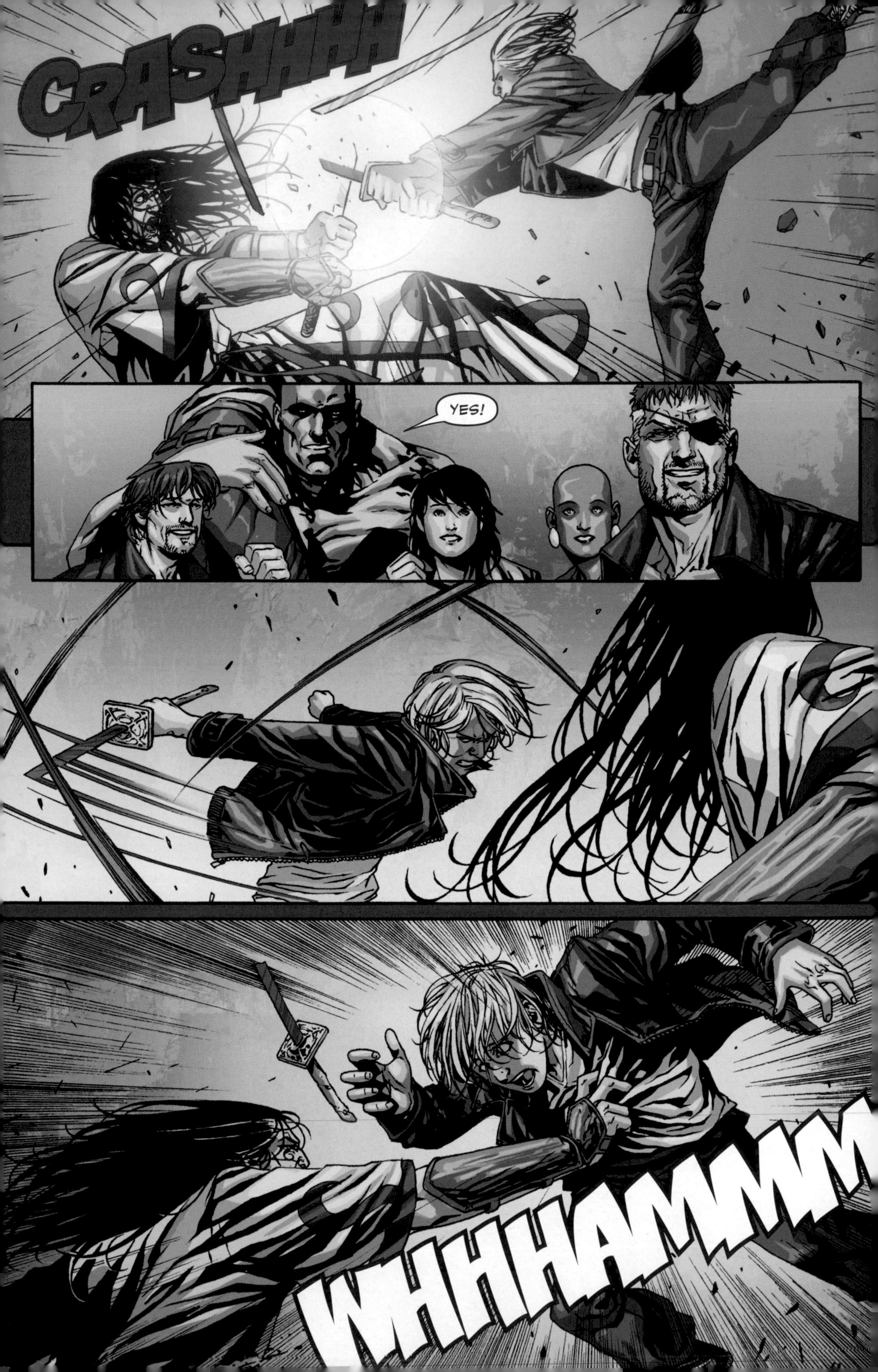

CRASHHHH
YES!
WHHHAMMM

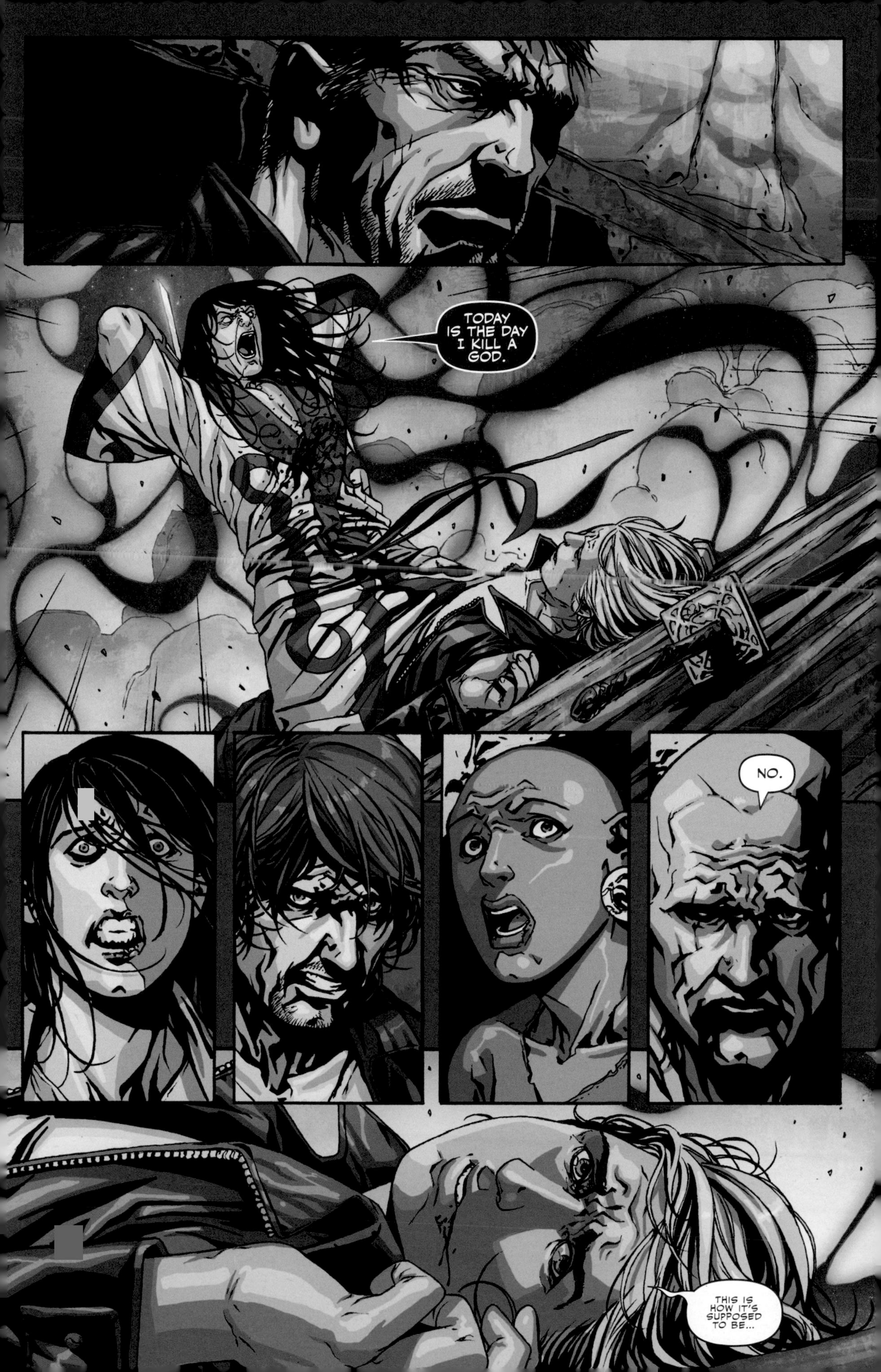
TODAY IS THE DAY I KILL A GOD.
NO.
THIS IS HOW IT'S SUPPOSED TO BE...

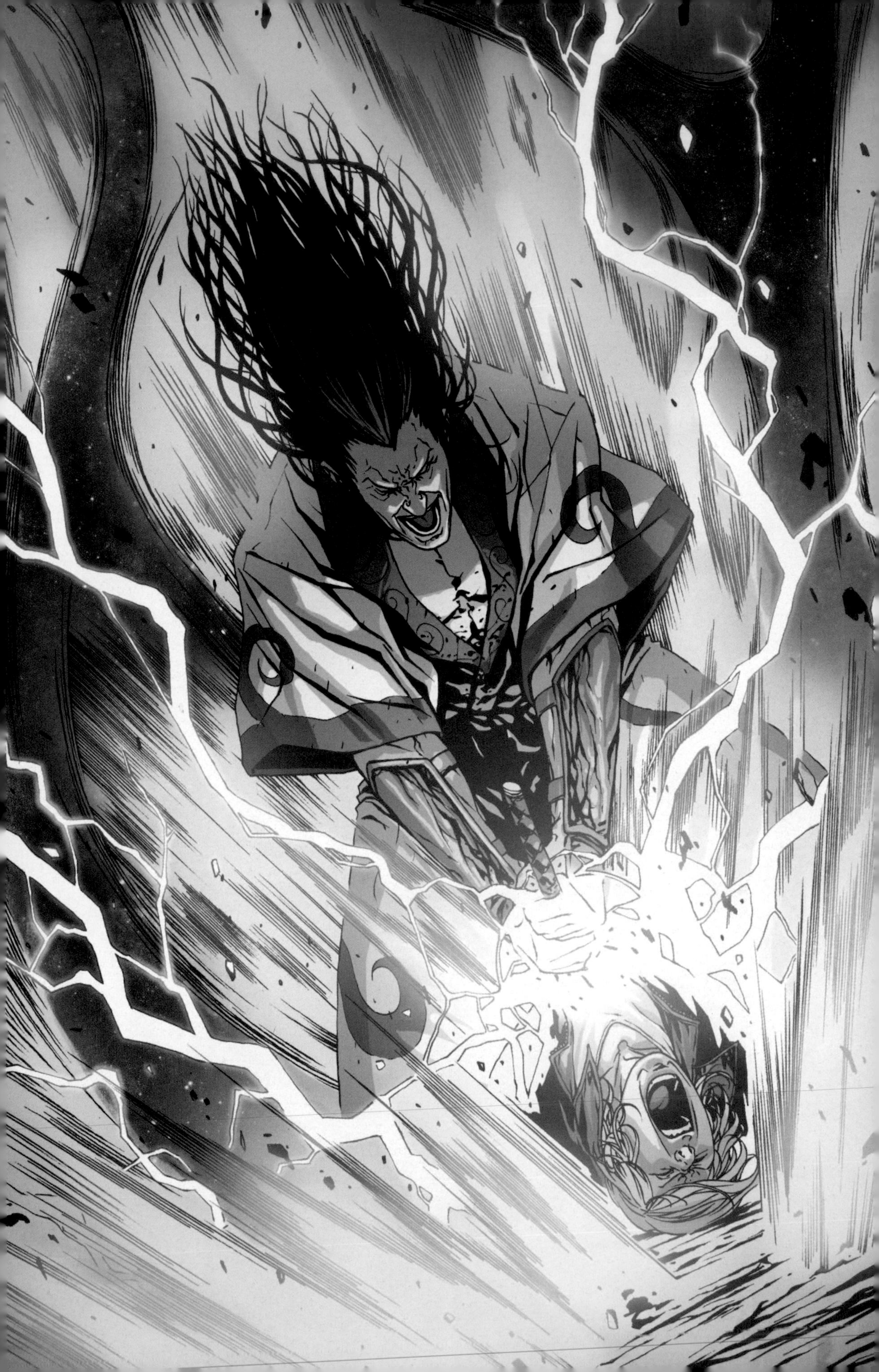

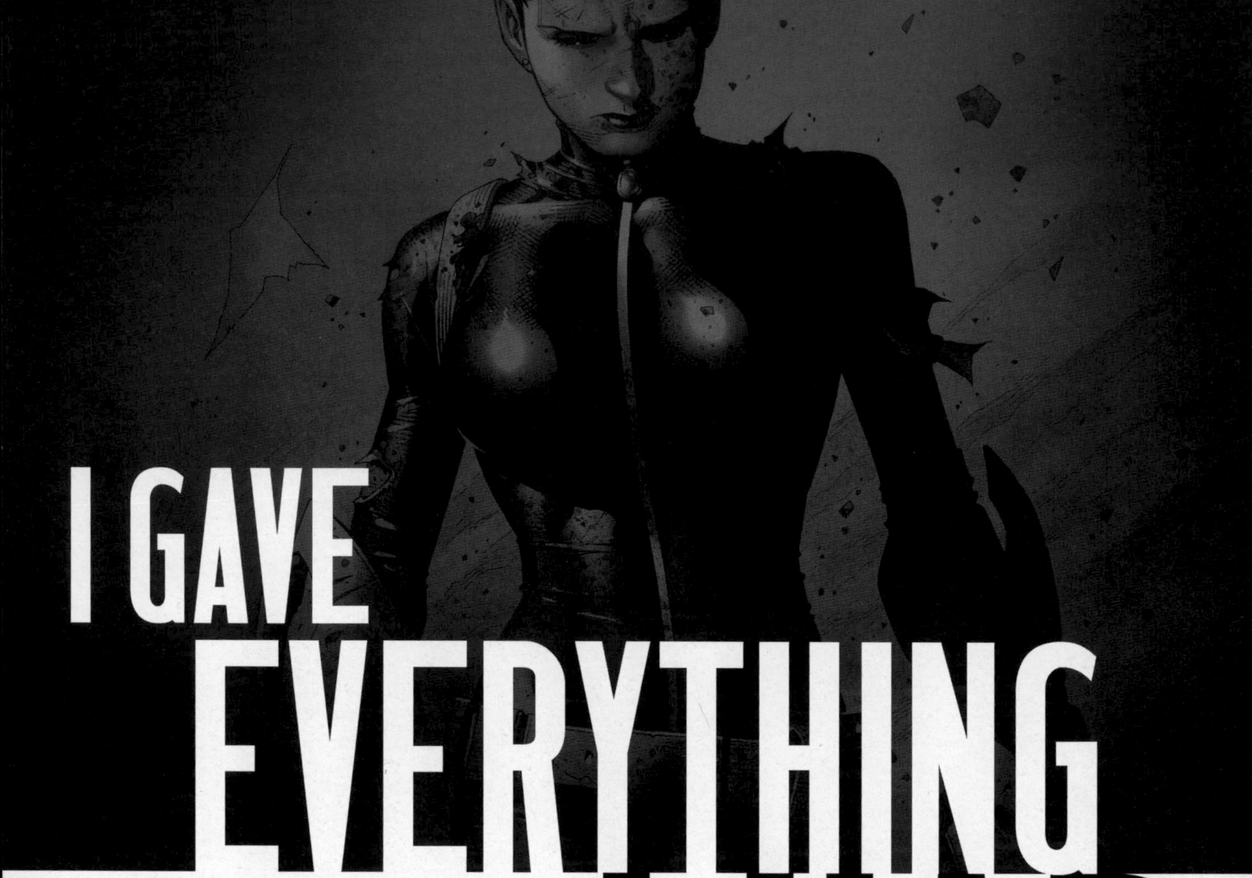

# I GAVE
# EVERYTHING
# I HAD

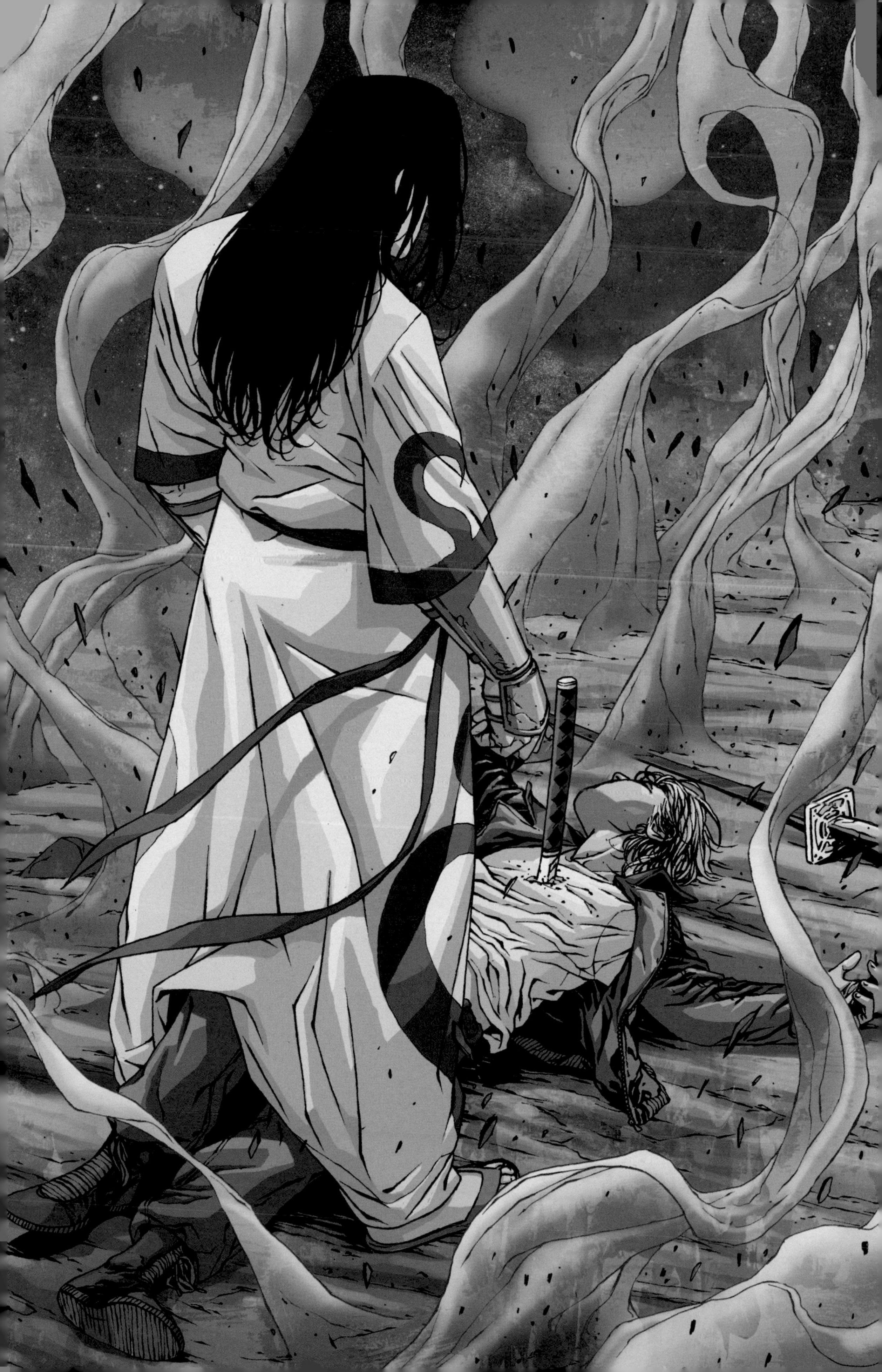

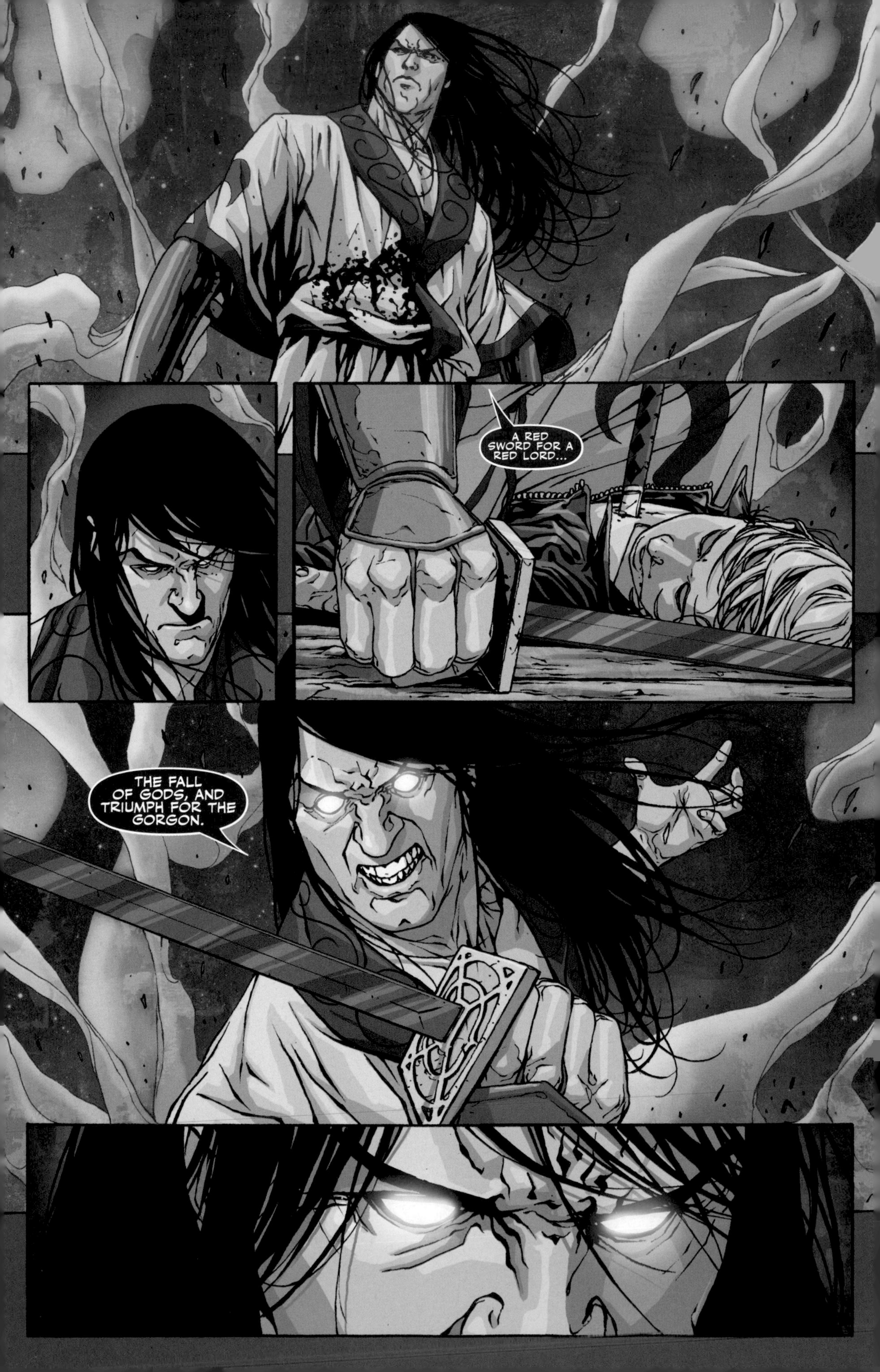
A RED SWORD FOR A RED LORD...
THE FALL OF GODS, AND TRIUMPH FOR THE GORGON.

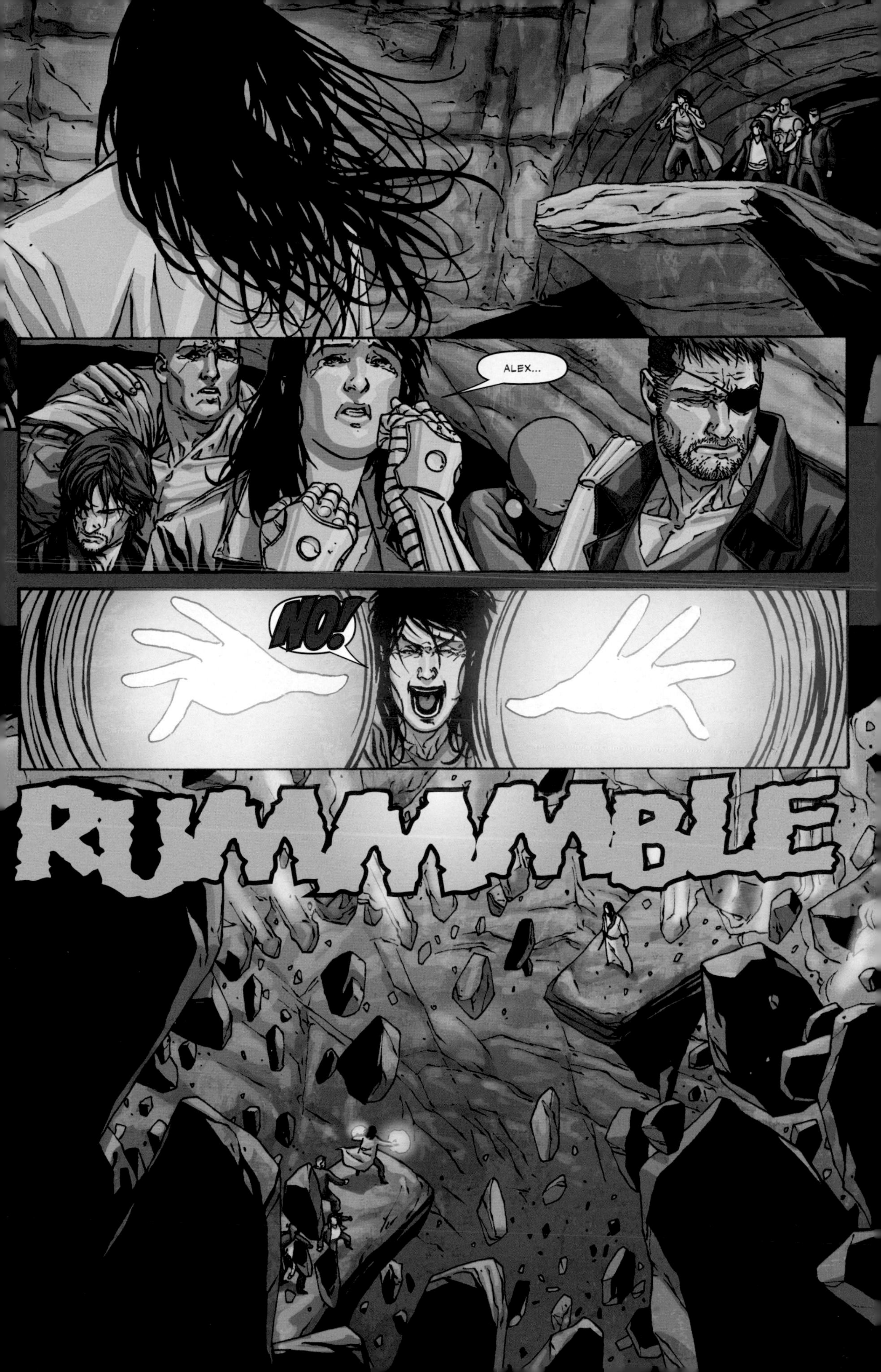
ALEX...
NO!
RUMMMBLE

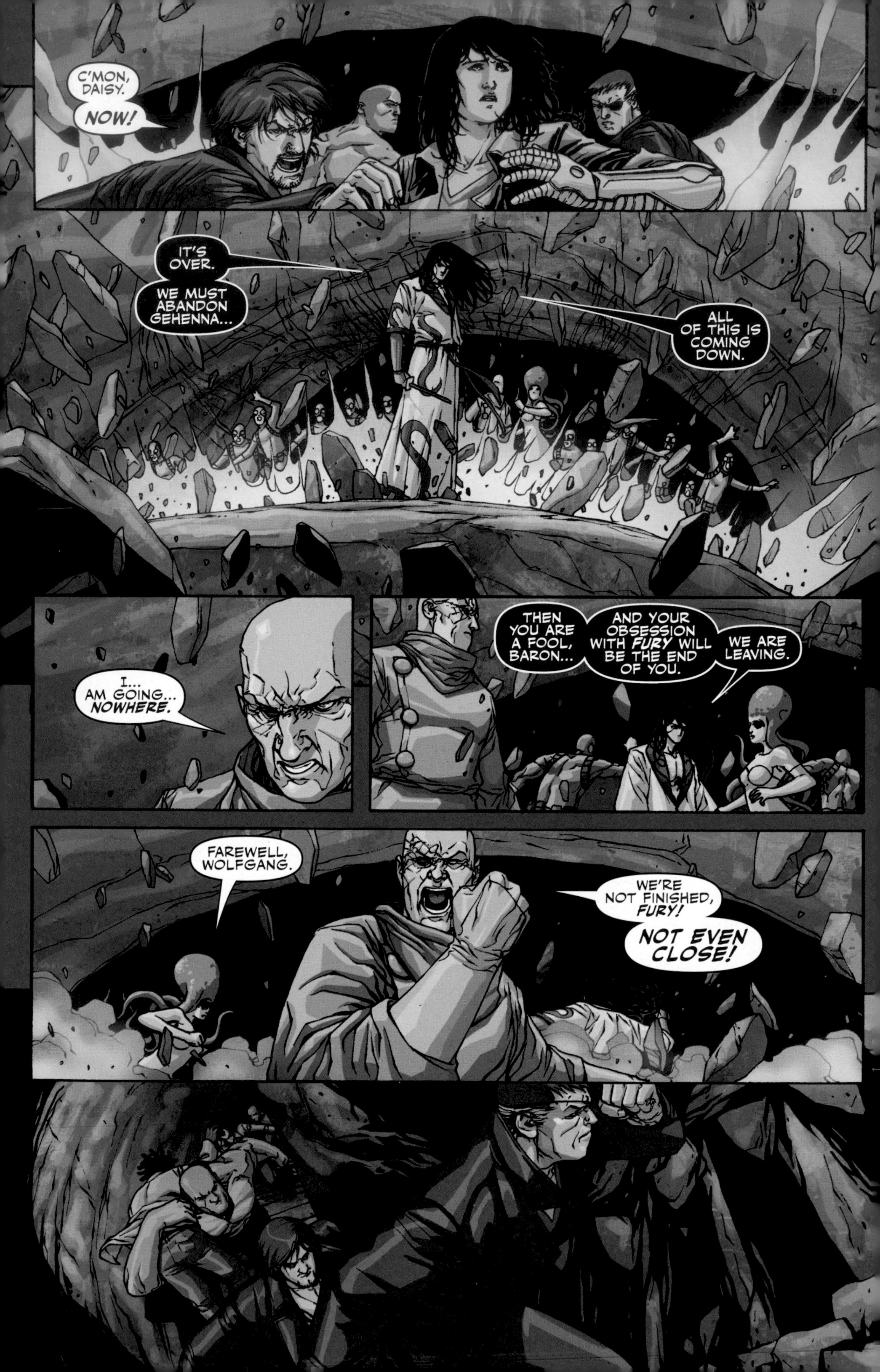
C'MON, DAISY.
NOW!
IT'S OVER.
WE MUST ABANDON GEHENNA...
ALL OF THIS IS COMING DOWN.
I... AM GOING... NOWHERE.
THEN YOU ARE A FOOL, BARON...
AND YOUR OBSESSION WITH FURY WILL BE THE END OF YOU.
WE ARE LEAVING.
FAREWELL, WOLFGANG.
WE'RE NOT FINISHED, FURY!
NOT EVEN CLOSE!

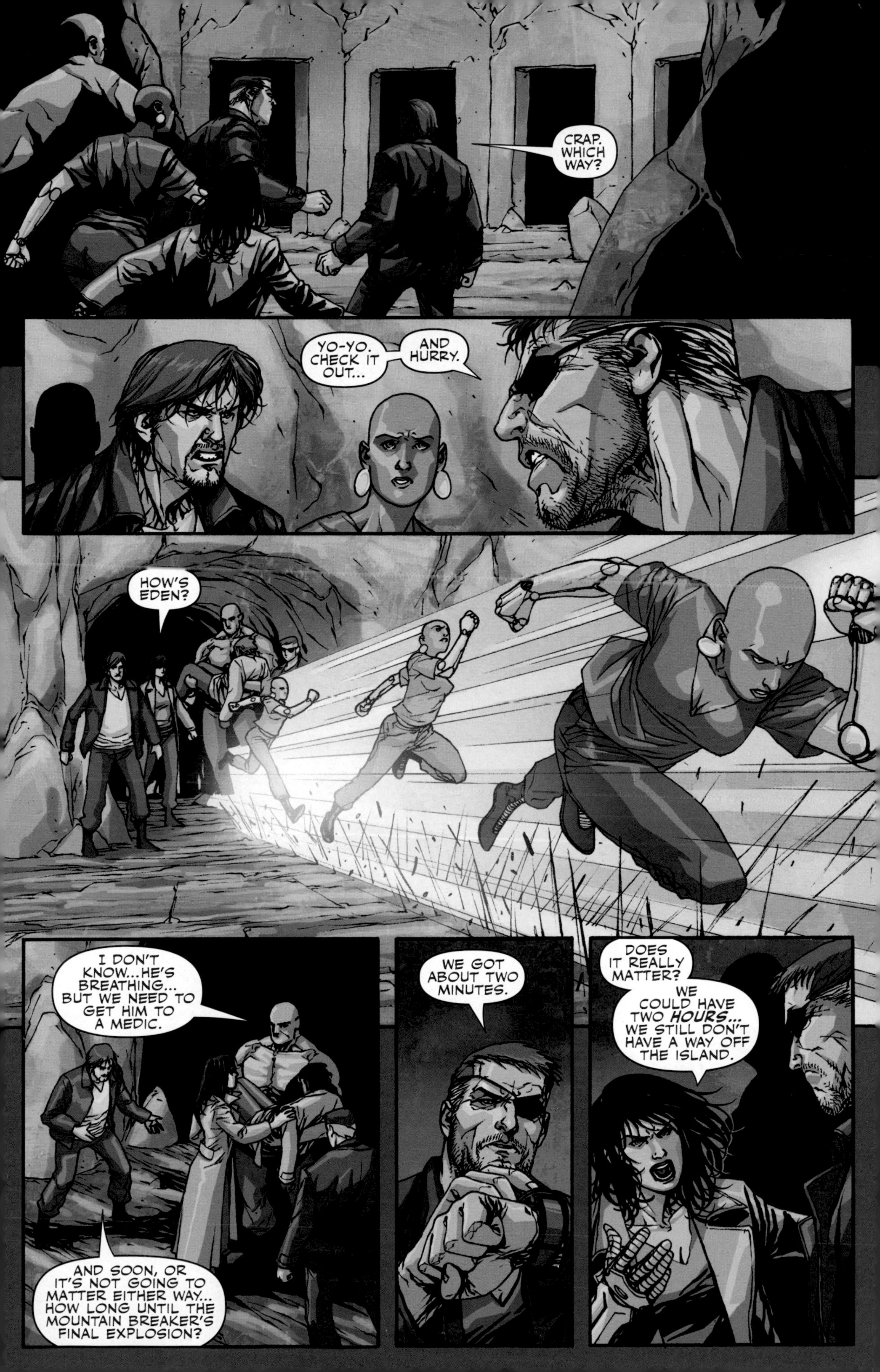
CRAP. WHICH WAY?
YO-YO. CHECK IT OUT...
AND HURRY.
HOW'S EDEN?
I DON'T KNOW...HE'S BREATHING... BUT WE NEED TO GET HIM TO A MEDIC.
AND SOON, OR IT'S NOT GOING TO MATTER EITHER WAY... HOW LONG UNTIL THE MOUNTAIN BREAKER'S FINAL EXPLOSION?
WE GOT ABOUT TWO MINUTES.
DOES IT REALLY MATTER?
WE COULD HAVE TWO HOURS... WE STILL DON'T HAVE A WAY OFF THE ISLAND.

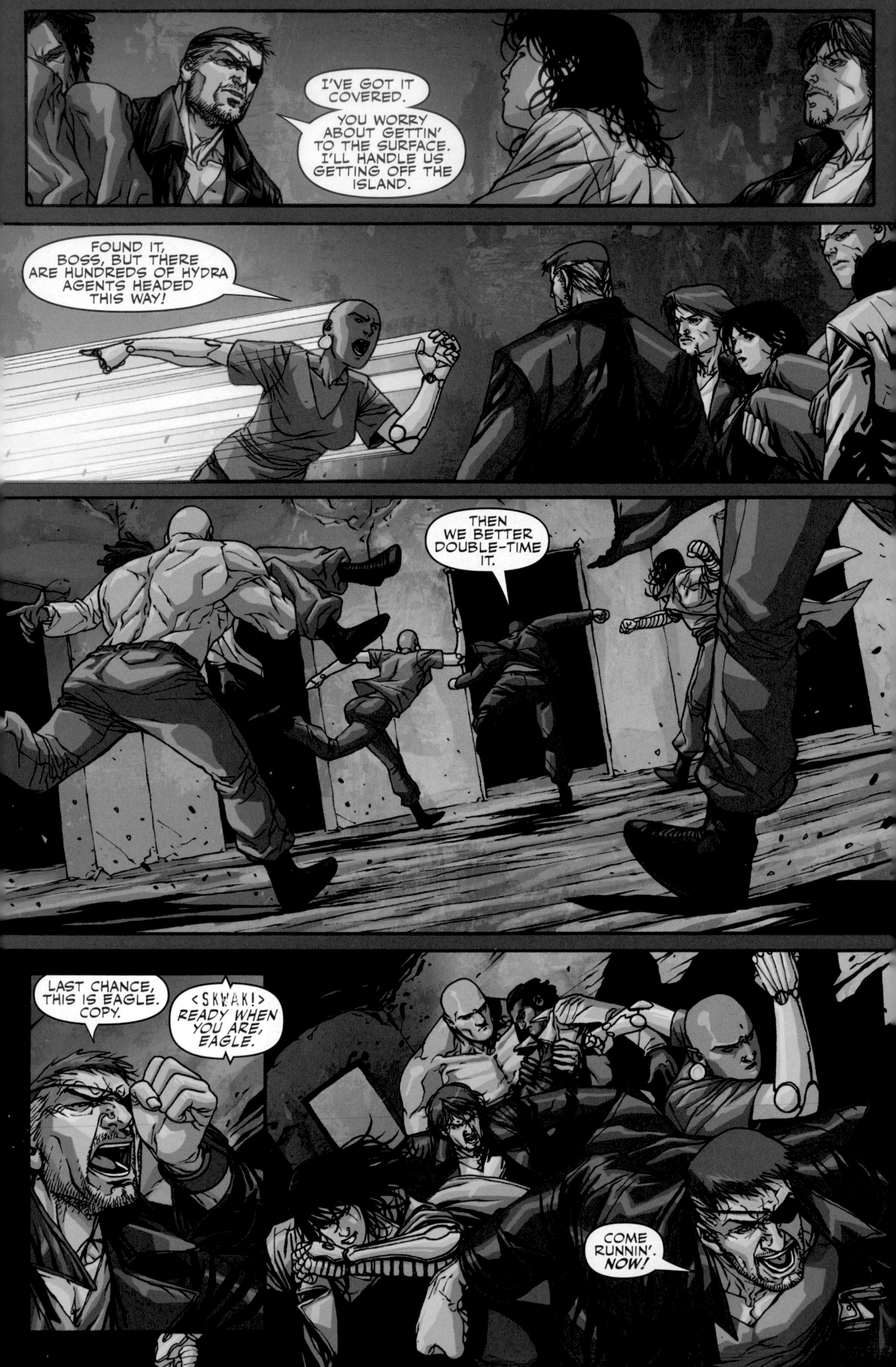
I'VE GOT IT COVERED.
YOU WORRY ABOUT GETTIN' TO THE SURFACE. I'LL HANDLE US GETTING OFF THE ISLAND.
FOUND IT, BOSS, BUT THERE ARE HUNDREDS OF HYDRA AGENTS HEADED THIS WAY!
THEN WE BETTER DOUBLE-TIME IT.
LAST CHANCE, THIS IS EAGLE. COPY.
<SKWAK!> READY WHEN YOU ARE, EAGLE.
COME RUNNIN'. NOW!

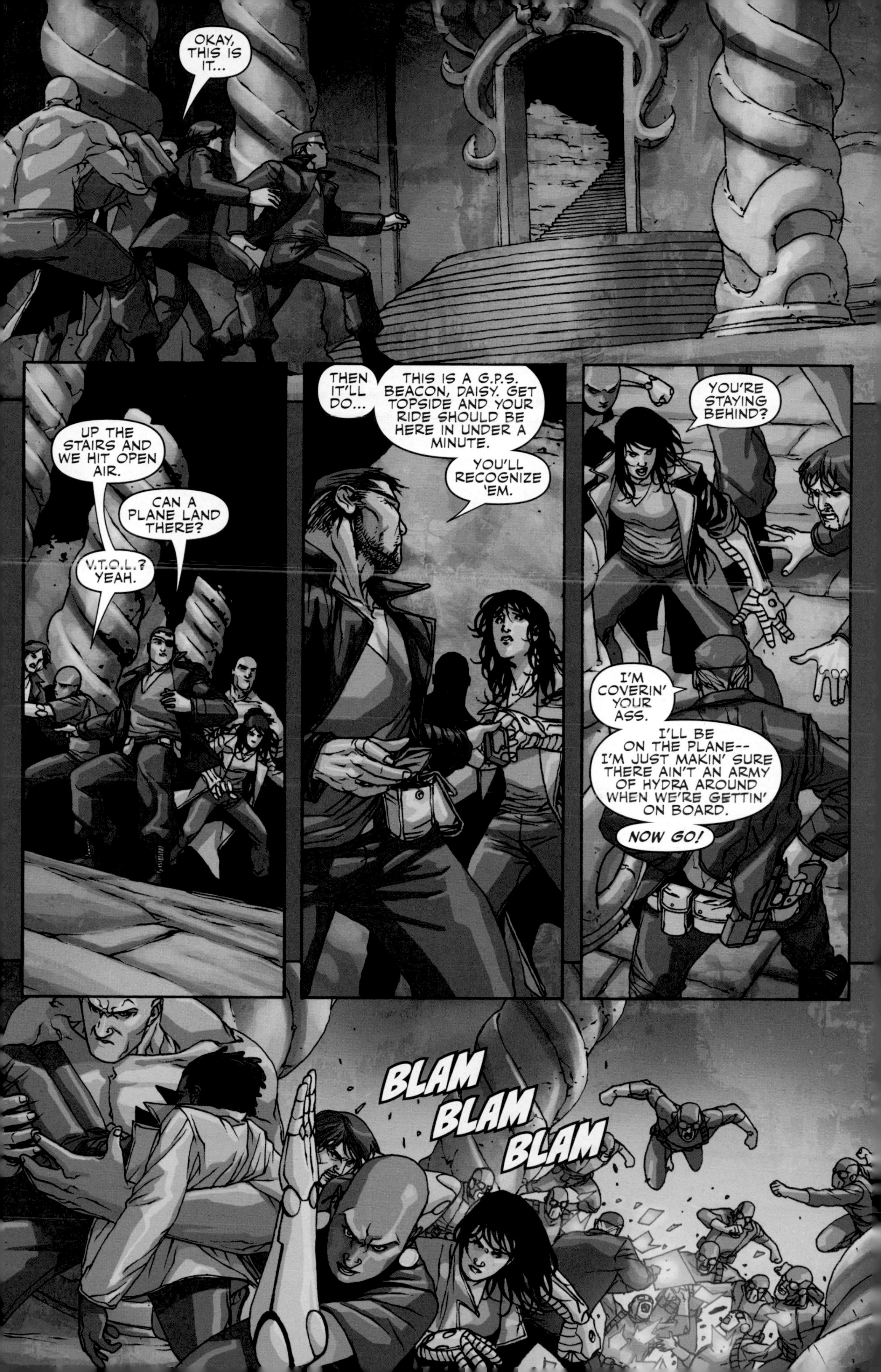
OKAY, THIS IS IT...
UP THE STAIRS AND WE HIT OPEN AIR.
CAN A PLANE LAND THERE?
V.T.O.L.? YEAH.
THEN IT'LL DO...
THIS IS A G.P.S. BEACON, DAISY. GET TOPSIDE AND YOUR RIDE SHOULD BE HERE IN UNDER A MINUTE.
YOU'LL RECOGNIZE 'EM.
YOU'RE STAYING BEHIND?
I'M COVERIN' YOUR ASS.
I'LL BE ON THE PLANE-- I'M JUST MAKIN' SURE THERE AIN'T AN ARMY OF HYDRA AROUND WHEN WE'RE GETTIN' ON BOARD.
NOW GO!
BLAM
BLAM
BLAM

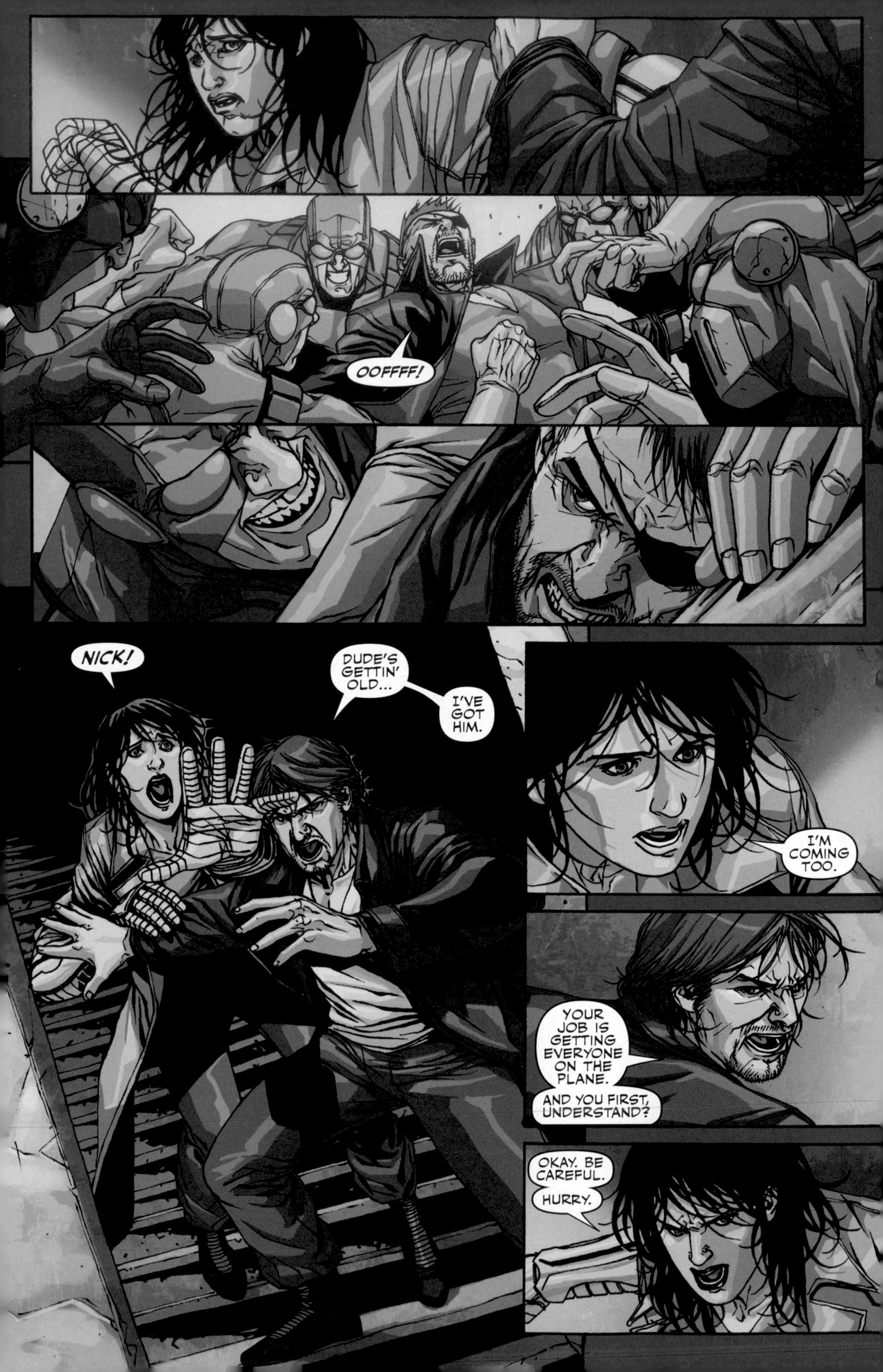
OOFFFF!
NICK!
DUDE'S GETTIN' OLD...
I'VE GOT HIM.
I'M COMING TOO.
YOUR JOB IS GETTING EVERYONE ON THE PLANE.
AND YOU FIRST, UNDERSTAND?
OKAY. BE CAREFUL.
HURRY.

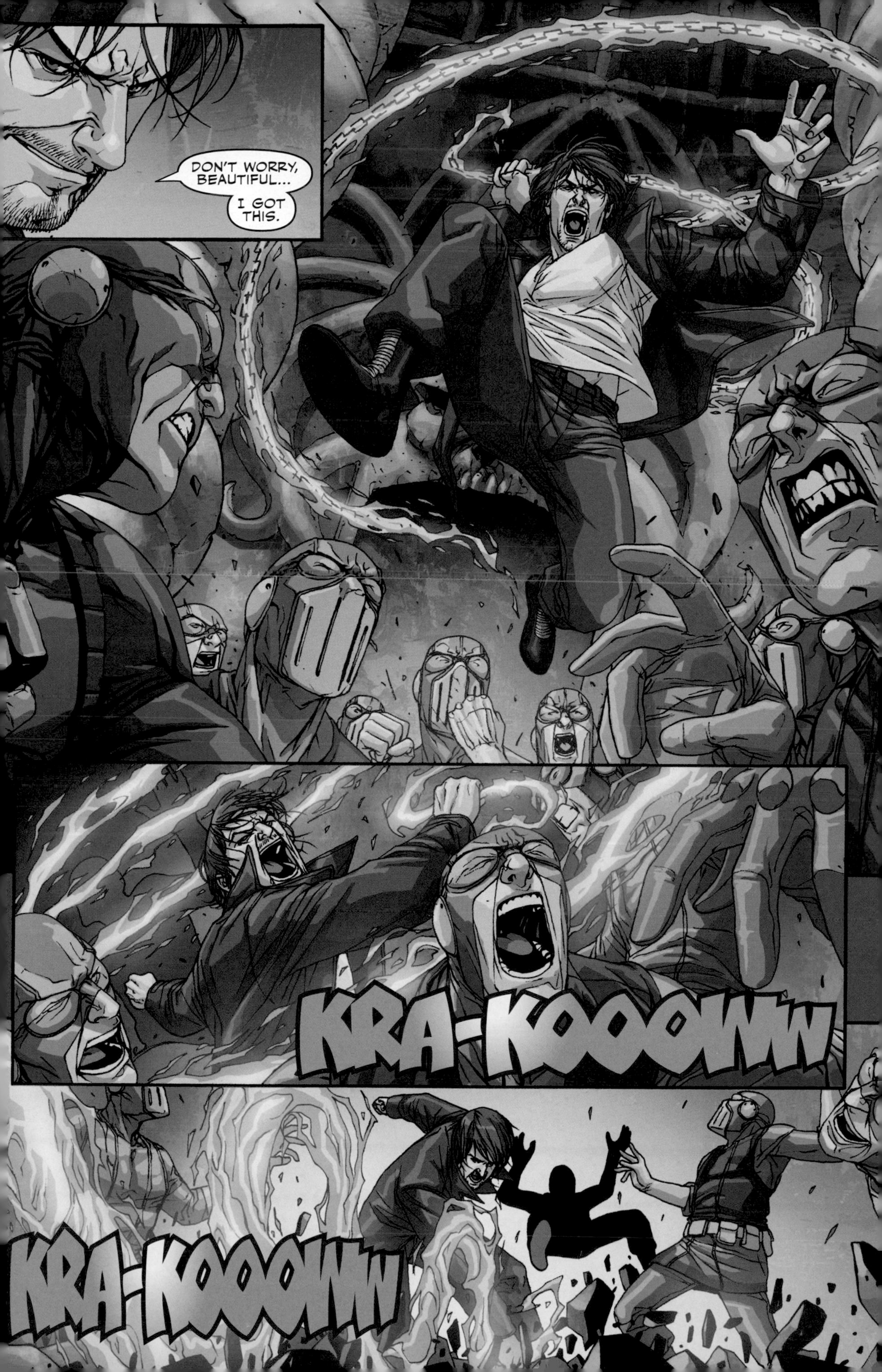
DON'T WORRY, BEAUTIFUL...
I GOT THIS.
KRA-KOOOMW
KRA-KOOOMW

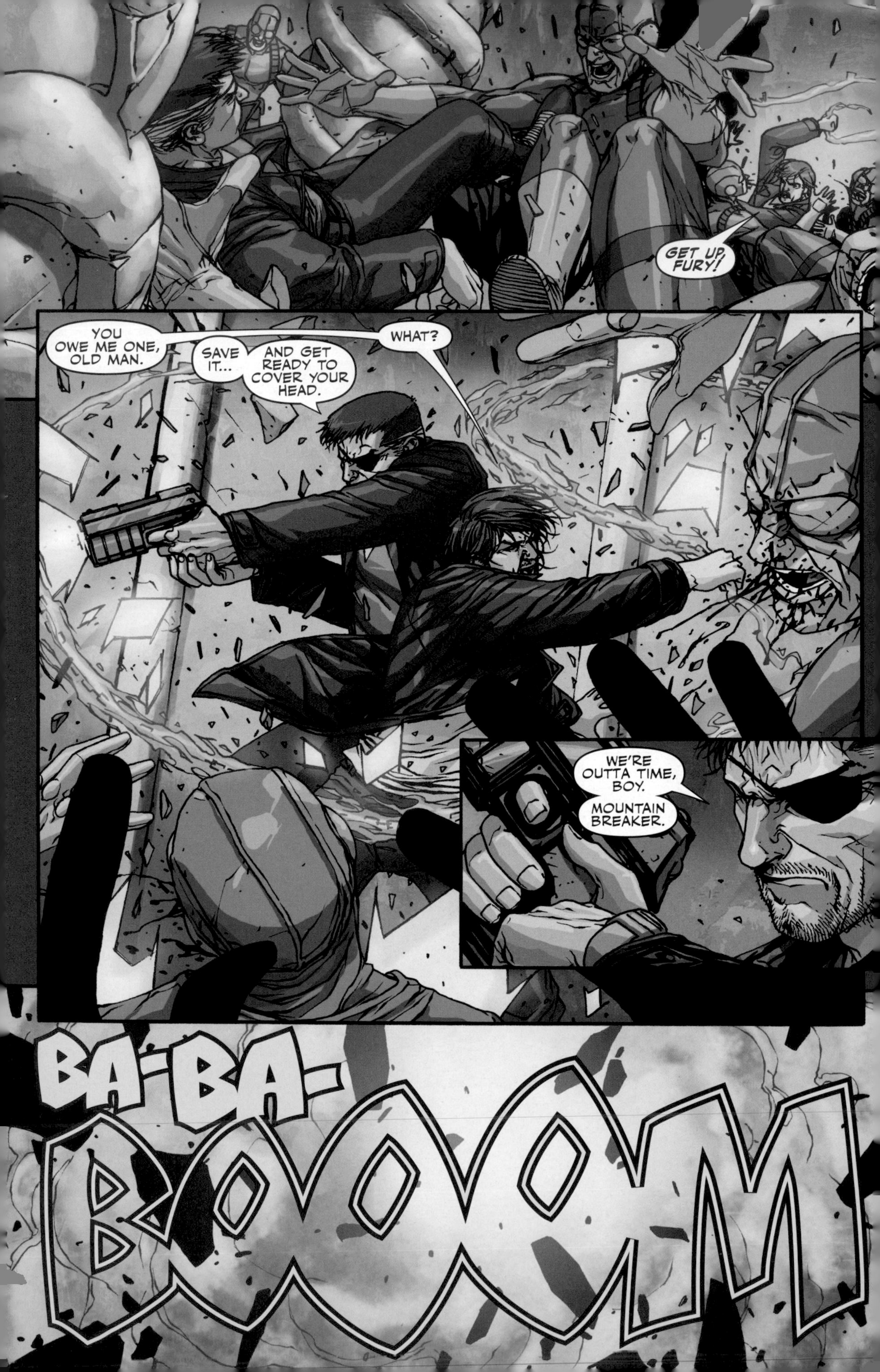
GET UP, FURY!
YOU OWE ME ONE, OLD MAN.
WHAT?
SAVE IT...
AND GET READY TO COVER YOUR HEAD.
WE'RE OUTTA TIME, BOY.
MOUNTAIN BREAKER.
BA-BA-BOOOM

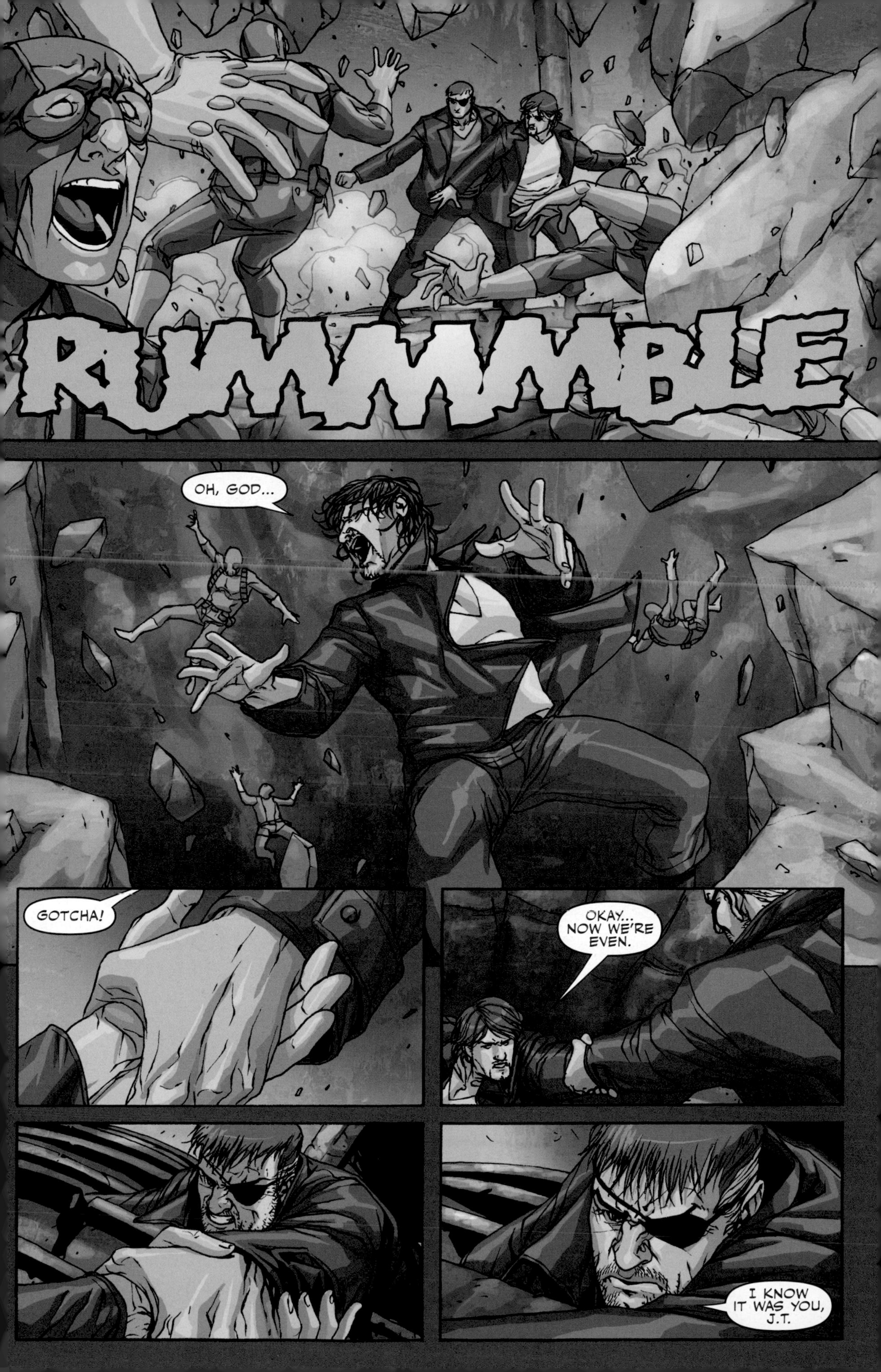
RUMMMBLE
OH, GOD...
GOTCHA!
OKAY... NOW WE'RE EVEN.
I KNOW IT WAS YOU, J.T.

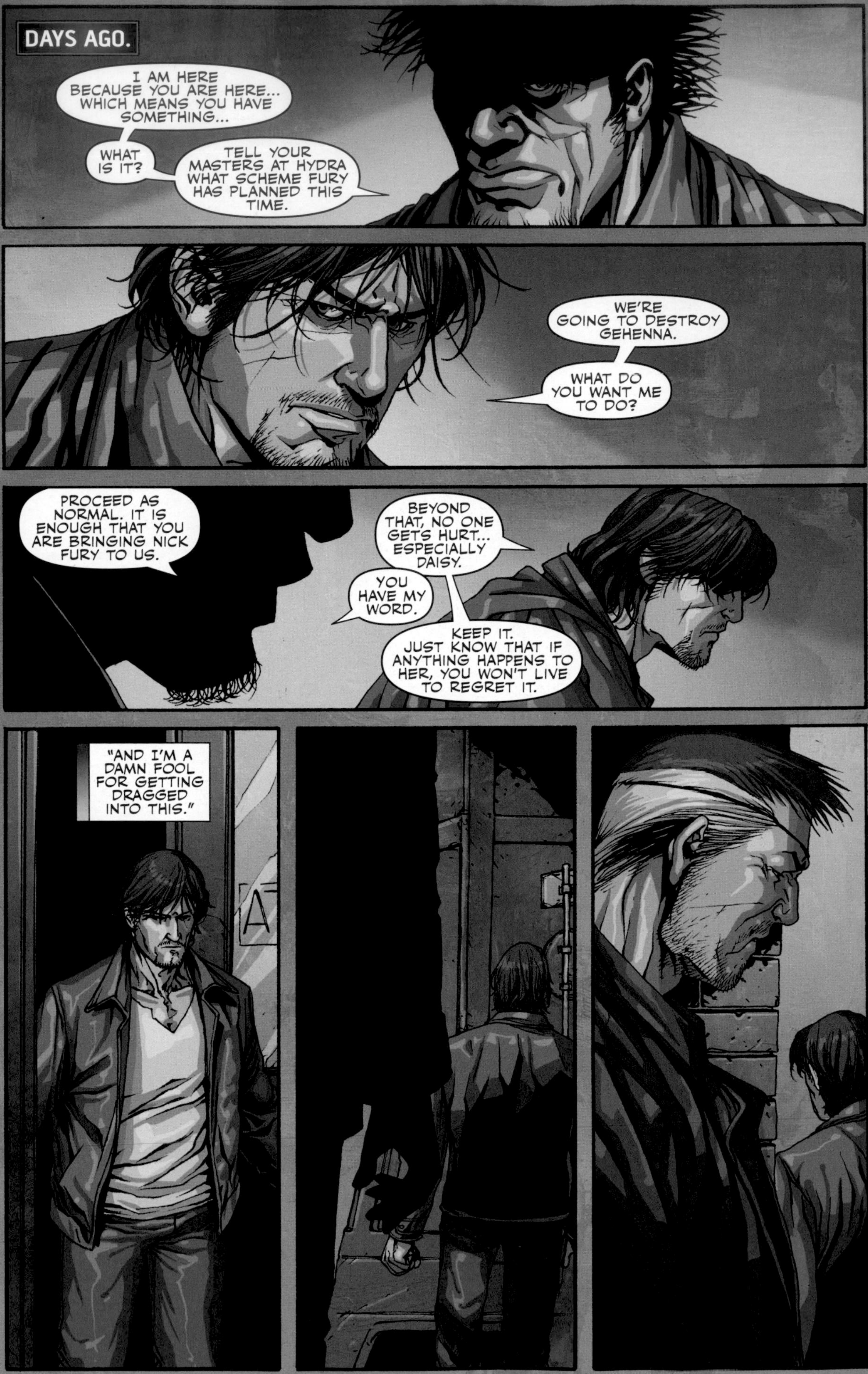

DAYS AGO.
I AM HERE BECAUSE YOU ARE HERE... WHICH MEANS YOU HAVE SOMETHING...
WHAT IS IT?
TELL YOUR MASTERS AT HYDRA WHAT SCHEME FURY HAS PLANNED THIS TIME.
WE'RE GOING TO DESTROY GEHENNA.
WHAT DO YOU WANT ME TO DO?
PROCEED AS NORMAL. IT IS ENOUGH THAT YOU ARE BRINGING NICK FURY TO US.
BEYOND THAT, NO ONE GETS HURT... ESPECIALLY DAISY.
YOU HAVE MY WORD.
KEEP IT. JUST KNOW THAT IF ANYTHING HAPPENS TO HER, YOU WON'T LIVE TO REGRET IT.
"AND I'M A DAMN FOOL FOR GETTING DRAGGED INTO THIS."

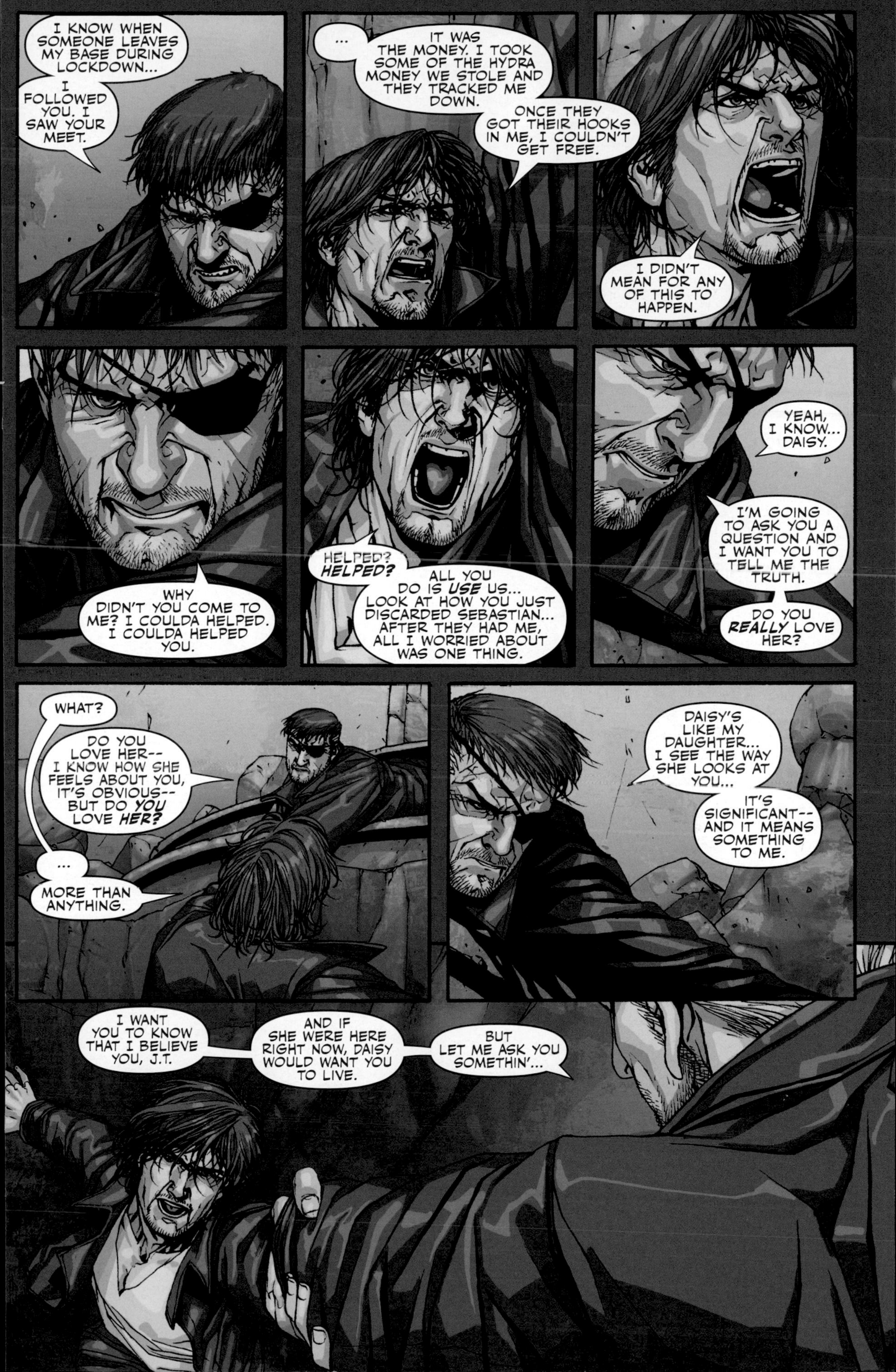

I KNOW WHEN SOMEONE LEAVES MY BASE DURING LOCKDOWN...
I FOLLOWED YOU. I SAW YOUR MEET.
...
IT WAS THE MONEY. I TOOK SOME OF THE HYDRA MONEY WE STOLE AND THEY TRACKED ME DOWN.
ONCE THEY GOT THEIR HOOKS IN ME, I COULDN'T GET FREE.
I DIDN'T MEAN FOR ANY OF THIS TO HAPPEN.
WHY DIDN'T YOU COME TO ME? I COULDA HELPED. I COULDA HELPED YOU.
HELPED? *HELPED?*
ALL YOU DO IS *USE* US... LOOK AT HOW YOU JUST DISCARDED SEBASTIAN... AFTER THEY HAD ME, ALL I WORRIED ABOUT WAS ONE THING.
YEAH, I KNOW... DAISY.
I'M GOING TO ASK YOU A QUESTION AND I WANT YOU TO TELL ME THE TRUTH.
DO YOU *REALLY* LOVE HER?
WHAT?
DO YOU LOVE HER-- I KNOW HOW SHE FEELS ABOUT YOU, IT'S OBVIOUS-- BUT DO *YOU* LOVE *HER?*
...
MORE THAN ANYTHING.
DAISY'S LIKE MY DAUGHTER... I SEE THE WAY SHE LOOKS AT YOU...
IT'S SIGNIFICANT-- AND IT MEANS SOMETHING TO ME.
I WANT YOU TO KNOW THAT I BELIEVE YOU, J.T.
AND IF SHE WERE HERE RIGHT NOW, DAISY WOULD WANT YOU TO LIVE.
BUT LET ME ASK YOU SOMETHIN'...

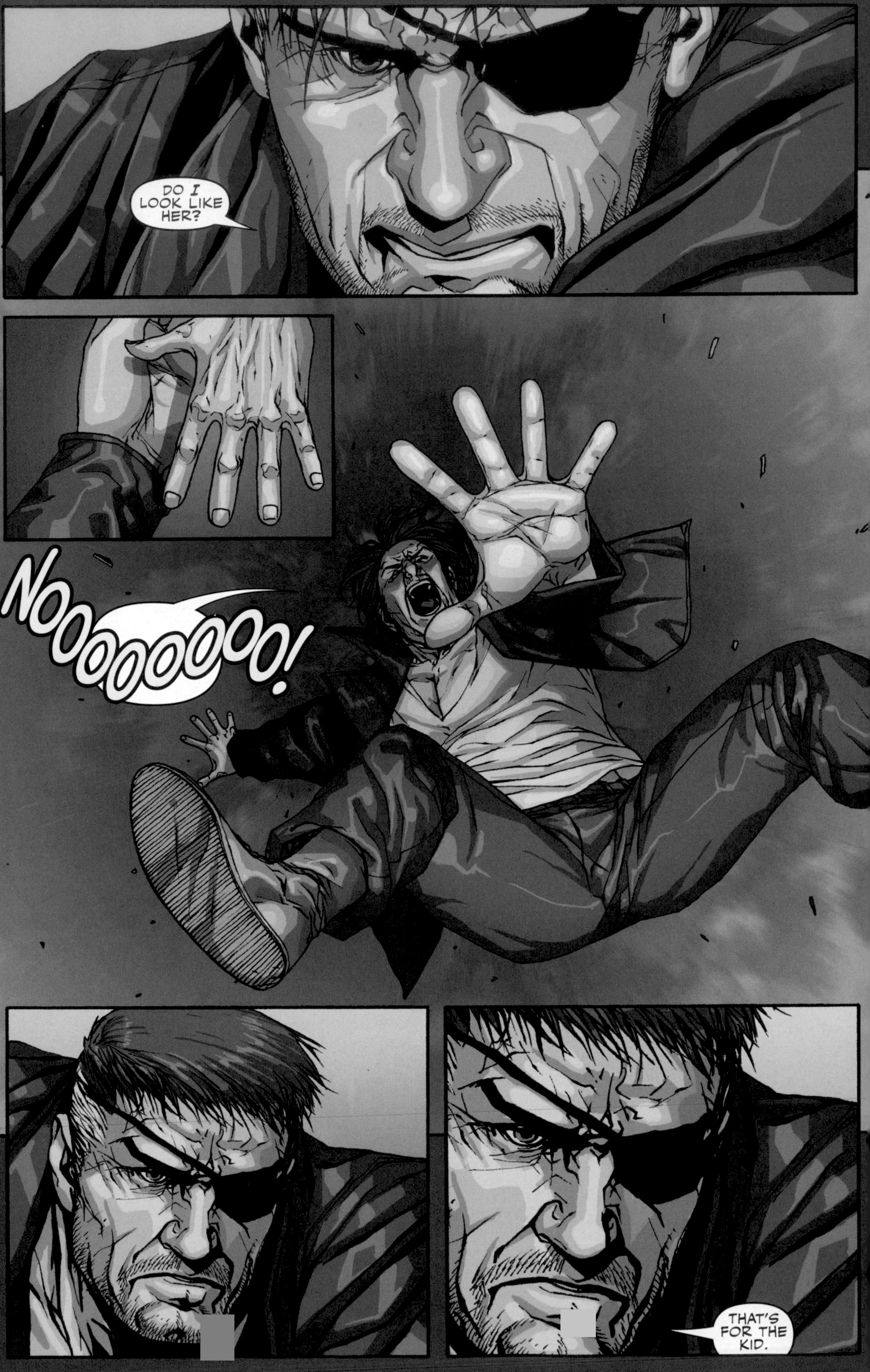
DO I LOOK LIKE HER?
NOOOOOOOO!
THAT'S FOR THE KID.

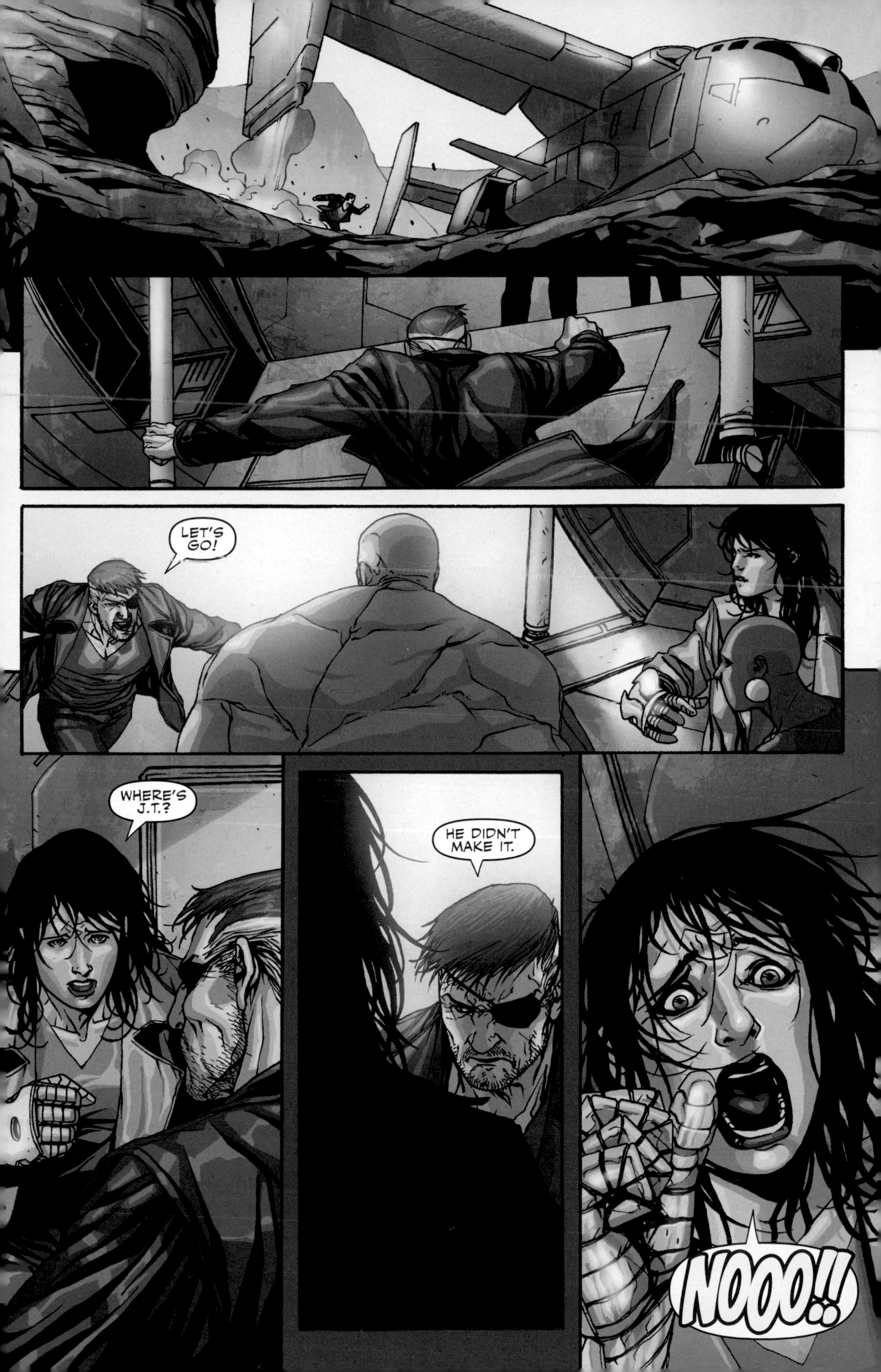
LET'S GO!
WHERE'S J.T.?
HE DIDN'T MAKE IT.
NOOO!!

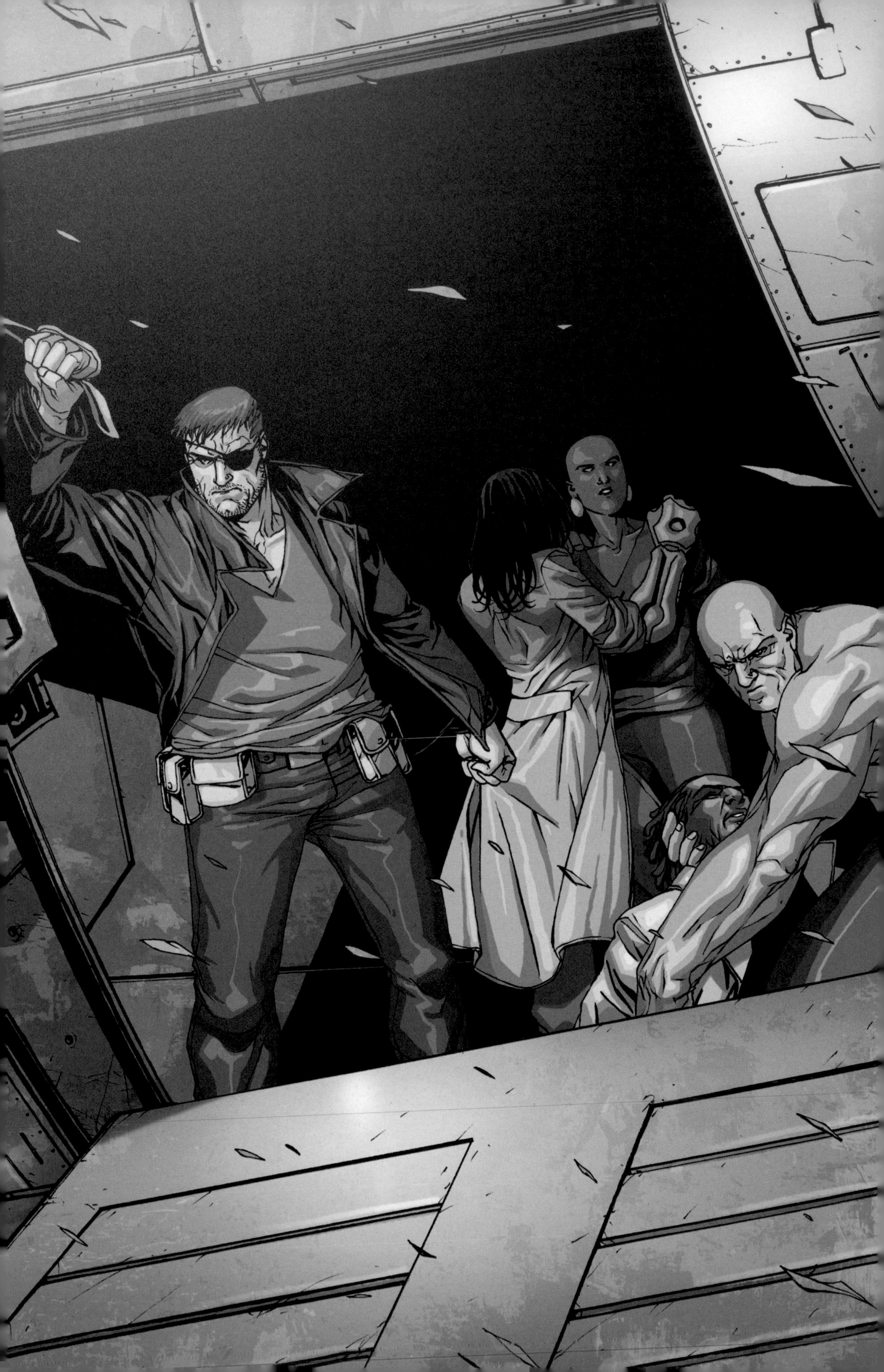

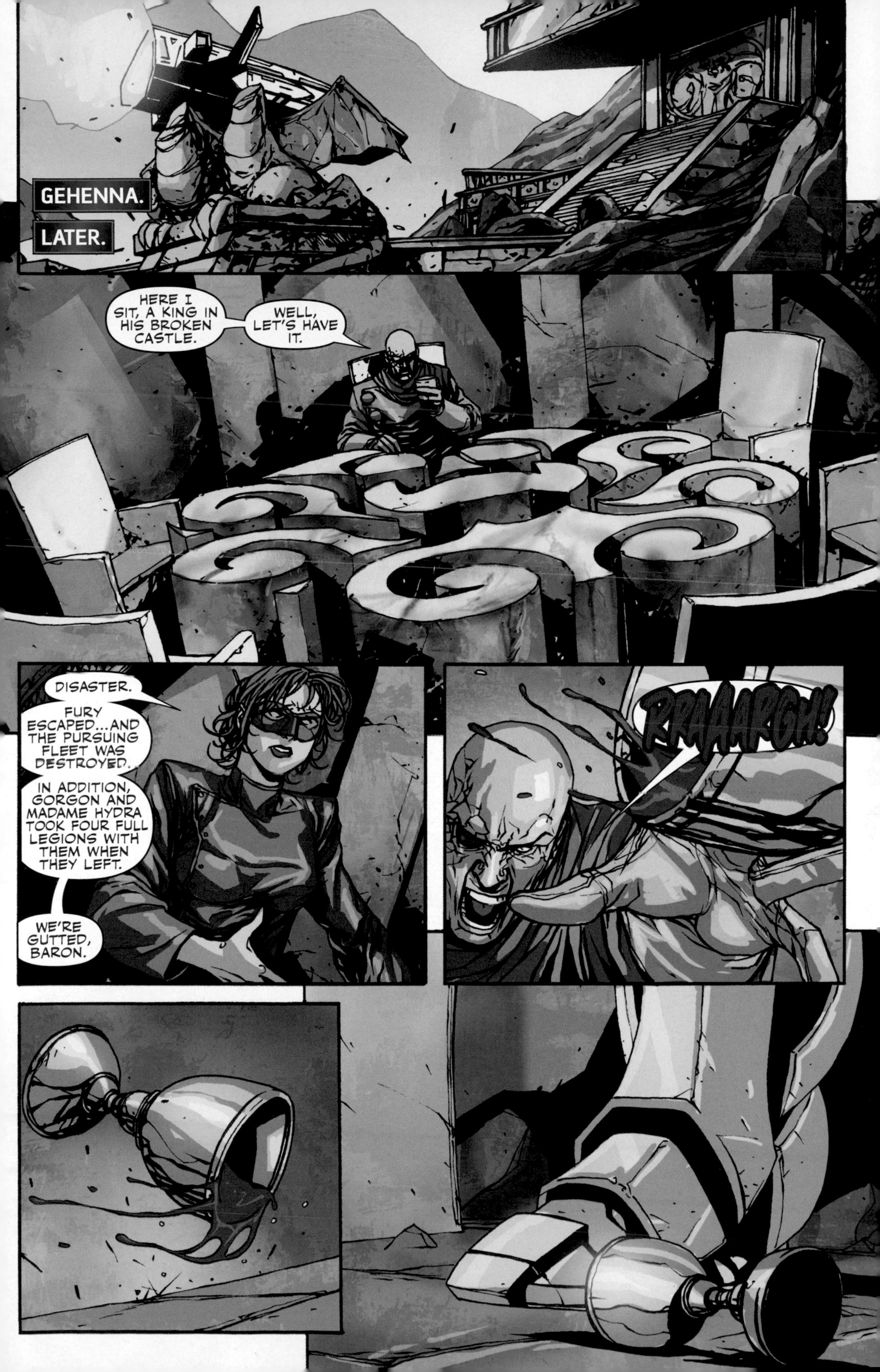
GEHENNA.
LATER.
HERE I SIT, A KING IN HIS BROKEN CASTLE.
WELL, LET'S HAVE IT.
DISASTER.
FURY ESCAPED...AND THE PURSUING FLEET WAS DESTROYED.
IN ADDITION, GORGON AND MADAME HYDRA TOOK FOUR FULL LEGIONS WITH THEM WHEN THEY LEFT.
WE'RE GUTTED, BARON.
RRAAARGH!

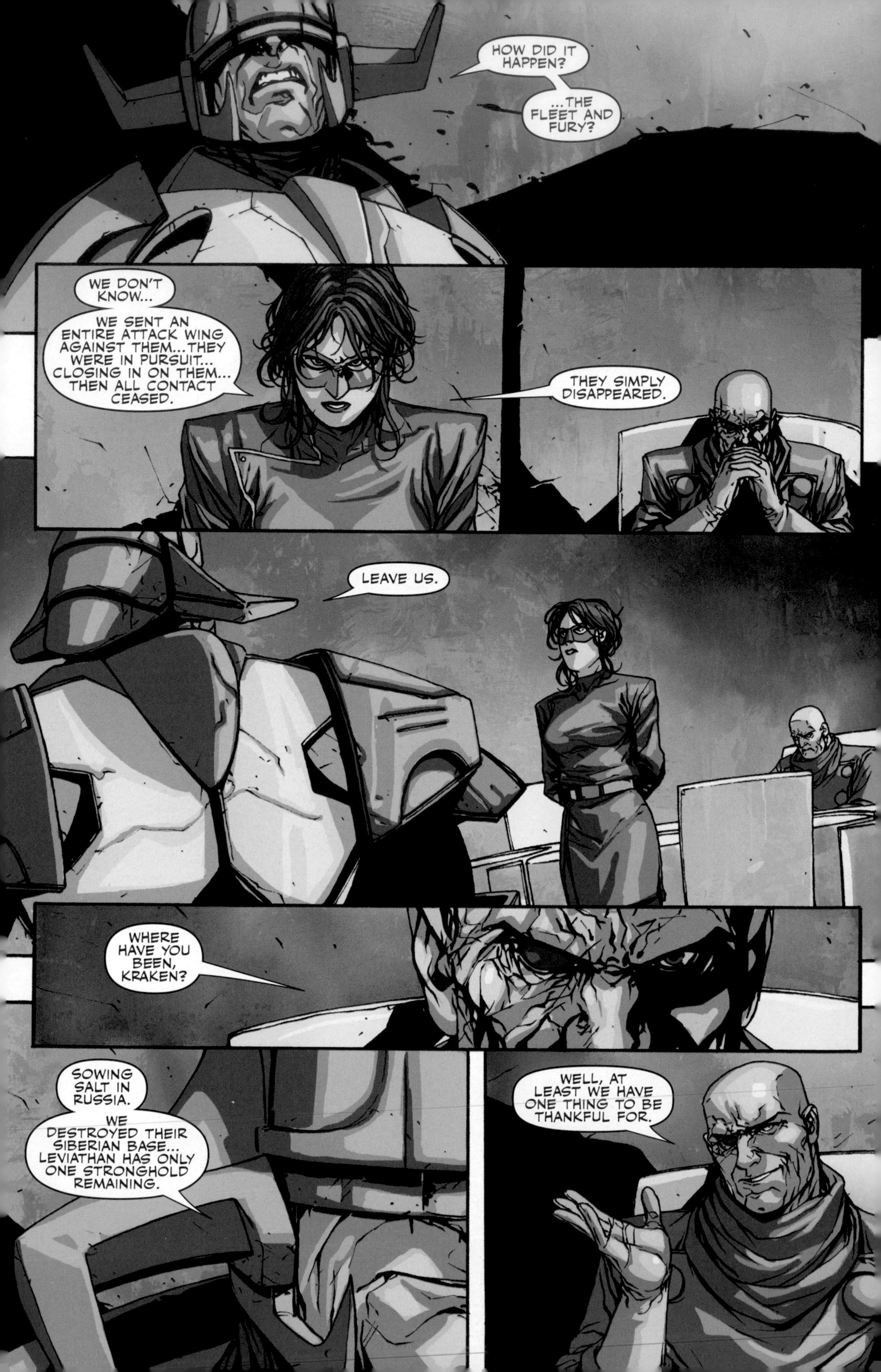
HOW DID IT HAPPEN?
...THE FLEET AND FURY?
WE DON'T KNOW...
WE SENT AN ENTIRE ATTACK WING AGAINST THEM...THEY WERE IN PURSUIT... CLOSING IN ON THEM... THEN ALL CONTACT CEASED.
THEY SIMPLY DISAPPEARED.
LEAVE US.
WHERE HAVE YOU BEEN, KRAKEN?
SOWING SALT IN RUSSIA.
WE DESTROYED THEIR SIBERIAN BASE... LEVIATHAN HAS ONLY ONE STRONGHOLD REMAINING.
WELL, AT LEAST WE HAVE ONE THING TO BE THANKFUL FOR.

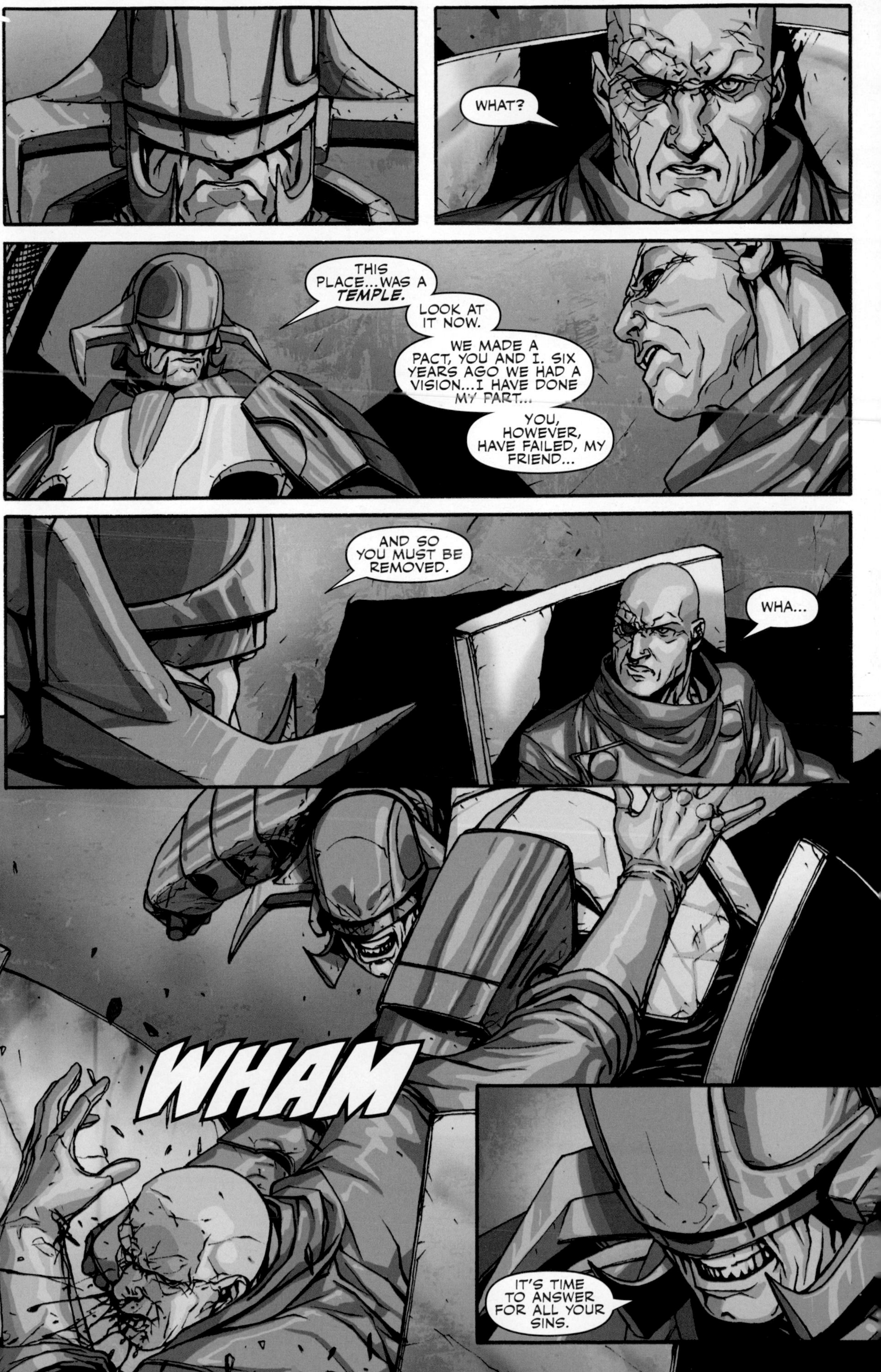
WHAT?
THIS PLACE...WAS A TEMPLE.
LOOK AT IT NOW.
WE MADE A PACT, YOU AND I. SIX YEARS AGO WE HAD A VISION...I HAVE DONE MY PART...
YOU, HOWEVER, HAVE FAILED, MY FRIEND...
AND SO YOU MUST BE REMOVED.
WHA...
WHAM
IT'S TIME TO ANSWER FOR ALL YOUR SINS.

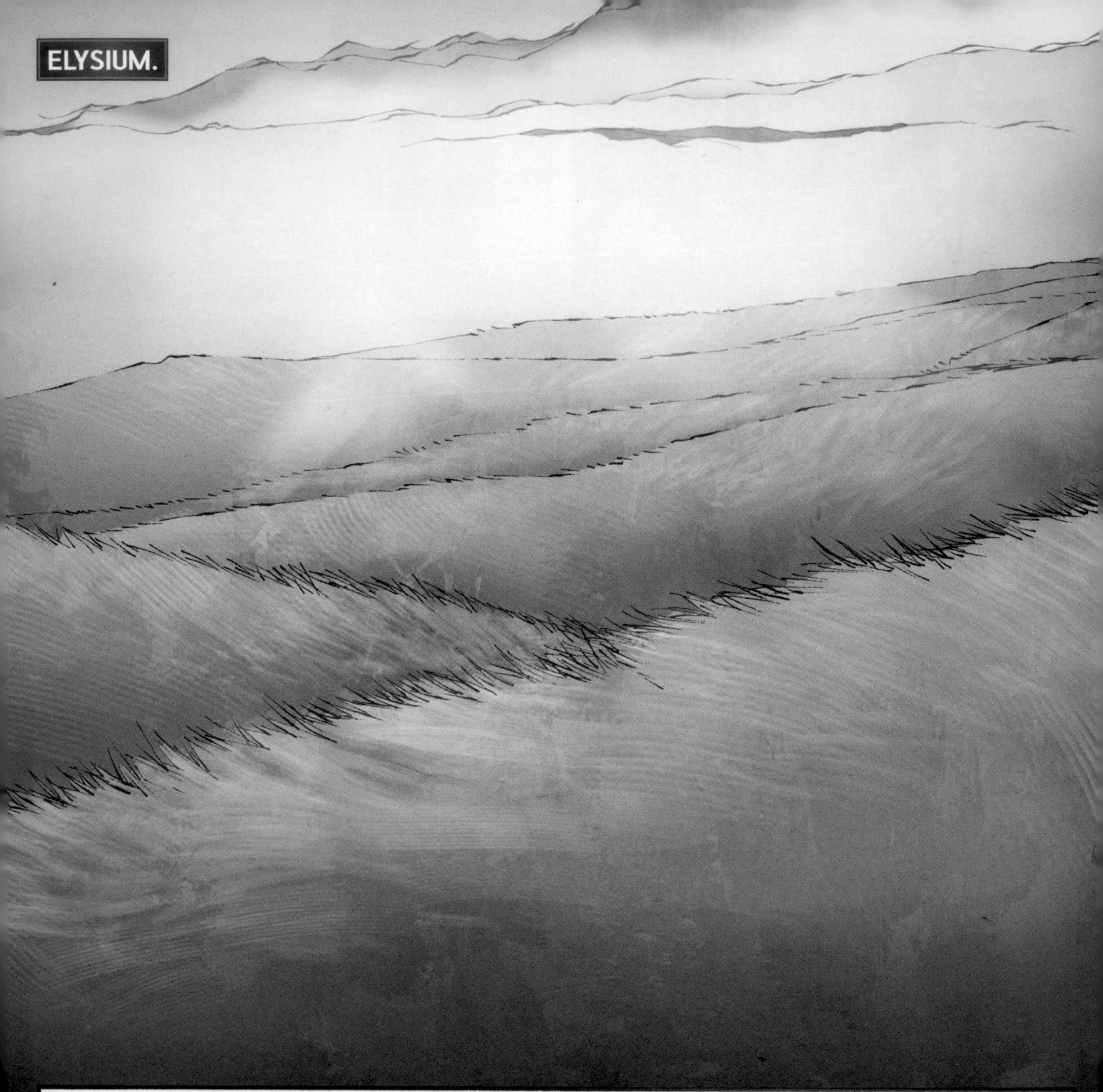
ELYSIUM.

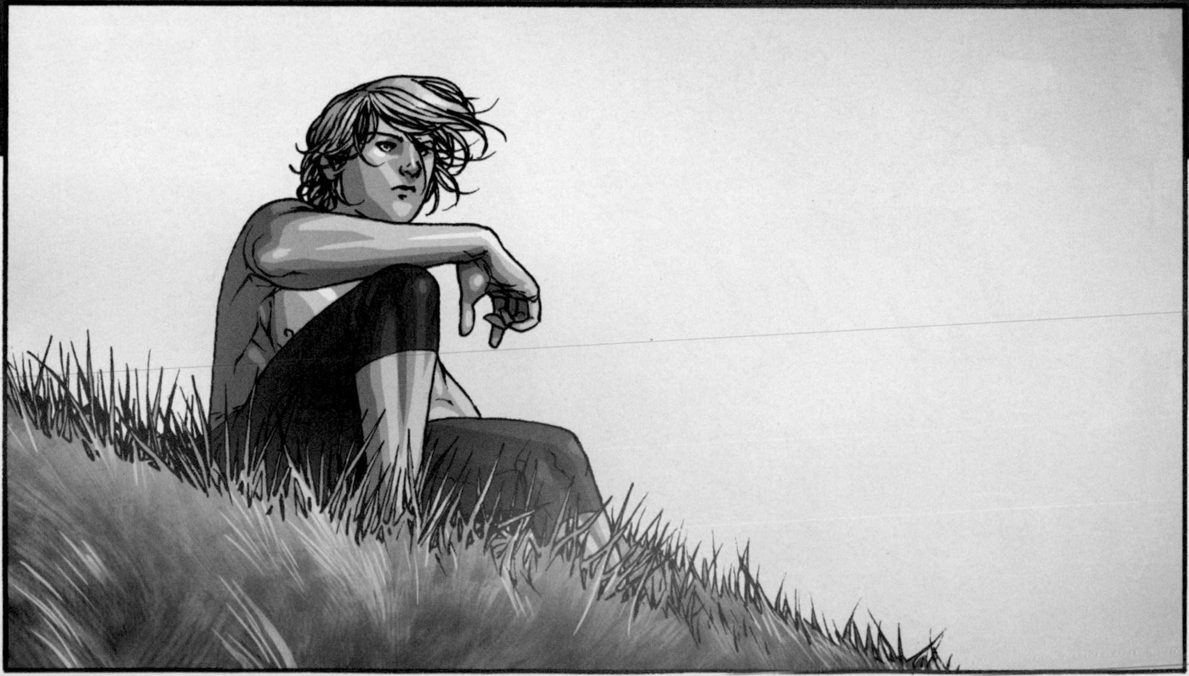

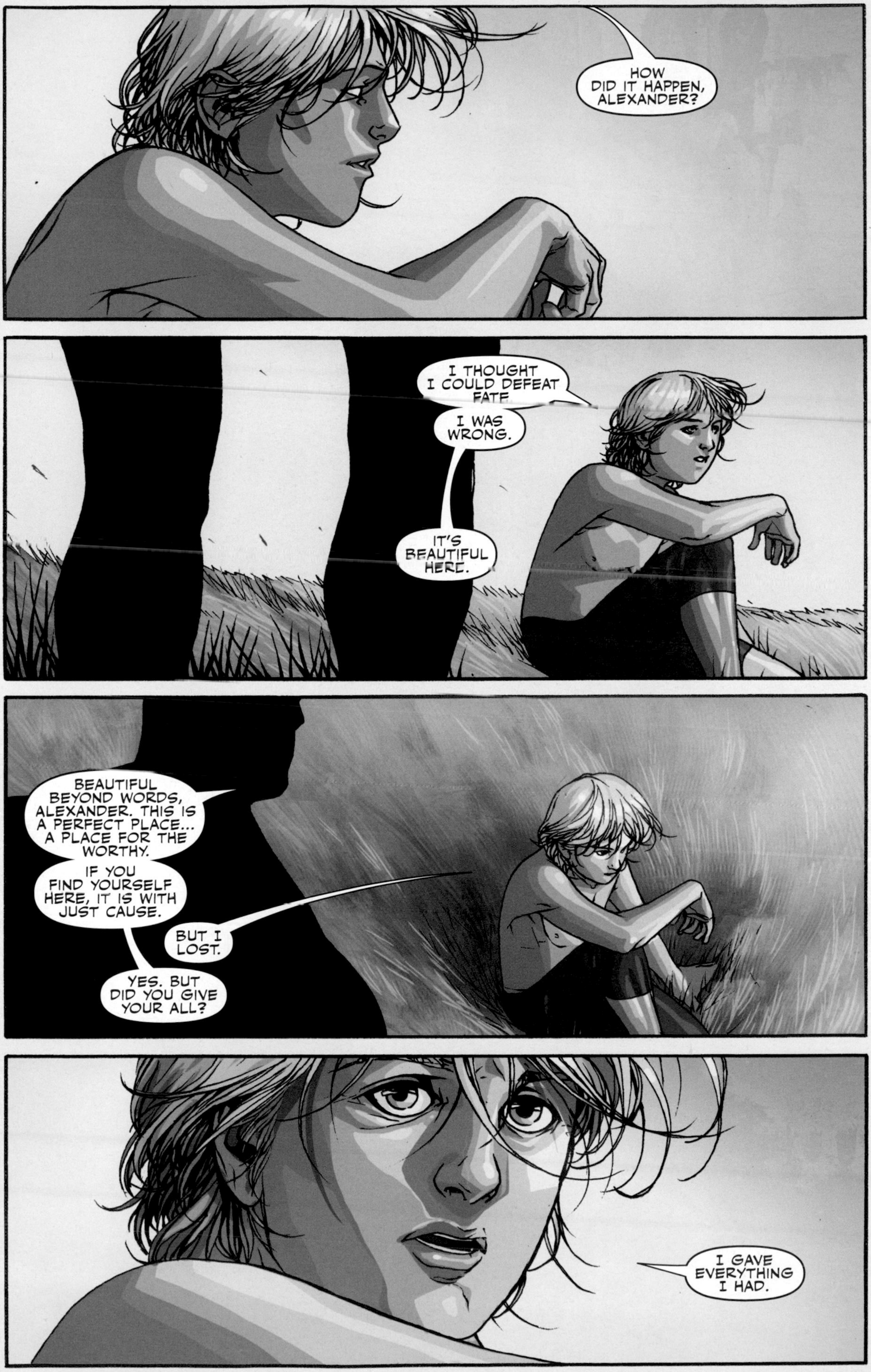

HOW DID IT HAPPEN, ALEXANDER?
I THOUGHT I COULD DEFEAT FATE.
I WAS WRONG.
IT'S BEAUTIFUL HERE.
BEAUTIFUL BEYOND WORDS, ALEXANDER. THIS IS A PERFECT PLACE... A PLACE FOR THE WORTHY.
IF YOU FIND YOURSELF HERE, IT IS WITH JUST CAUSE.
BUT I LOST.
YES. BUT DID YOU GIVE YOUR ALL?
I GAVE EVERYTHING I HAD.

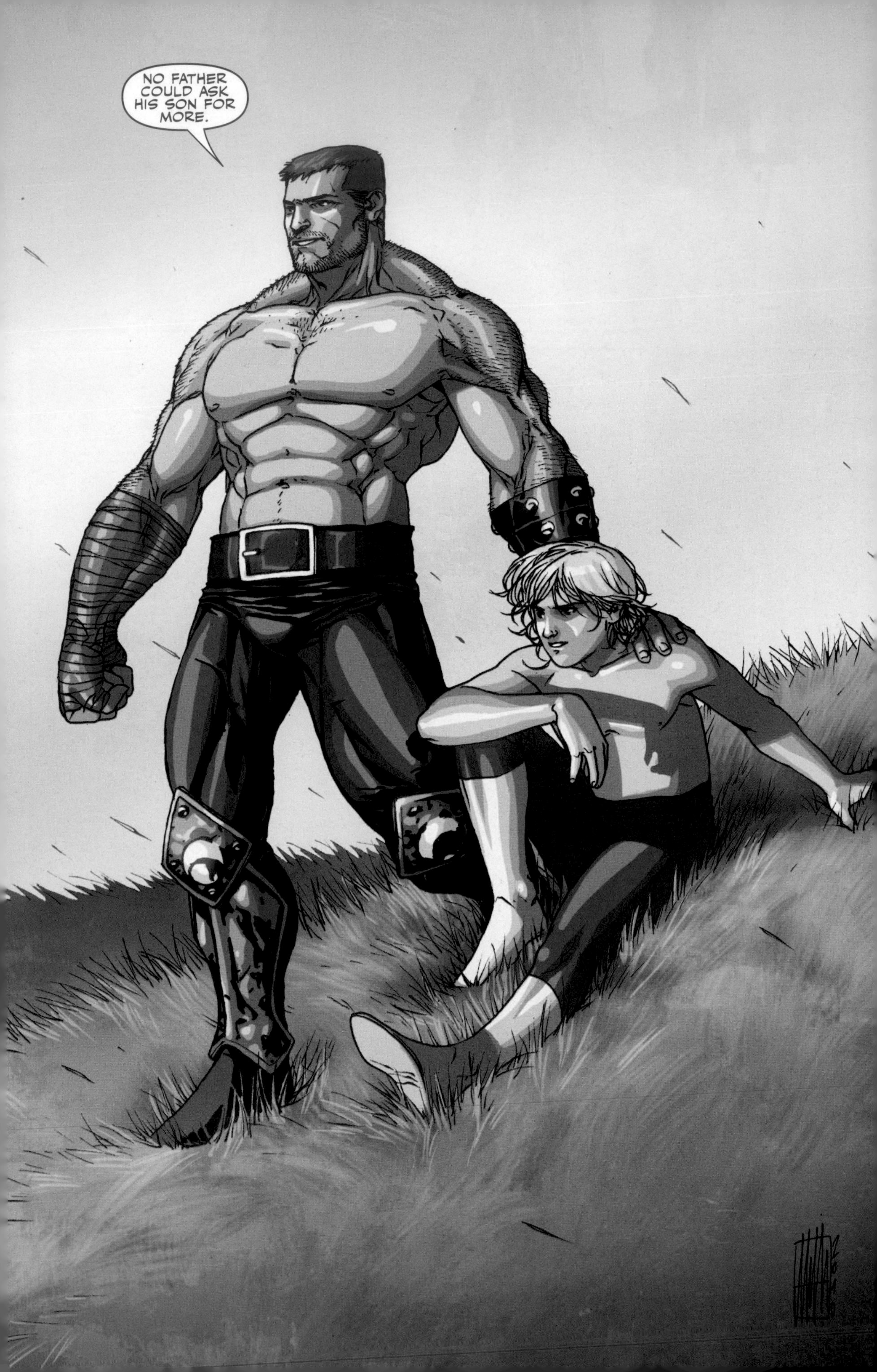
NO FATHER COULD ASK HIS SON FOR MORE.

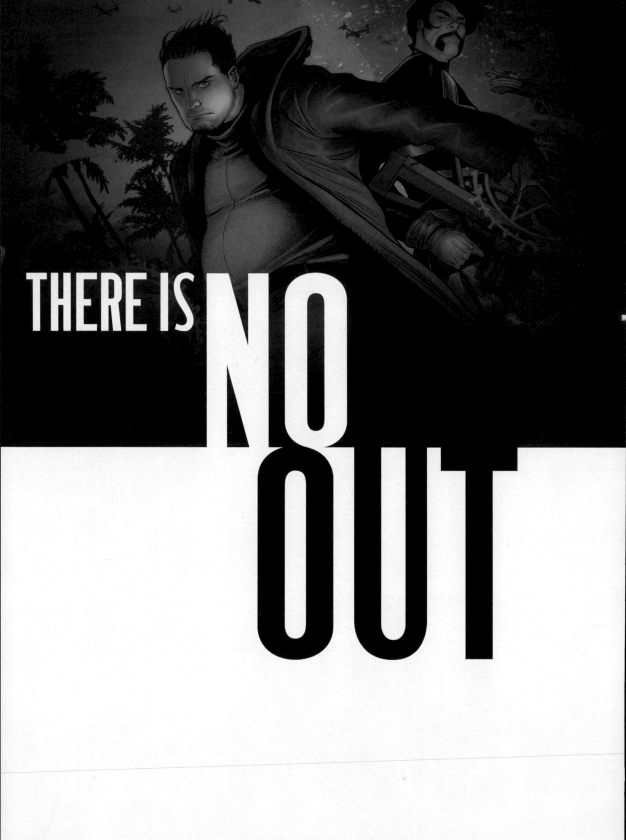

# THERE IS NO OUT

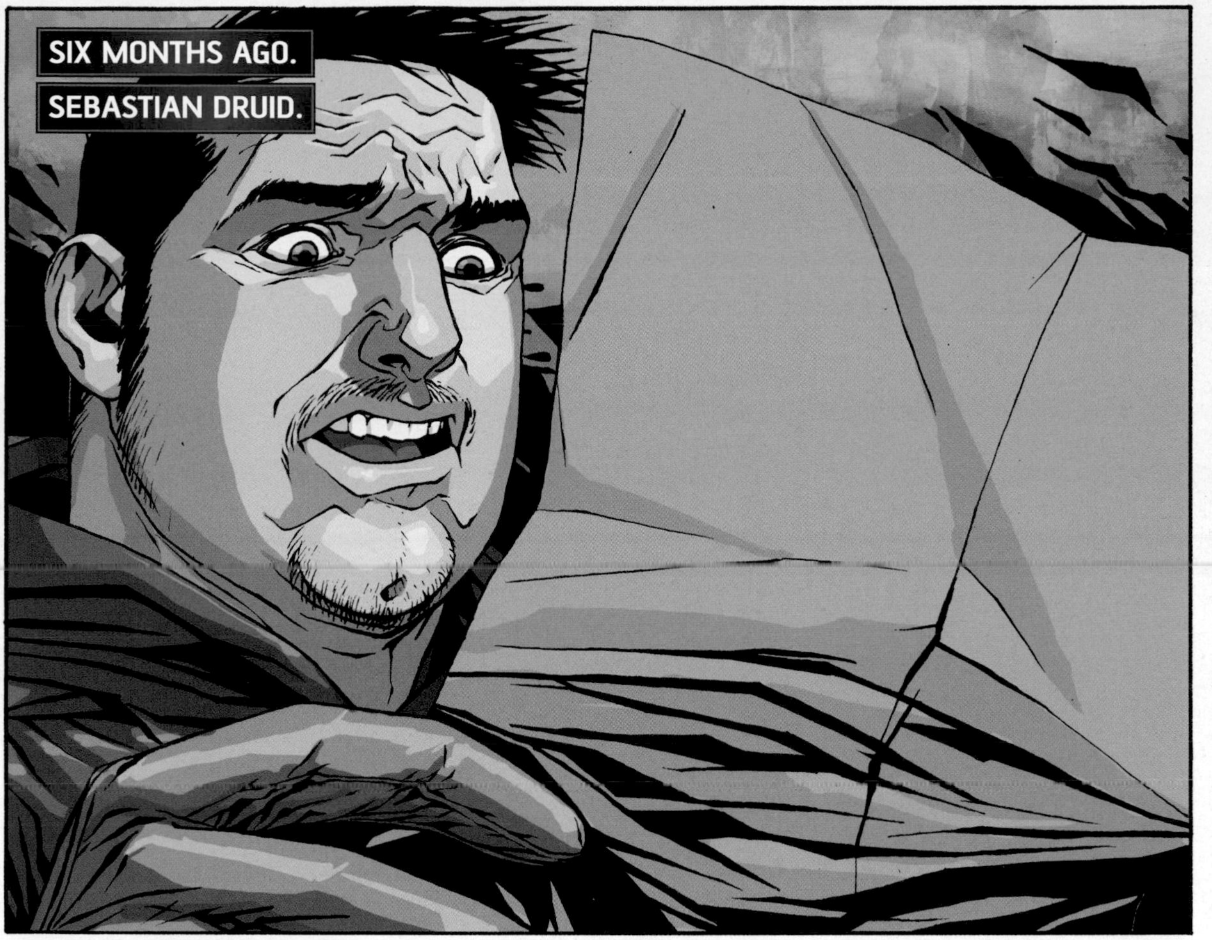
SIX MONTHS AGO.
SEBASTIAN DRUID.

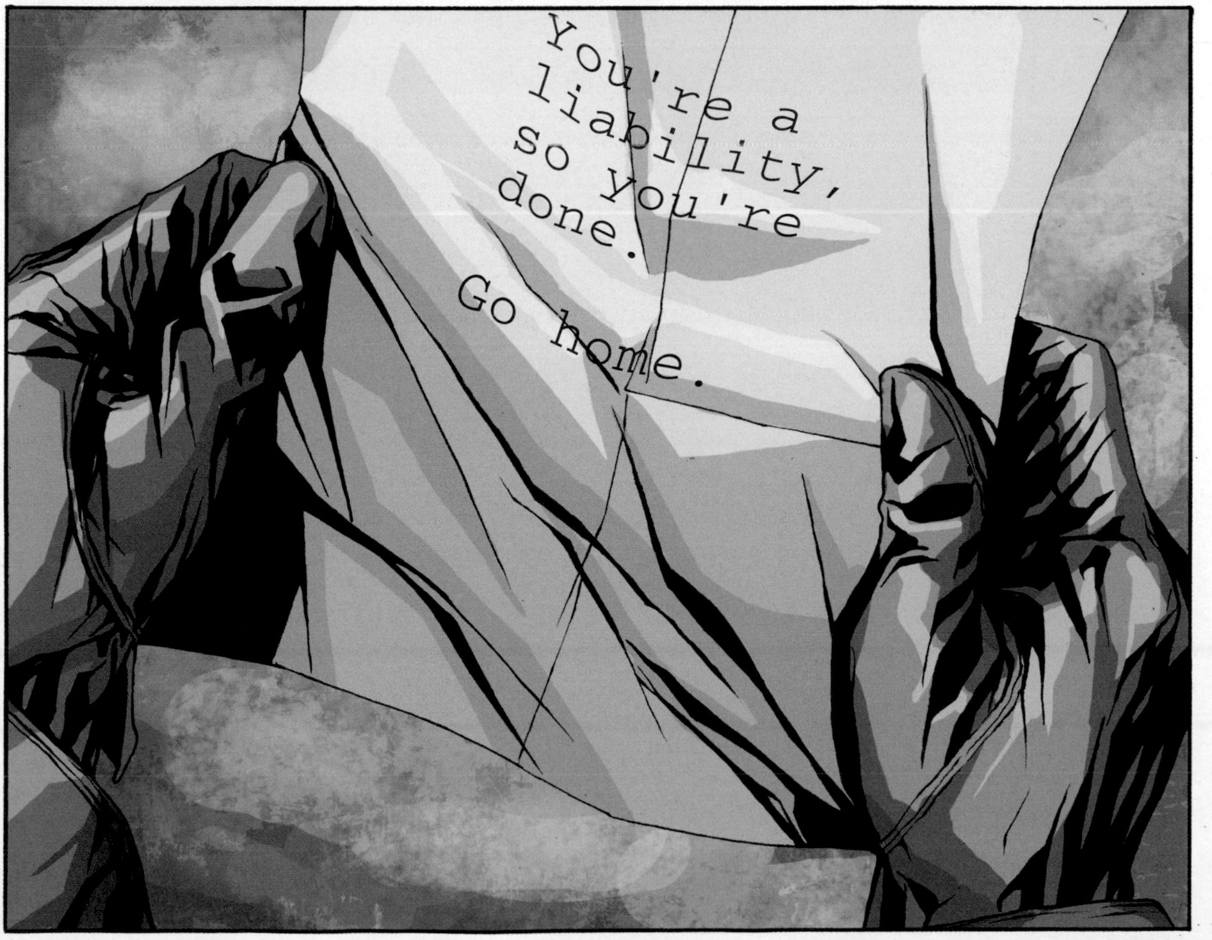
You're a liability, so you're done.
Go home.

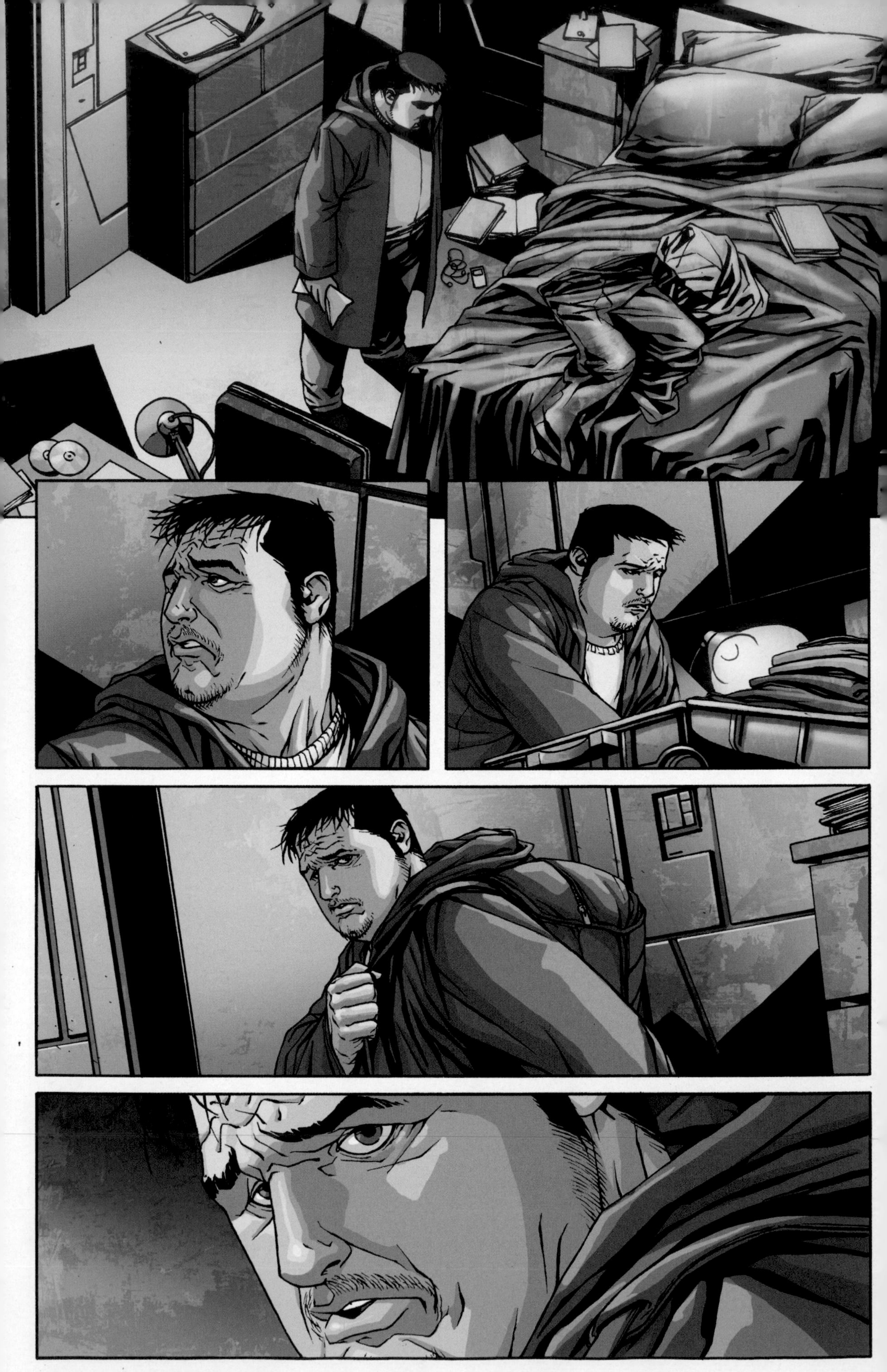

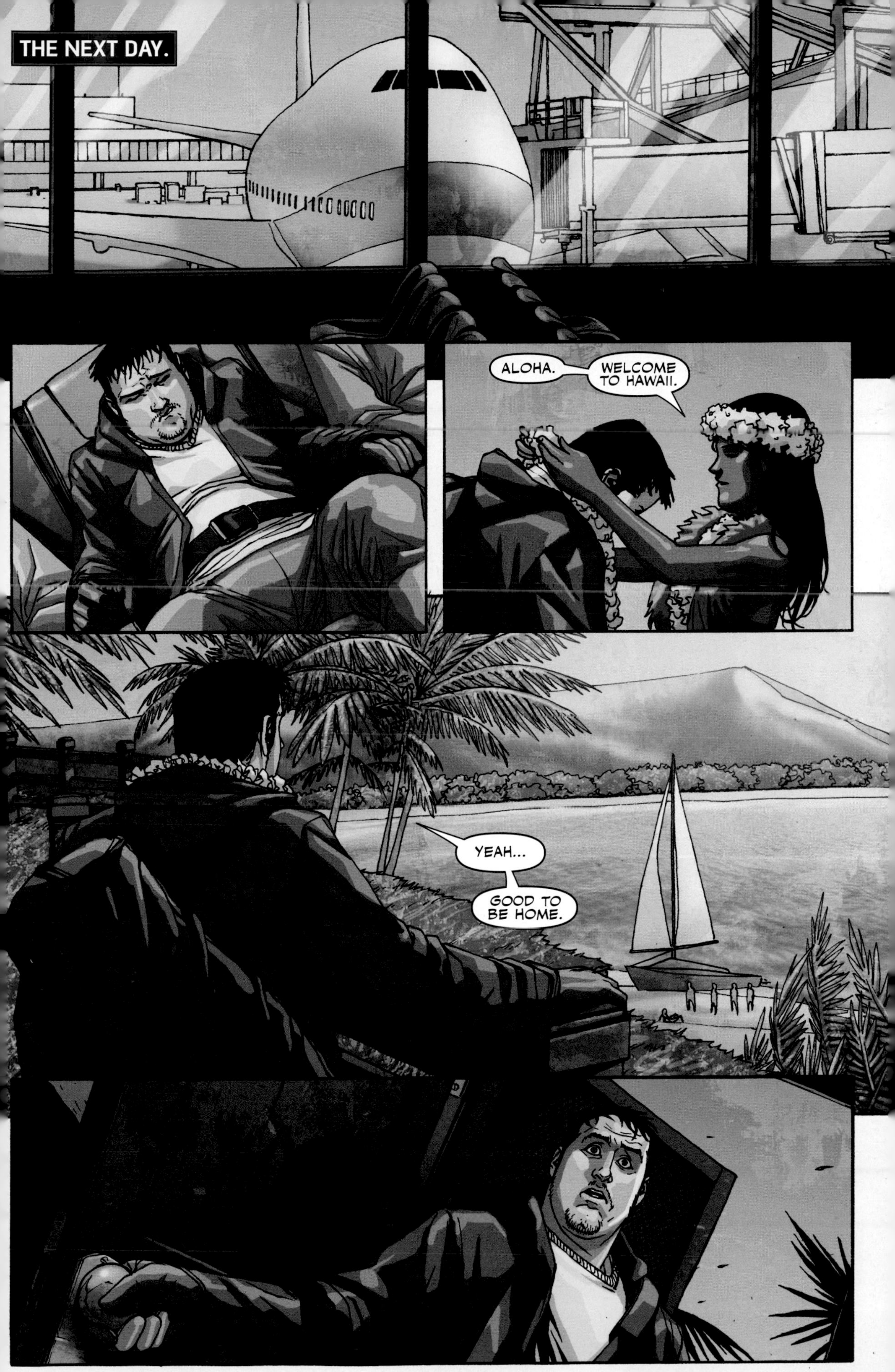
THE NEXT DAY.
ALOHA.
WELCOME TO HAWAII.
YEAH...
GOOD TO BE HOME.

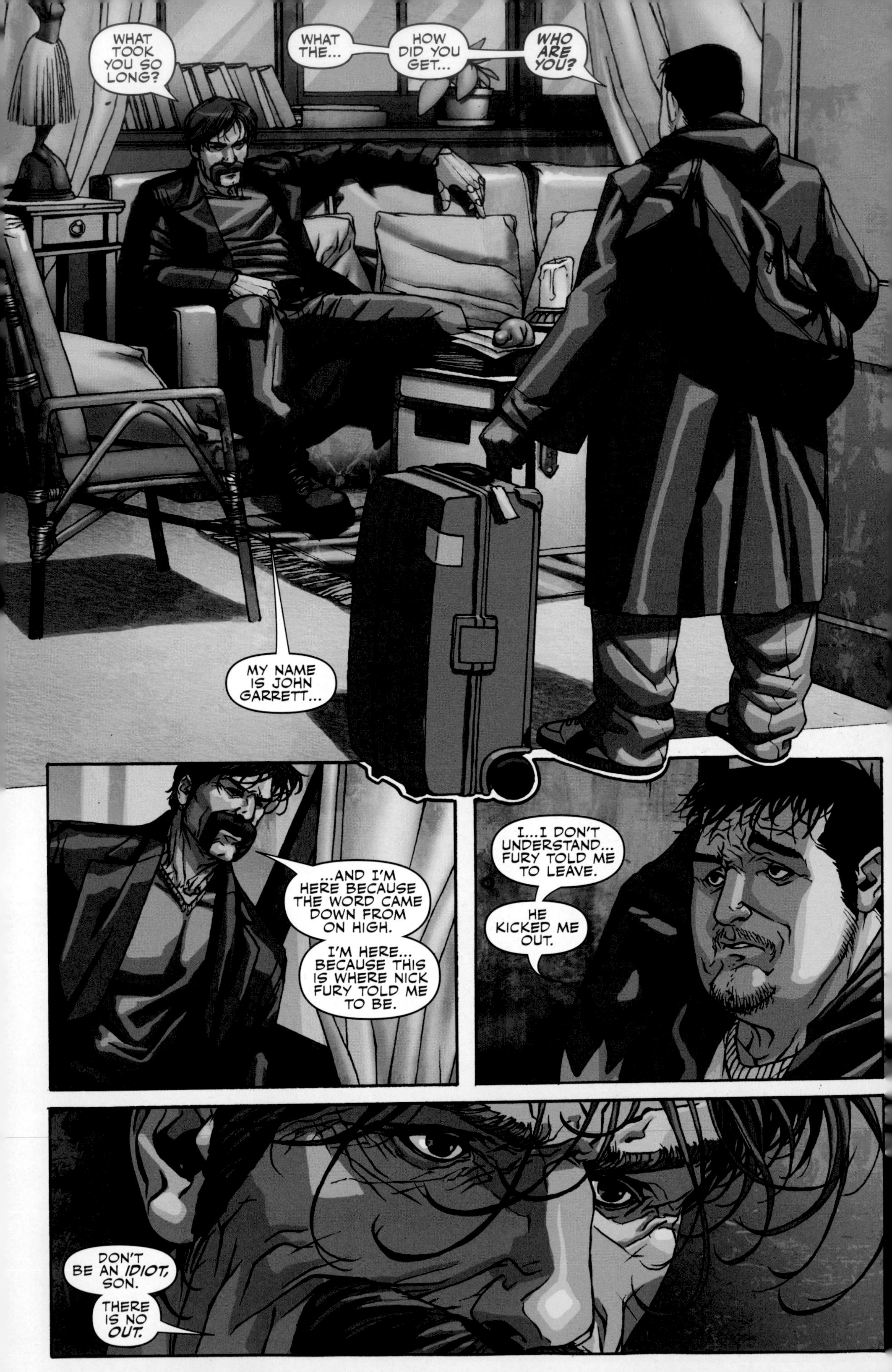
WHAT TOOK YOU SO LONG?
WHAT THE...
HOW DID YOU GET...
WHO ARE YOU?
MY NAME IS JOHN GARRETT...
...AND I'M HERE BECAUSE THE WORD CAME DOWN FROM ON HIGH.
I'M HERE... BECAUSE THIS IS WHERE NICK FURY TOLD ME TO BE.
I...I DON'T UNDERSTAND... FURY TOLD ME TO LEAVE.
HE KICKED ME OUT.
DON'T BE AN *IDIOT,* SON.
THERE IS NO *OUT.*

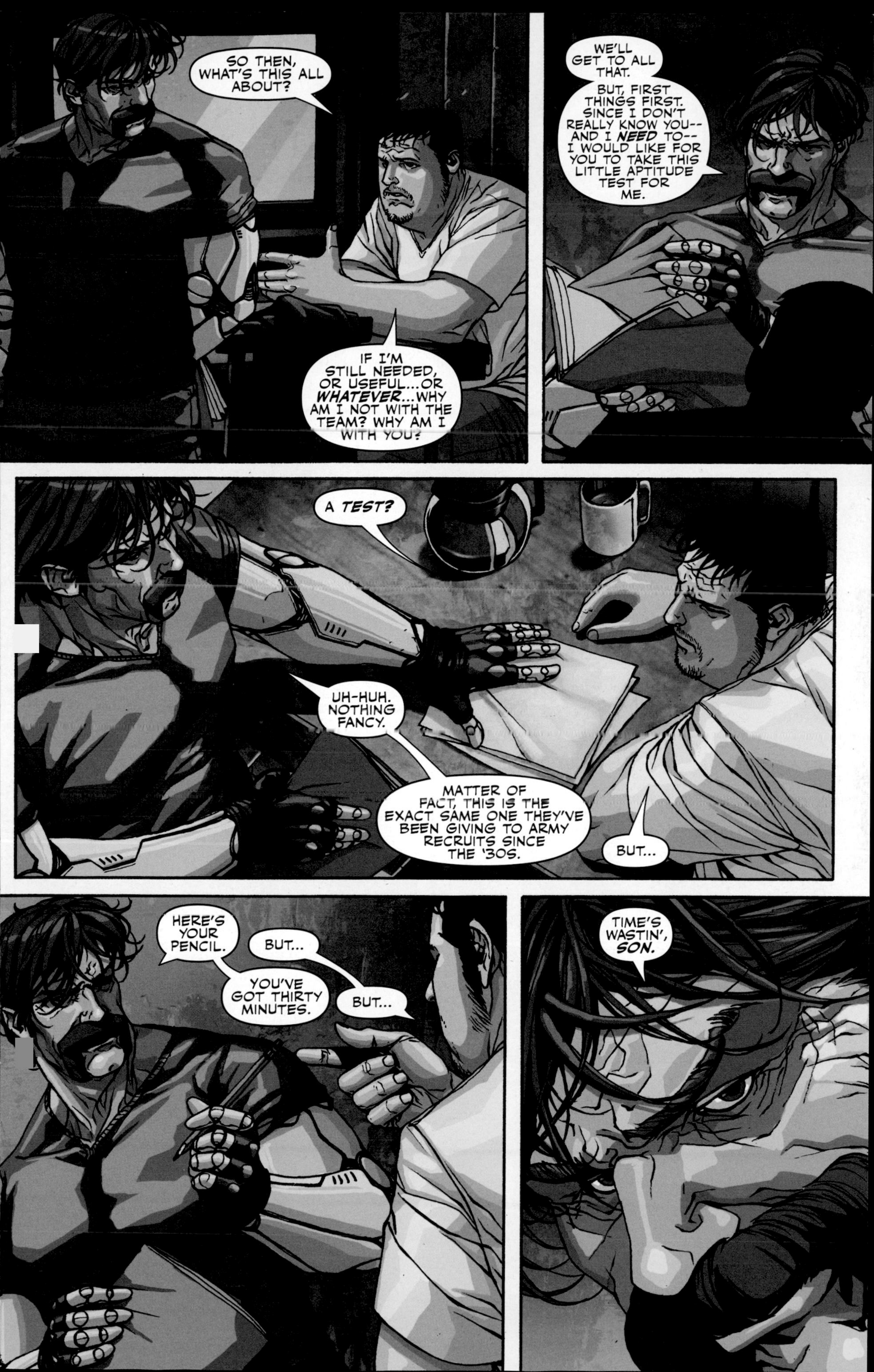
SO THEN, WHAT'S THIS ALL ABOUT?
IF I'M STILL NEEDED, OR USEFUL...OR *WHATEVER*...WHY AM I NOT WITH THE TEAM? WHY AM I WITH YOU?
WE'LL GET TO ALL THAT.
BUT, FIRST THINGS FIRST. SINCE I DON'T REALLY KNOW YOU-- AND I *NEED* TO-- I WOULD LIKE FOR YOU TO TAKE THIS LITTLE APTITUDE TEST FOR ME.
A *TEST?*
UH-HUH. NOTHING FANCY.
MATTER OF FACT, THIS IS THE EXACT SAME ONE THEY'VE BEEN GIVING TO ARMY RECRUITS SINCE THE '30S.
BUT...
HERE'S YOUR PENCIL.
BUT...
YOU'VE GOT THIRTY MINUTES.
BUT...
TIME'S WASTIN', *SON.*

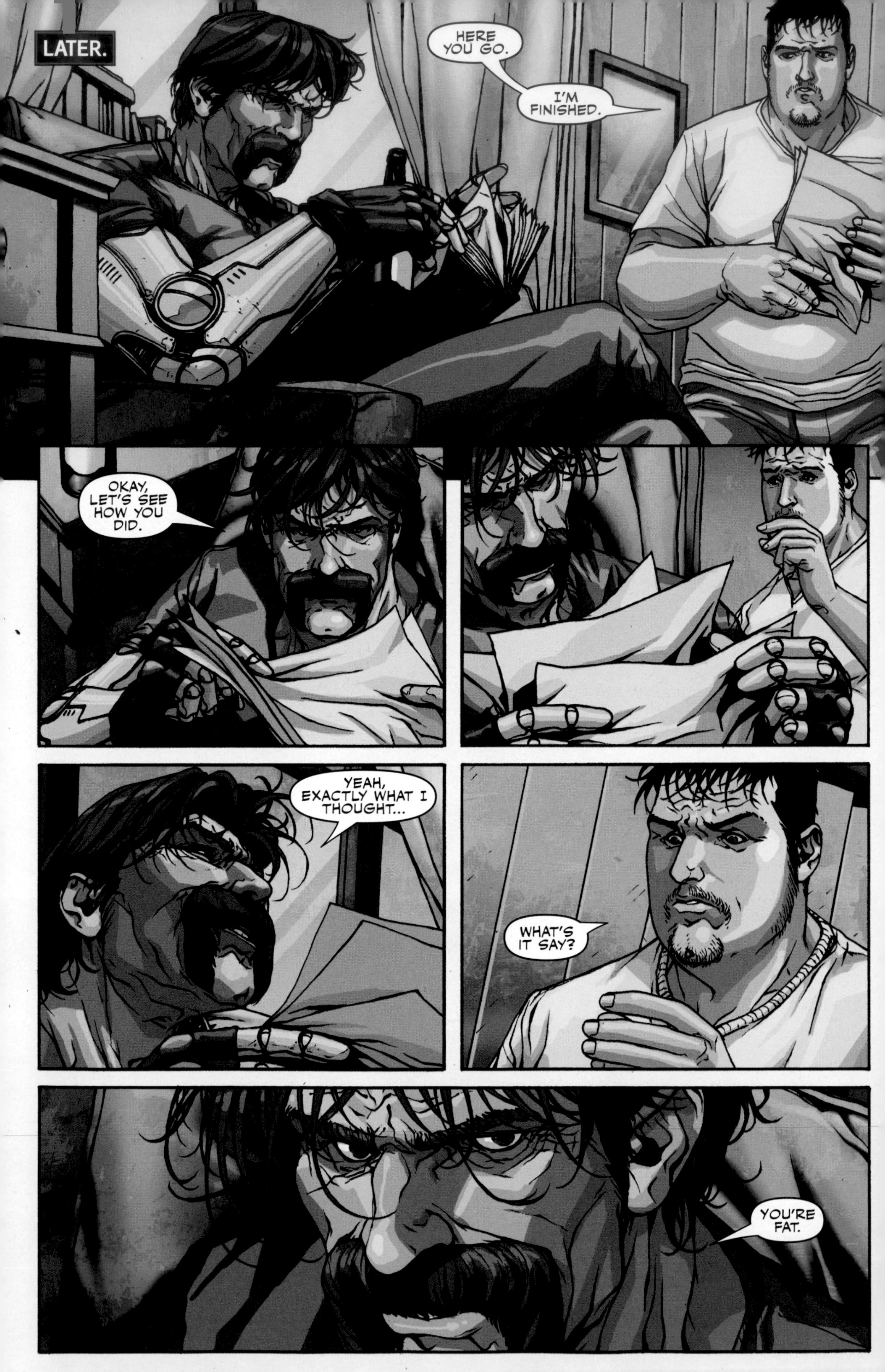
LATER.
HERE YOU GO.
I'M FINISHED.
OKAY, LET'S SEE HOW YOU DID.
YEAH, EXACTLY WHAT I THOUGHT...
WHAT'S IT SAY?
YOU'RE FAT.

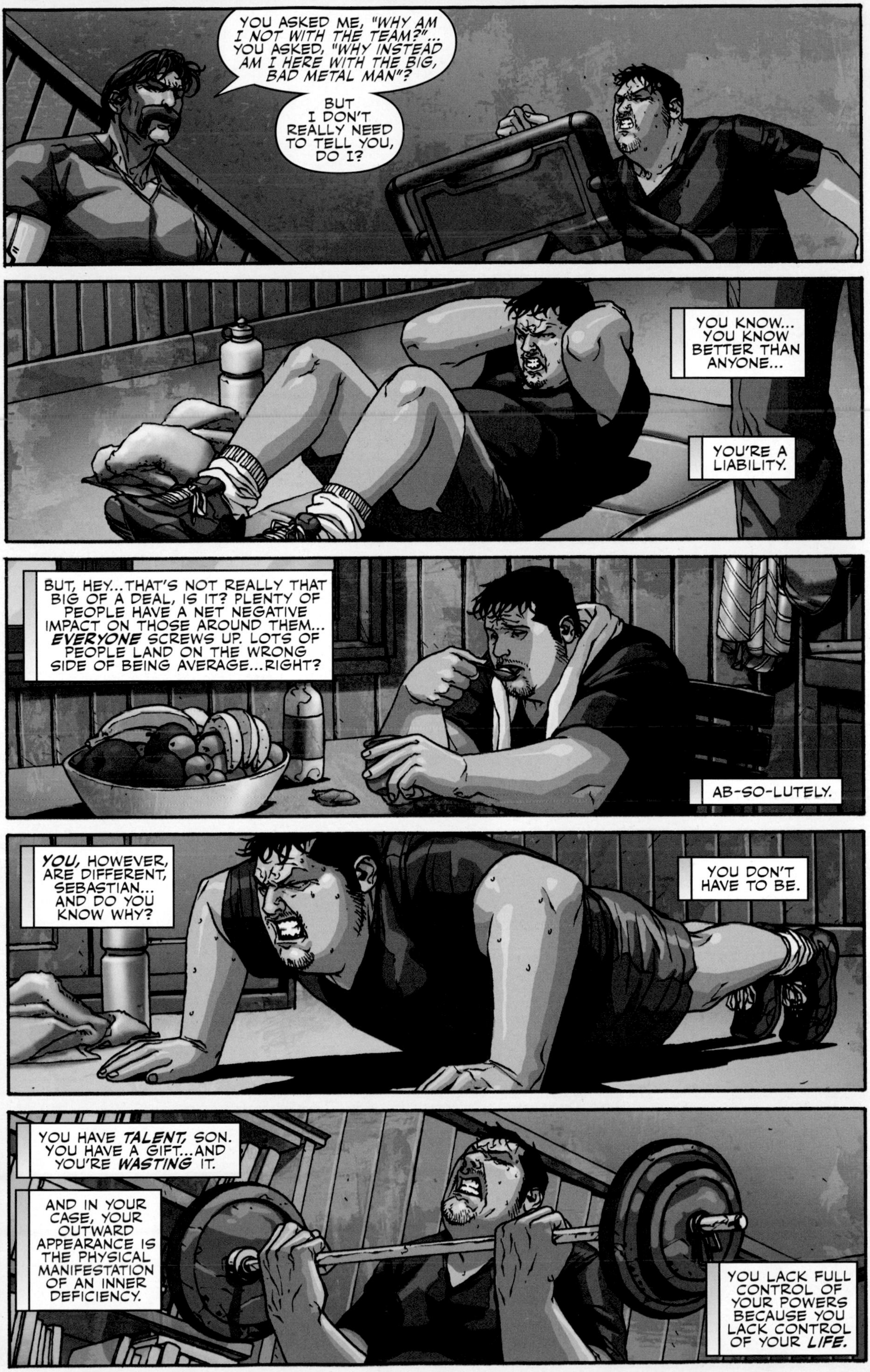
YOU ASKED ME, "WHY AM I NOT WITH THE TEAM?"... YOU ASKED, "WHY INSTEAD AM I HERE WITH THE BIG, BAD METAL MAN"?
BUT I DON'T REALLY NEED TO TELL YOU, DO I?
YOU KNOW... YOU KNOW BETTER THAN ANYONE...
YOU'RE A LIABILITY.
BUT, HEY...THAT'S NOT REALLY THAT BIG OF A DEAL, IS IT? PLENTY OF PEOPLE HAVE A NET NEGATIVE IMPACT ON THOSE AROUND THEM... EVERYONE SCREWS UP. LOTS OF PEOPLE LAND ON THE WRONG SIDE OF BEING AVERAGE...RIGHT?
AB-SO-LUTELY.
YOU, HOWEVER, ARE DIFFERENT, SEBASTIAN... AND DO YOU KNOW WHY?
YOU DON'T HAVE TO BE.
YOU HAVE TALENT, SON. YOU HAVE A GIFT...AND YOU'RE WASTING IT.
AND IN YOUR CASE, YOUR OUTWARD APPEARANCE IS THE PHYSICAL MANIFESTATION OF AN INNER DEFICIENCY.
YOU LACK FULL CONTROL OF YOUR POWERS BECAUSE YOU LACK CONTROL OF YOUR LIFE.

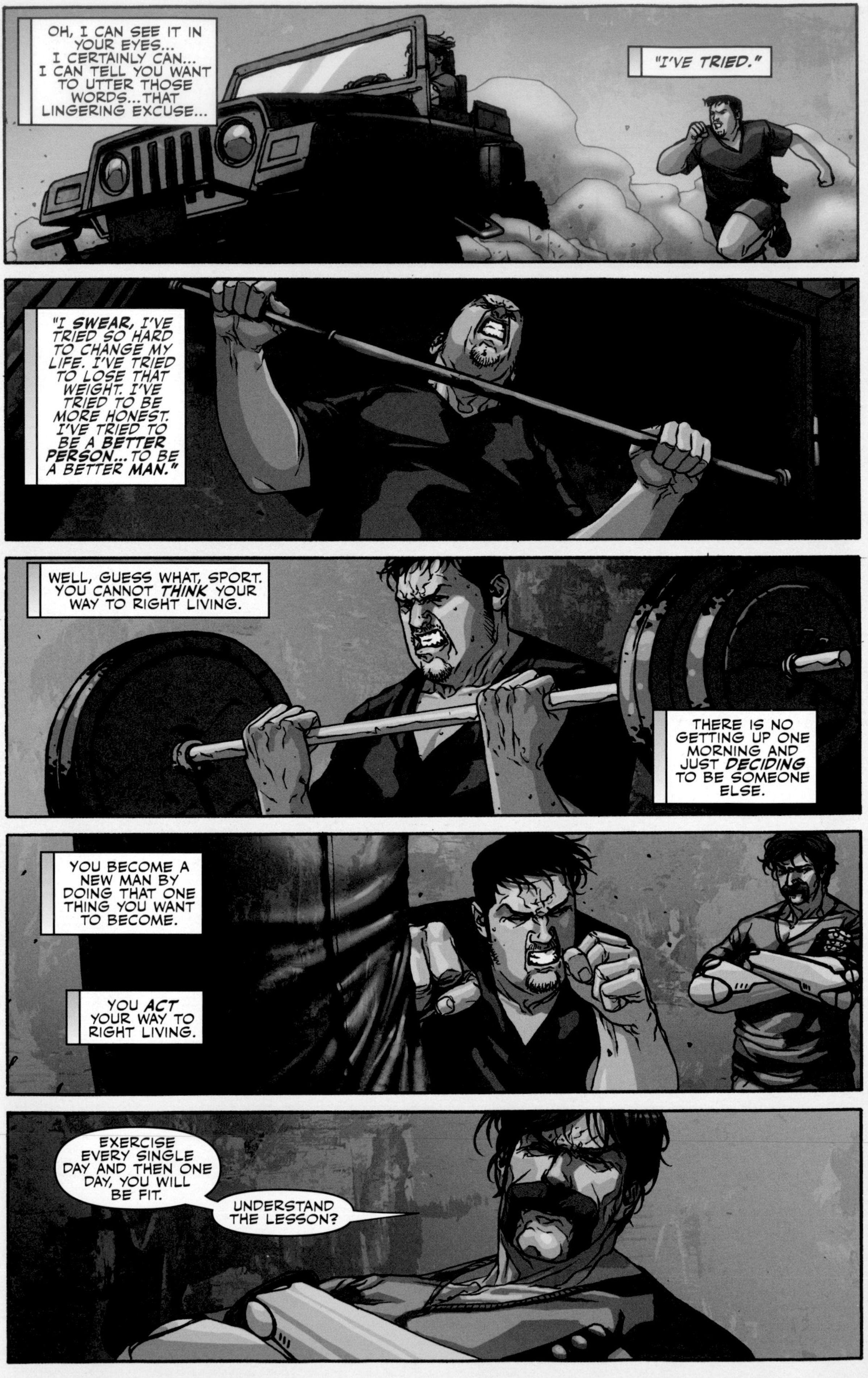
OH, I CAN SEE IT IN YOUR EYES... I CERTAINLY CAN... I CAN TELL YOU WANT TO UTTER THOSE WORDS...THAT LINGERING EXCUSE...
"I'VE TRIED."
"I SWEAR, I'VE TRIED SO HARD TO CHANGE MY LIFE. I'VE TRIED TO LOSE THAT WEIGHT. I'VE TRIED TO BE MORE HONEST. I'VE TRIED TO BE A BETTER PERSON...TO BE A BETTER MAN."
WELL, GUESS WHAT, SPORT. YOU CANNOT THINK YOUR WAY TO RIGHT LIVING.
THERE IS NO GETTING UP ONE MORNING AND JUST DECIDING TO BE SOMEONE ELSE.
YOU BECOME A NEW MAN BY DOING THAT ONE THING YOU WANT TO BECOME.
YOU ACT YOUR WAY TO RIGHT LIVING.
EXERCISE EVERY SINGLE DAY AND THEN ONE DAY, YOU WILL BE FIT.
UNDERSTAND THE LESSON?

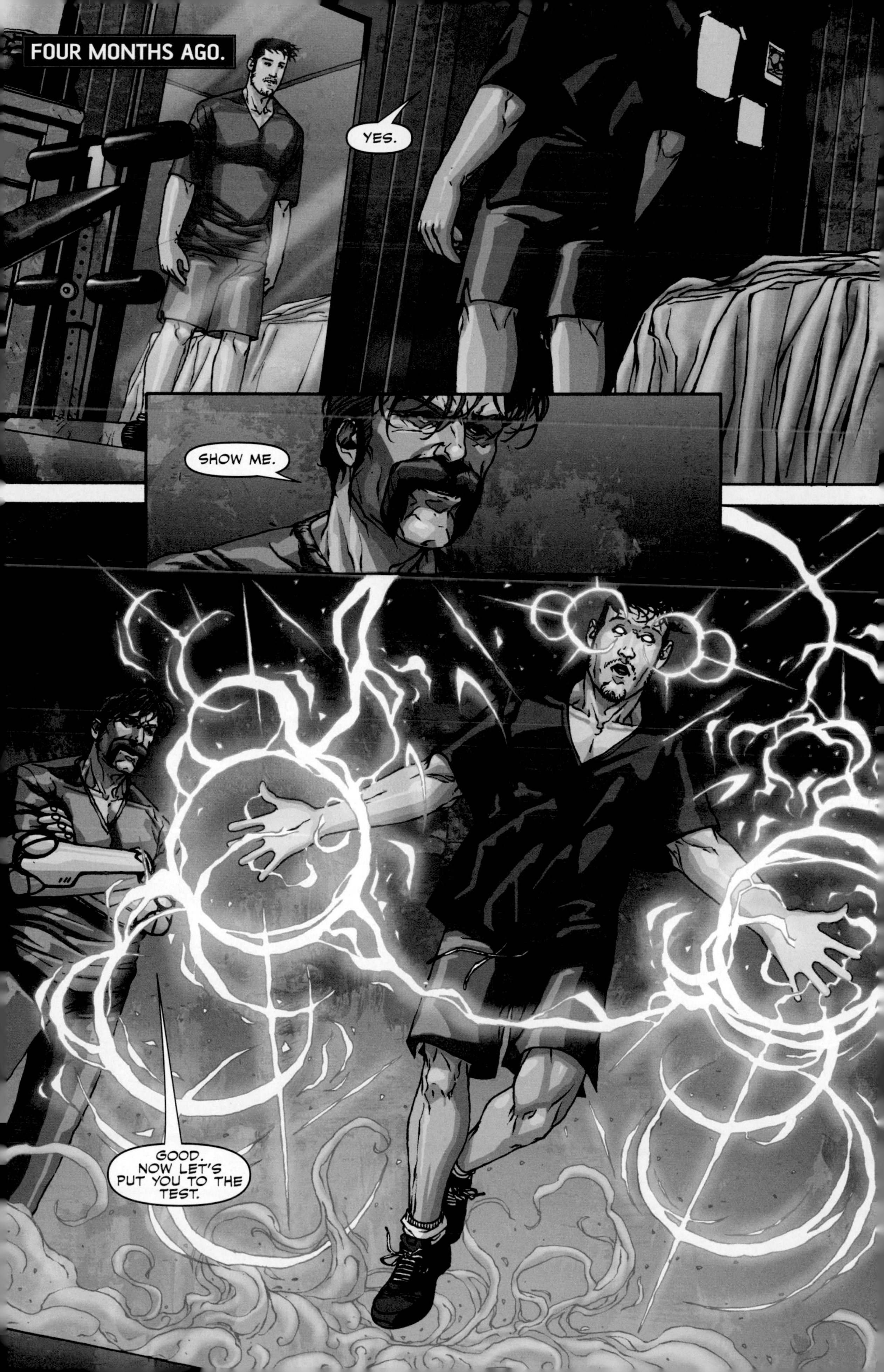
FOUR MONTHS AGO.
YES.
SHOW ME.
GOOD. NOW LET'S PUT YOU TO THE TEST.

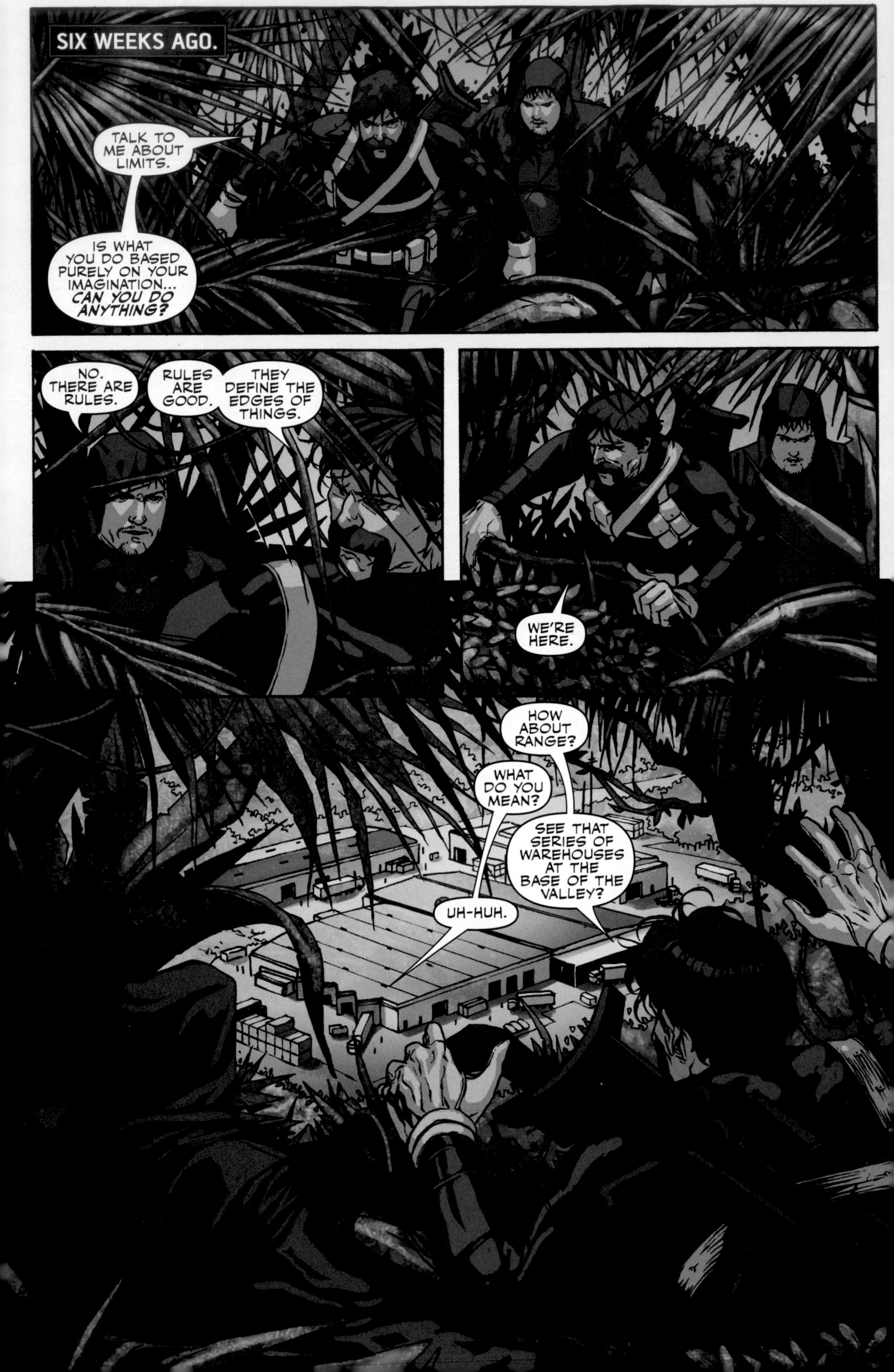

SIX WEEKS AGO.
TALK TO ME ABOUT LIMITS.
IS WHAT YOU DO BASED PURELY ON YOUR IMAGINATION... *CAN YOU DO ANYTHING?*
NO. THERE ARE RULES.
RULES ARE GOOD.
THEY DEFINE THE EDGES OF THINGS.
WE'RE HERE.
HOW ABOUT RANGE?
WHAT DO YOU MEAN?
SEE THAT SERIES OF WAREHOUSES AT THE BASE OF THE VALLEY?
UH-HUH.

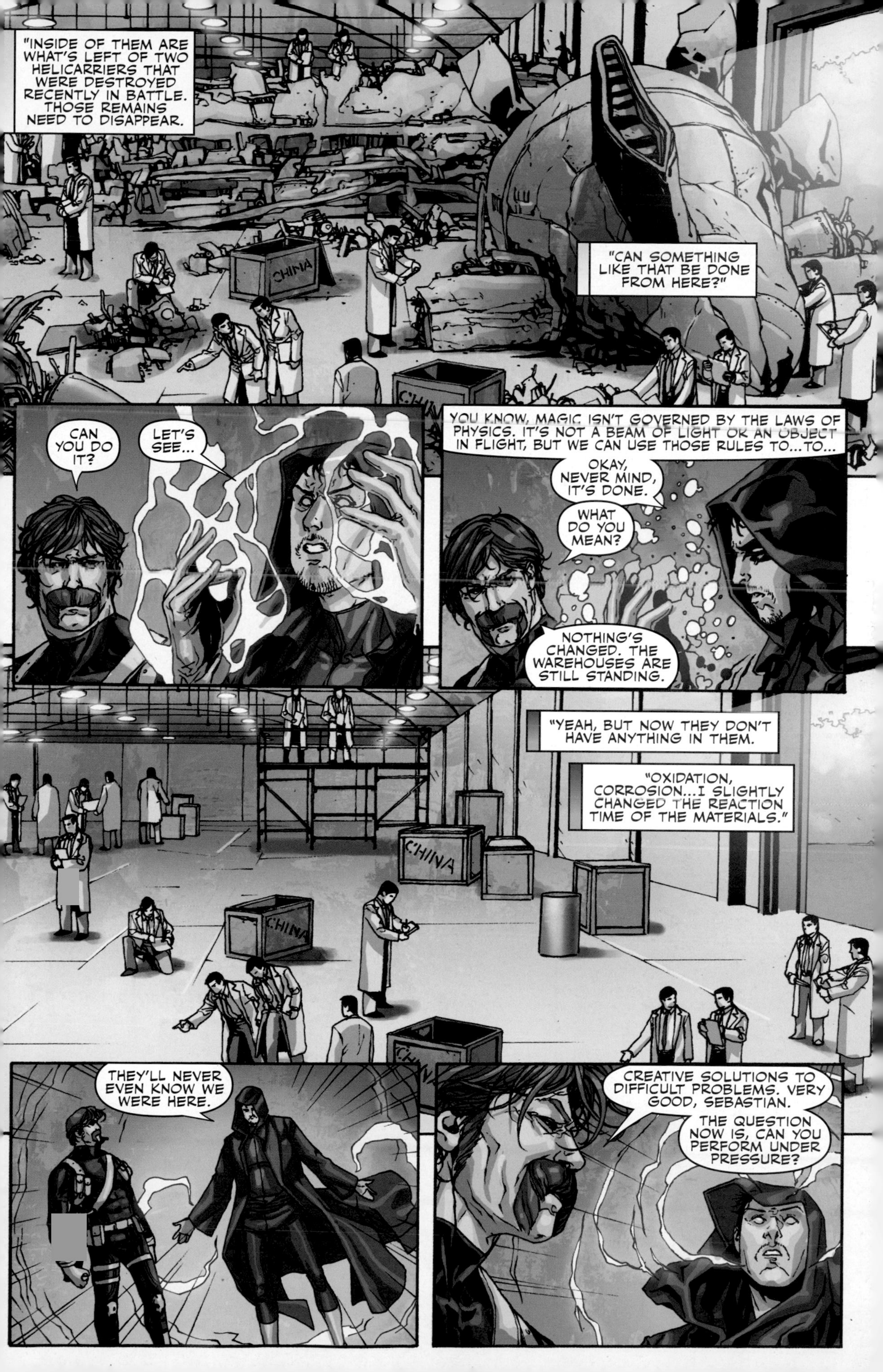
"INSIDE OF THEM ARE WHAT'S LEFT OF TWO HELICARRIERS THAT WERE DESTROYED RECENTLY IN BATTLE. THOSE REMAINS NEED TO DISAPPEAR.
CHINA
"CAN SOMETHING LIKE THAT BE DONE FROM HERE?"
CAN YOU DO IT?
LET'S SEE...
YOU KNOW, MAGIC ISN'T GOVERNED BY THE LAWS OF PHYSICS. IT'S NOT A BEAM OF LIGHT OR AN OBJECT IN FLIGHT, BUT WE CAN USE THOSE RULES TO...TO...
OKAY, NEVER MIND, IT'S DONE.
WHAT DO YOU MEAN?
NOTHING'S CHANGED. THE WAREHOUSES ARE STILL STANDING.
"YEAH, BUT NOW THEY DON'T HAVE ANYTHING IN THEM.
"OXIDATION, CORROSION...I SLIGHTLY CHANGED THE REACTION TIME OF THE MATERIALS."
CHINA
CHINA
THEY'LL NEVER EVEN KNOW WE WERE HERE.
CREATIVE SOLUTIONS TO DIFFICULT PROBLEMS. VERY GOOD, SEBASTIAN.
THE QUESTION NOW IS, CAN YOU PERFORM UNDER PRESSURE?

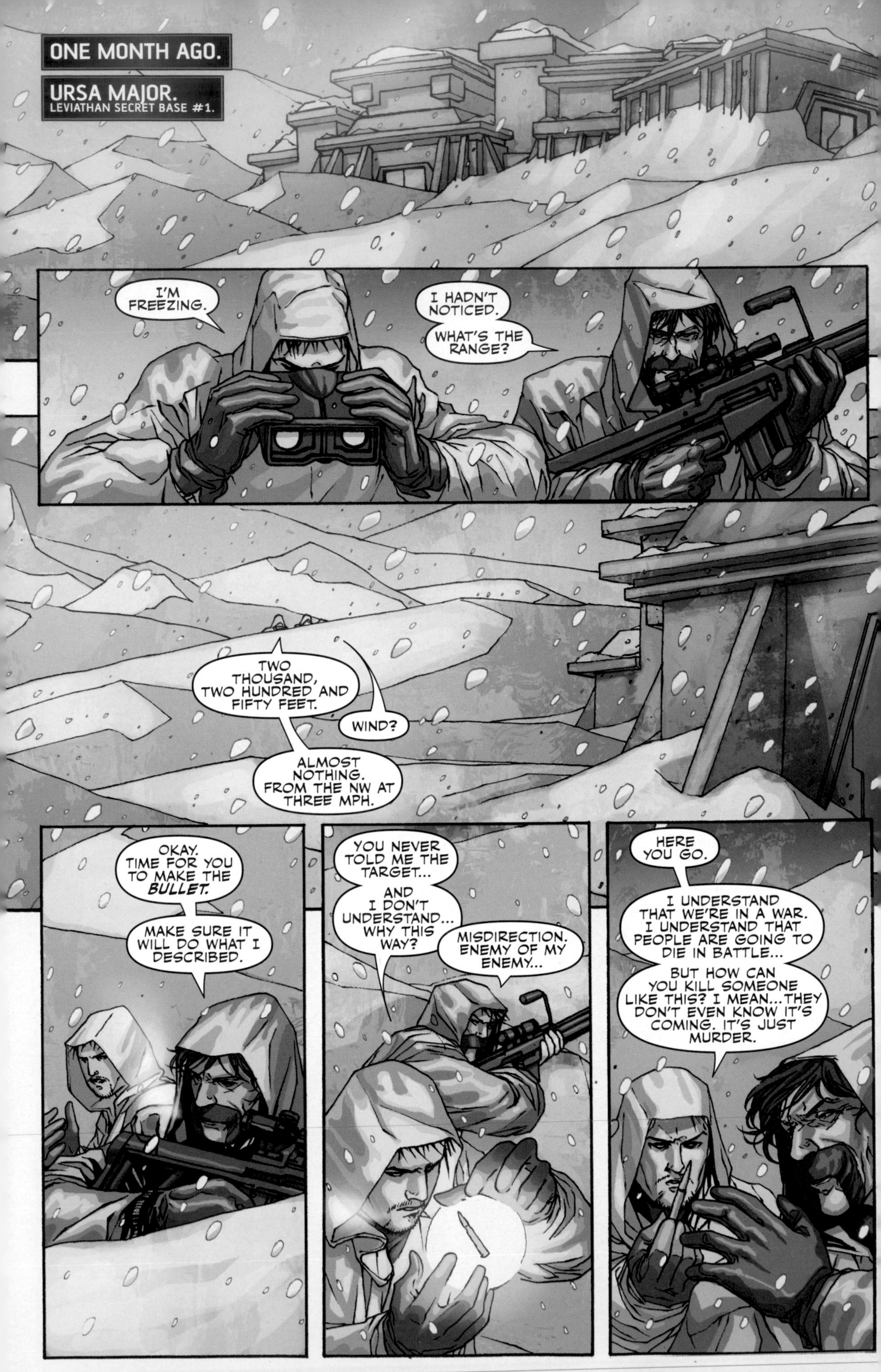
ONE MONTH AGO.
URSA MAJOR.
LEVIATHAN SECRET BASE #1.
I'M FREEZING.
I HADN'T NOTICED.
WHAT'S THE RANGE?
TWO THOUSAND, TWO HUNDRED AND FIFTY FEET.
WIND?
ALMOST NOTHING. FROM THE NW AT THREE MPH.
OKAY. TIME FOR YOU TO MAKE THE *BULLET.*
MAKE SURE IT WILL DO WHAT I DESCRIBED.
YOU NEVER TOLD ME THE TARGET...
AND I DON'T UNDERSTAND... WHY THIS WAY?
MISDIRECTION. ENEMY OF MY ENEMY...
HERE YOU GO.
I UNDERSTAND THAT WE'RE IN A WAR. I UNDERSTAND THAT PEOPLE ARE GOING TO DIE IN BATTLE...
BUT HOW CAN YOU KILL SOMEONE LIKE THIS? I MEAN...THEY DON'T EVEN KNOW IT'S COMING. IT'S JUST MURDER.

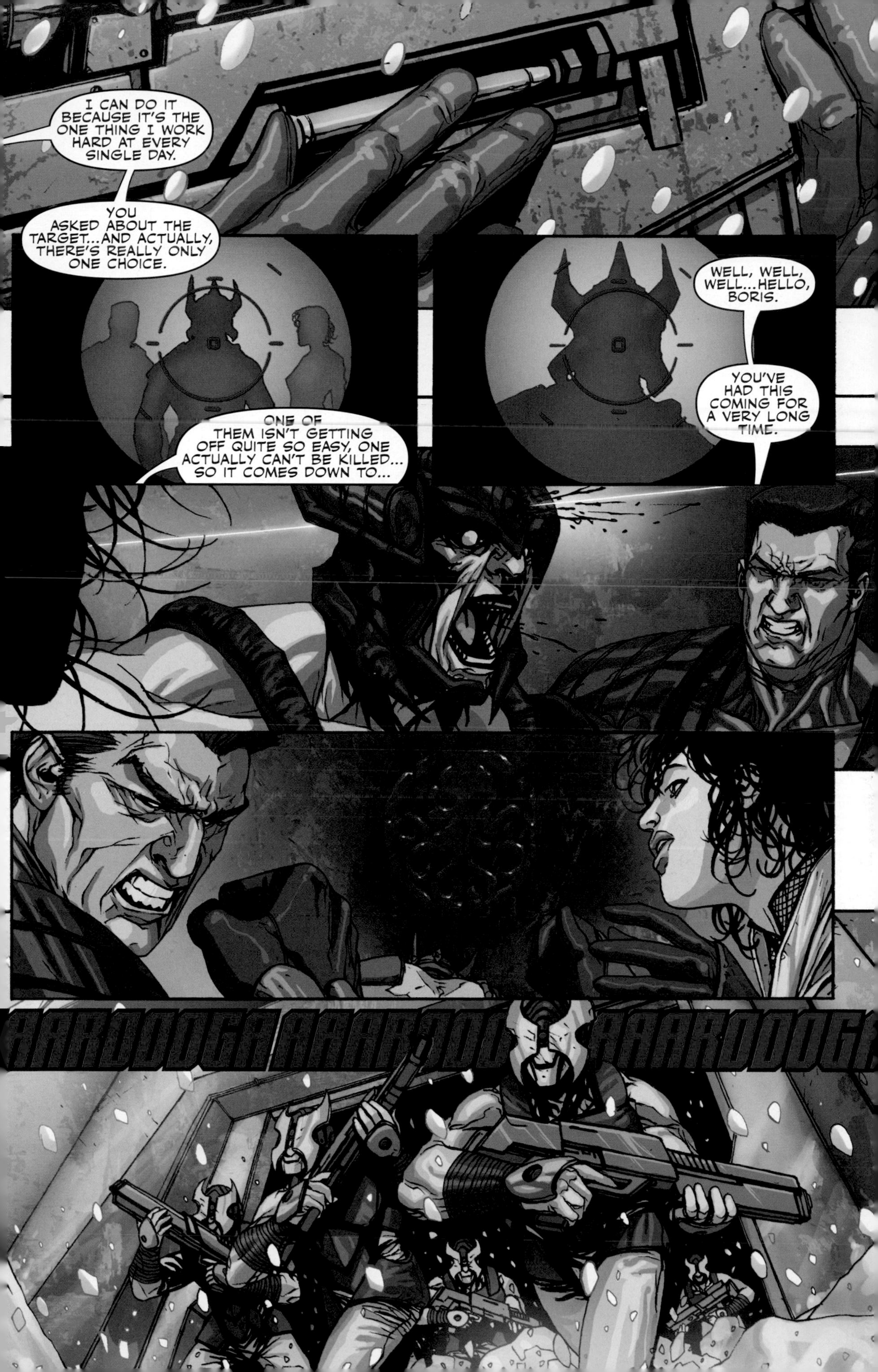
I CAN DO IT BECAUSE IT'S THE ONE THING I WORK HARD AT EVERY SINGLE DAY.
YOU ASKED ABOUT THE TARGET...AND ACTUALLY, THERE'S REALLY ONLY ONE CHOICE.
ONE OF THEM ISN'T GETTING OFF QUITE SO EASY, ONE ACTUALLY CAN'T BE KILLED... SO IT COMES DOWN TO...
WELL, WELL, WELL...HELLO, BORIS.
YOU'VE HAD THIS COMING FOR A VERY LONG TIME.
AARDOOGA

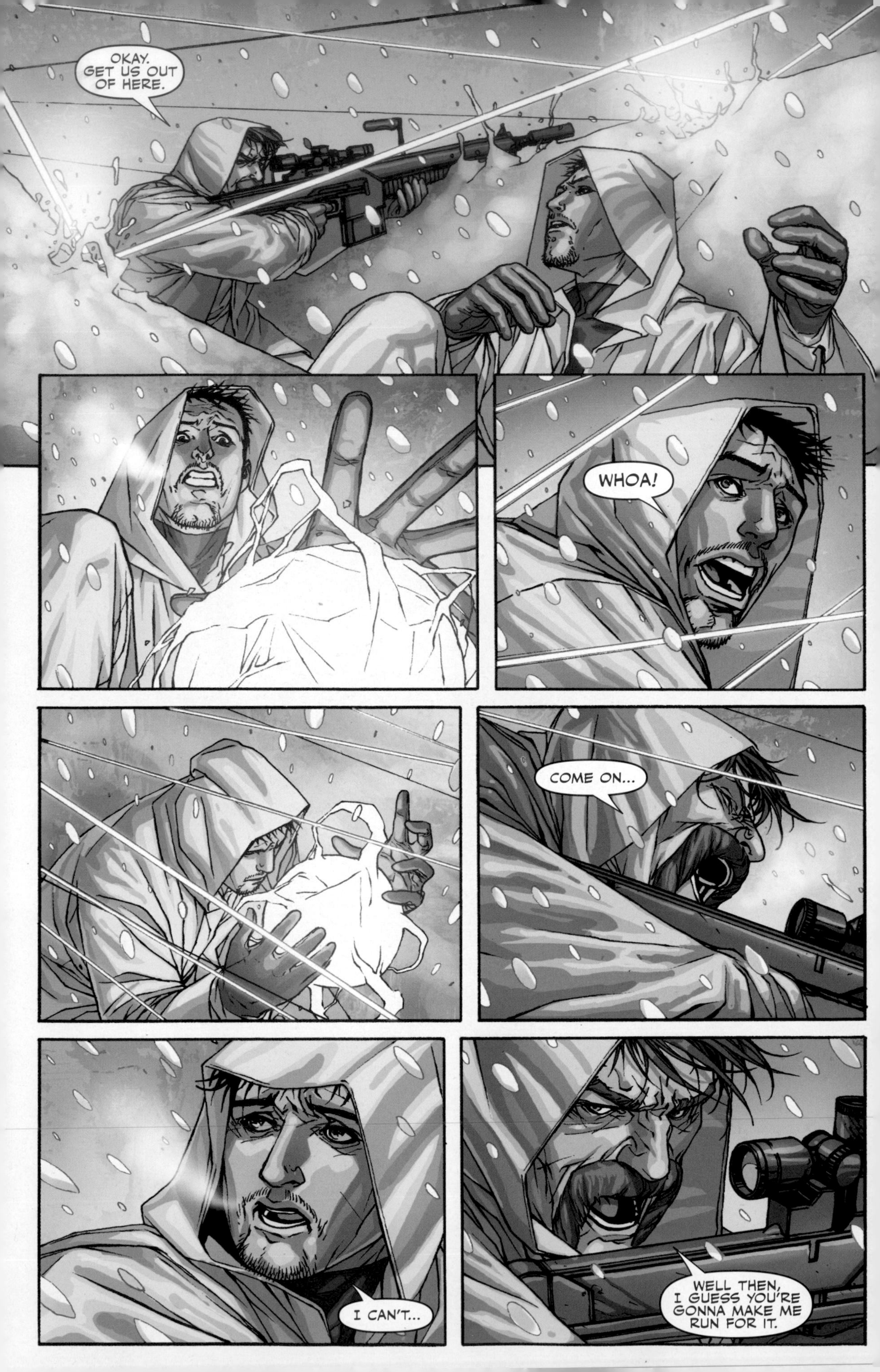
OKAY. GET US OUT OF HERE.
WHOA!
COME ON...
I CAN'T...
WELL THEN, I GUESS YOU'RE GONNA MAKE ME RUN FOR IT.

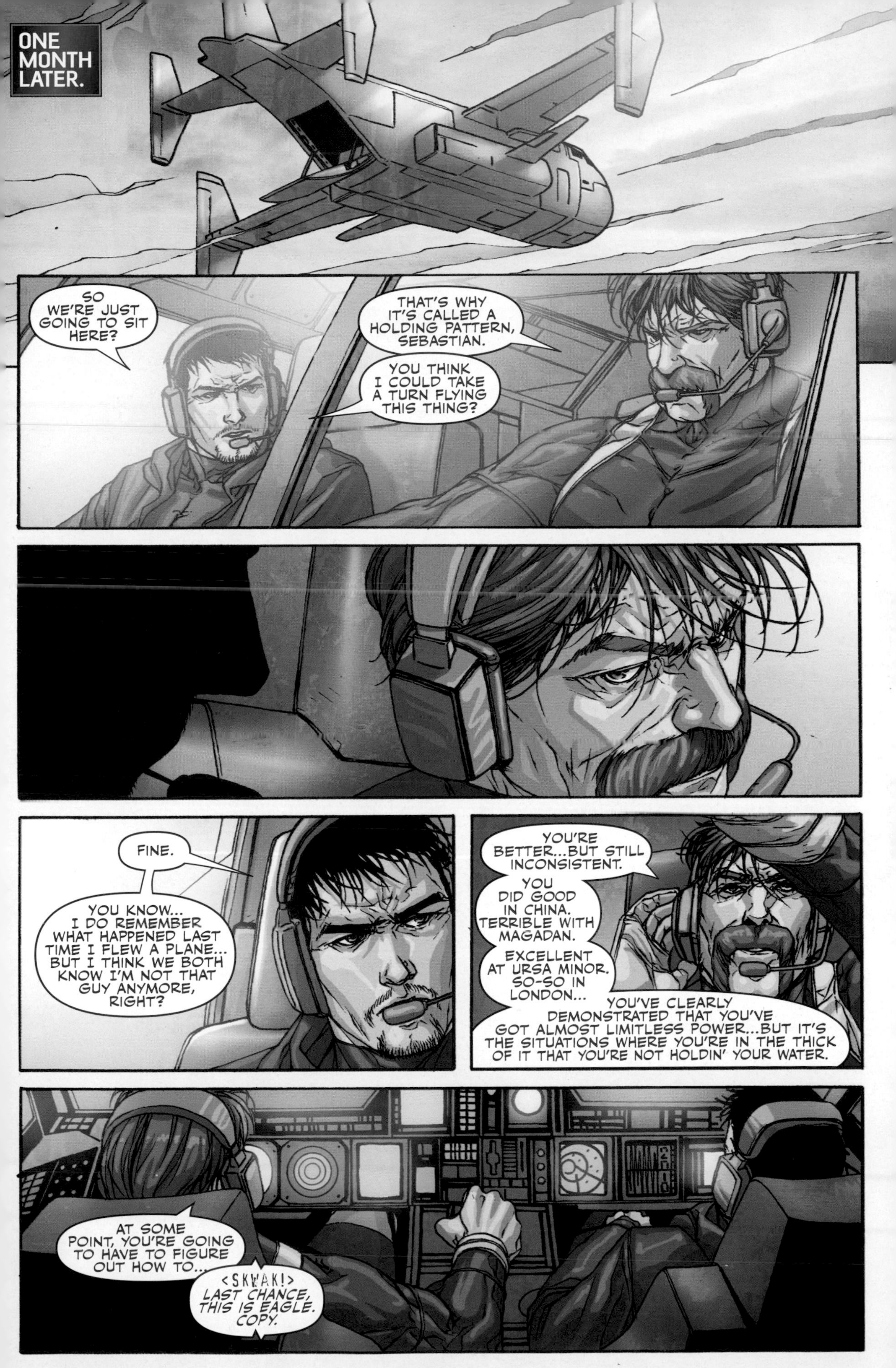
ONE MONTH LATER.
SO WE'RE JUST GOING TO SIT HERE?
THAT'S WHY IT'S CALLED A HOLDING PATTERN, SEBASTIAN.
YOU THINK I COULD TAKE A TURN FLYING THIS THING?
FINE.
YOU KNOW... I DO REMEMBER WHAT HAPPENED LAST TIME I FLEW A PLANE... BUT I THINK WE BOTH KNOW I'M NOT THAT GUY ANYMORE, RIGHT?
YOU'RE BETTER...BUT STILL INCONSISTENT.
YOU DID GOOD IN CHINA. TERRIBLE WITH MAGADAN.
EXCELLENT AT URSA MINOR. SO-SO IN LONDON...
YOU'VE CLEARLY DEMONSTRATED THAT YOU'VE GOT ALMOST LIMITLESS POWER...BUT IT'S THE SITUATIONS WHERE YOU'RE IN THE THICK OF IT THAT YOU'RE NOT HOLDIN' YOUR WATER.
AT SOME POINT, YOU'RE GOING TO HAVE TO FIGURE OUT HOW TO...
<SKWAK!> LAST CHANCE, THIS IS EAGLE. COPY.

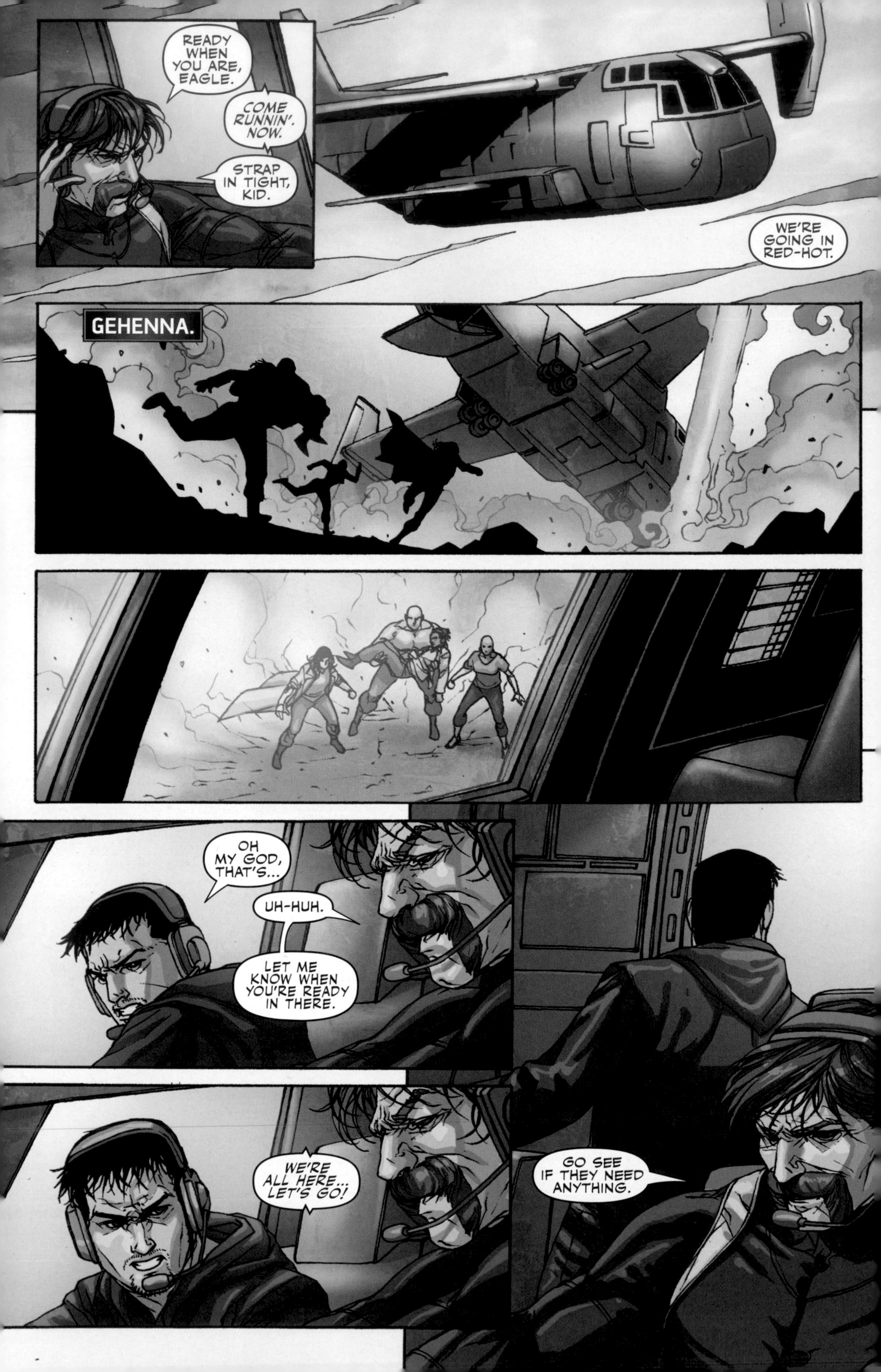
READY WHEN YOU ARE, EAGLE.
COME RUNNIN'. NOW.
STRAP IN TIGHT, KID.
WE'RE GOING IN RED-HOT.
GEHENNA.
OH MY GOD, THAT'S...
UH-HUH.
LET ME KNOW WHEN YOU'RE READY IN THERE.
WE'RE ALL HERE... LET'S GO!
GO SEE IF THEY NEED ANYTHING.

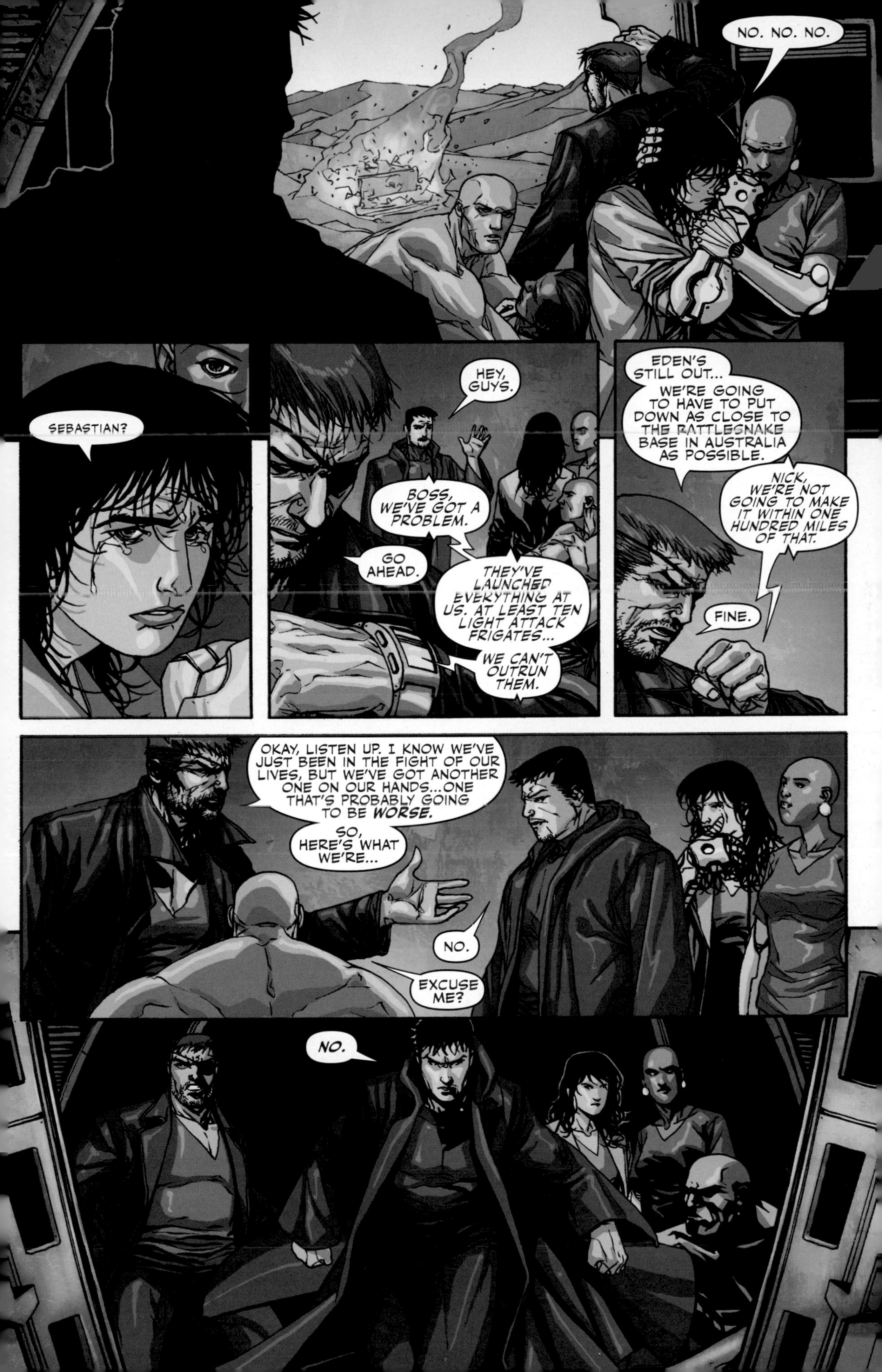
NO. NO. NO.
SEBASTIAN?
HEY, GUYS.
BOSS, WE'VE GOT A PROBLEM.
GO AHEAD.
THEY'VE LAUNCHED EVERYTHING AT US. AT LEAST TEN LIGHT ATTACK FRIGATES...
WE CAN'T OUTRUN THEM.
EDEN'S STILL OUT...
WE'RE GOING TO HAVE TO PUT DOWN AS CLOSE TO THE RATTLESNAKE BASE IN AUSTRALIA AS POSSIBLE.
NICK, WE'RE NOT GOING TO MAKE IT WITHIN ONE HUNDRED MILES OF THAT.
FINE.
OKAY, LISTEN UP. I KNOW WE'VE JUST BEEN IN THE FIGHT OF OUR LIVES, BUT WE'VE GOT ANOTHER ONE ON OUR HANDS...ONE THAT'S PROBABLY GOING TO BE WORSE.
SO, HERE'S WHAT WE'RE...
NO.
EXCUSE ME?
NO.

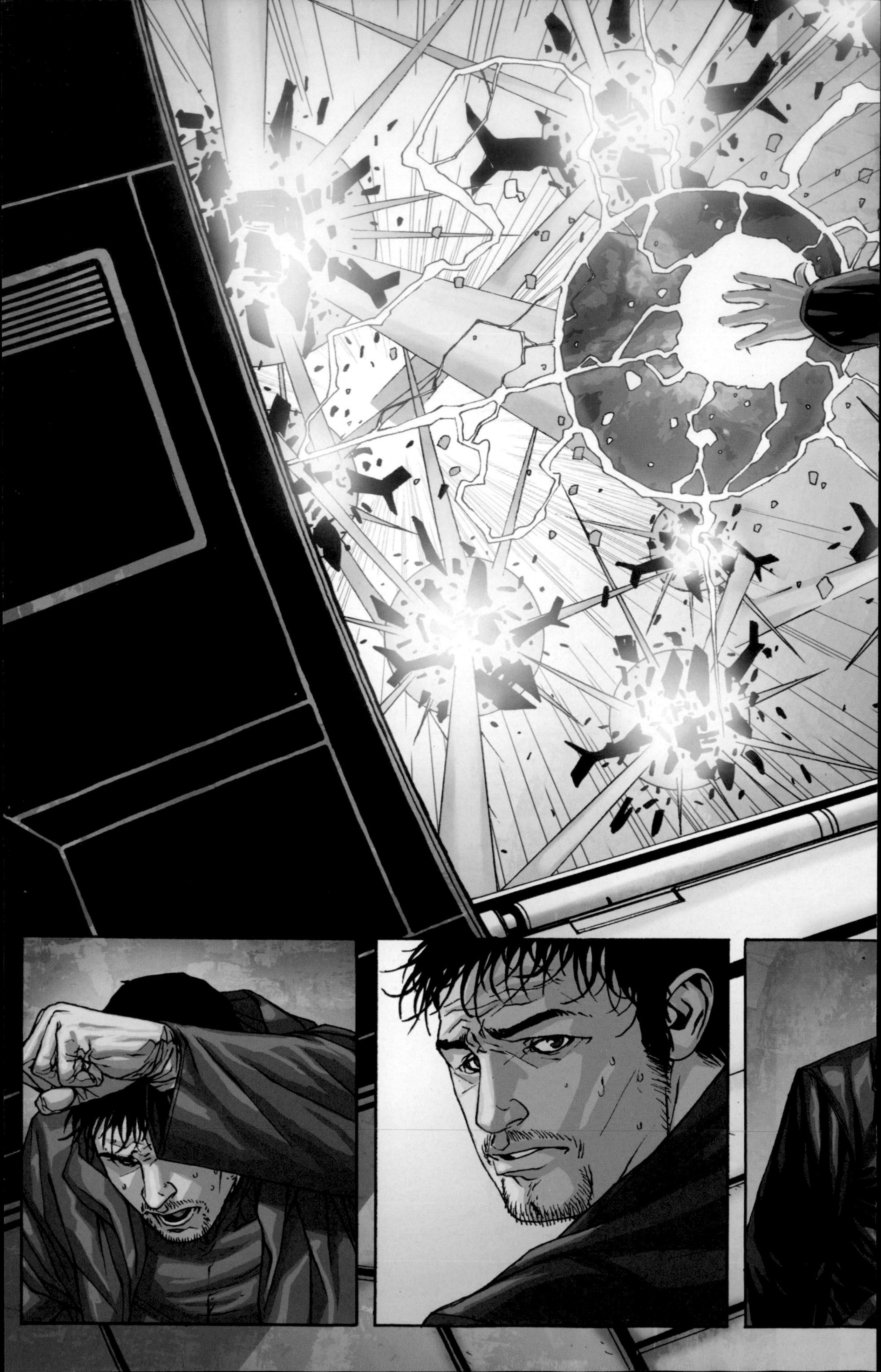

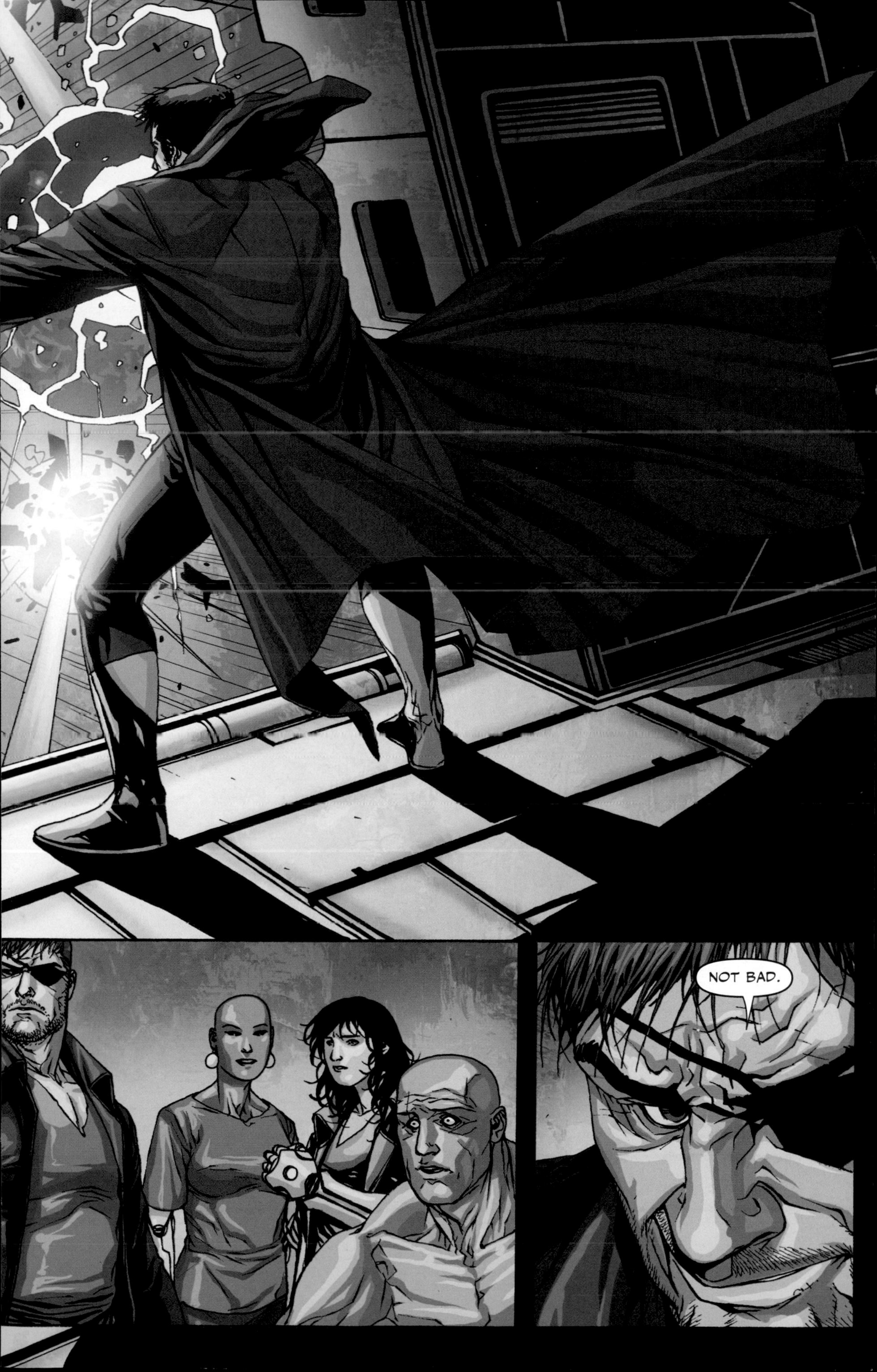
NOT BAD.

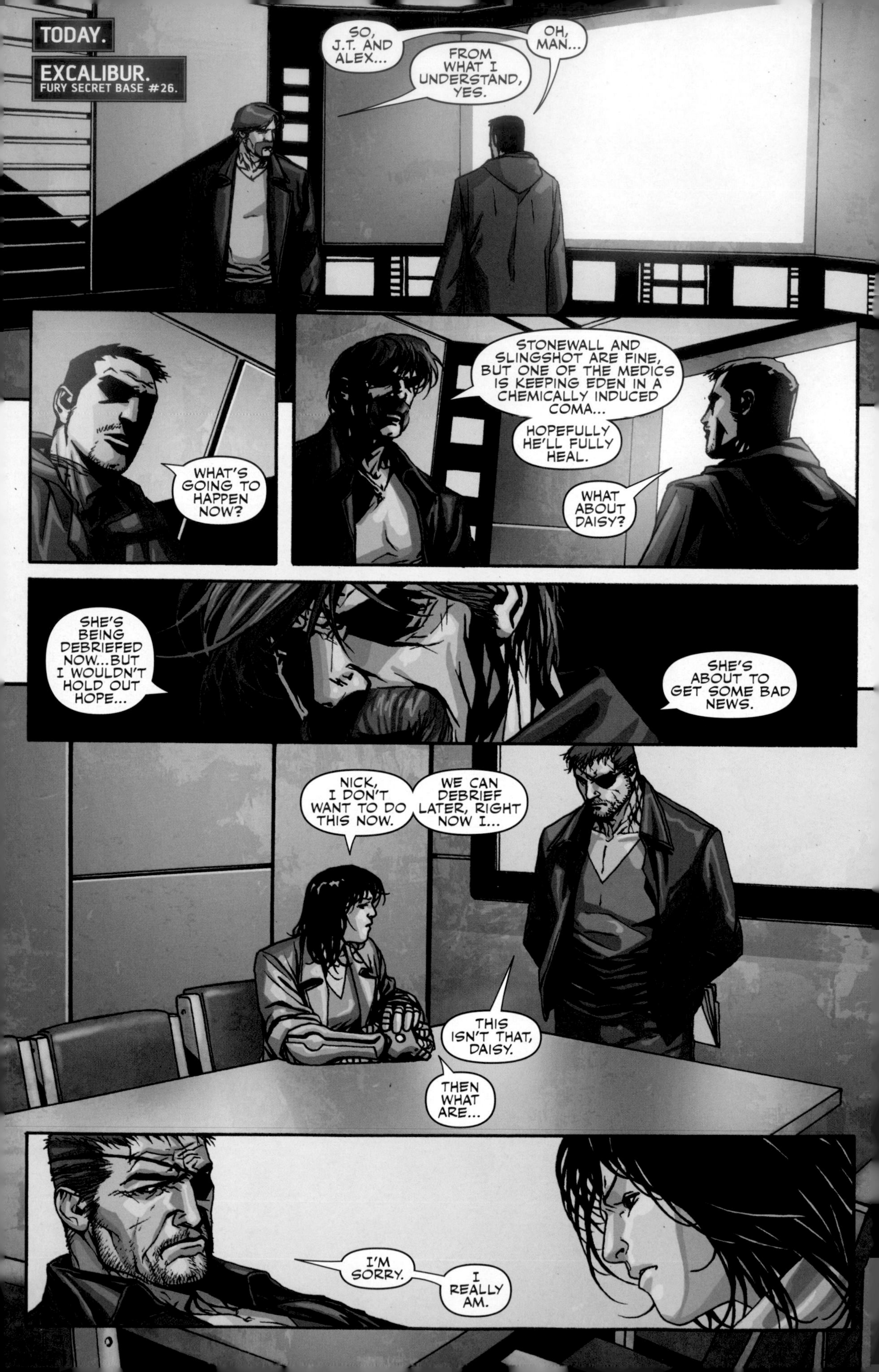

TODAY.
EXCALIBUR.
FURY SECRET BASE #26.
SO, J.T. AND ALEX...
FROM WHAT I UNDERSTAND, YES.
OH, MAN...
WHAT'S GOING TO HAPPEN NOW?
STONEWALL AND SLINGSHOT ARE FINE, BUT ONE OF THE MEDICS IS KEEPING EDEN IN A CHEMICALLY INDUCED COMA...
HOPEFULLY HE'LL FULLY HEAL.
WHAT ABOUT DAISY?
SHE'S BEING DEBRIEFED NOW...BUT I WOULDN'T HOLD OUT HOPE...
SHE'S ABOUT TO GET SOME BAD NEWS.
NICK, I DON'T WANT TO DO THIS NOW.
WE CAN DEBRIEF LATER, RIGHT NOW I...
THIS ISN'T THAT, DAISY.
THEN WHAT ARE...
I'M SORRY.
I REALLY AM.

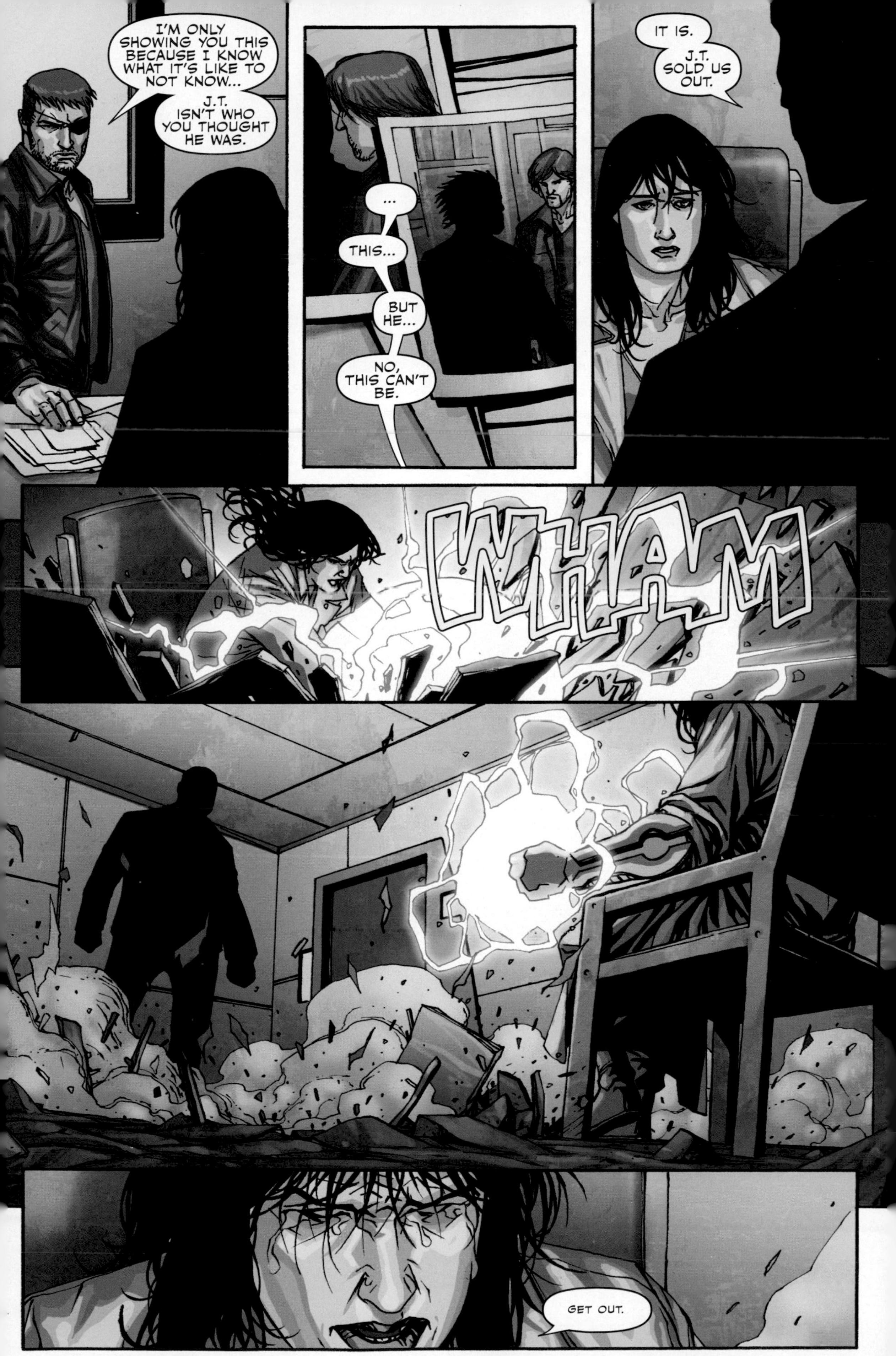
I'M ONLY SHOWING YOU THIS BECAUSE I KNOW WHAT IT'S LIKE TO NOT KNOW...
J.T. ISN'T WHO YOU THOUGHT HE WAS.
...
THIS...
BUT HE...
NO, THIS CAN'T BE.
IT IS.
J.T. SOLD US OUT.
WHAM
GET OUT.

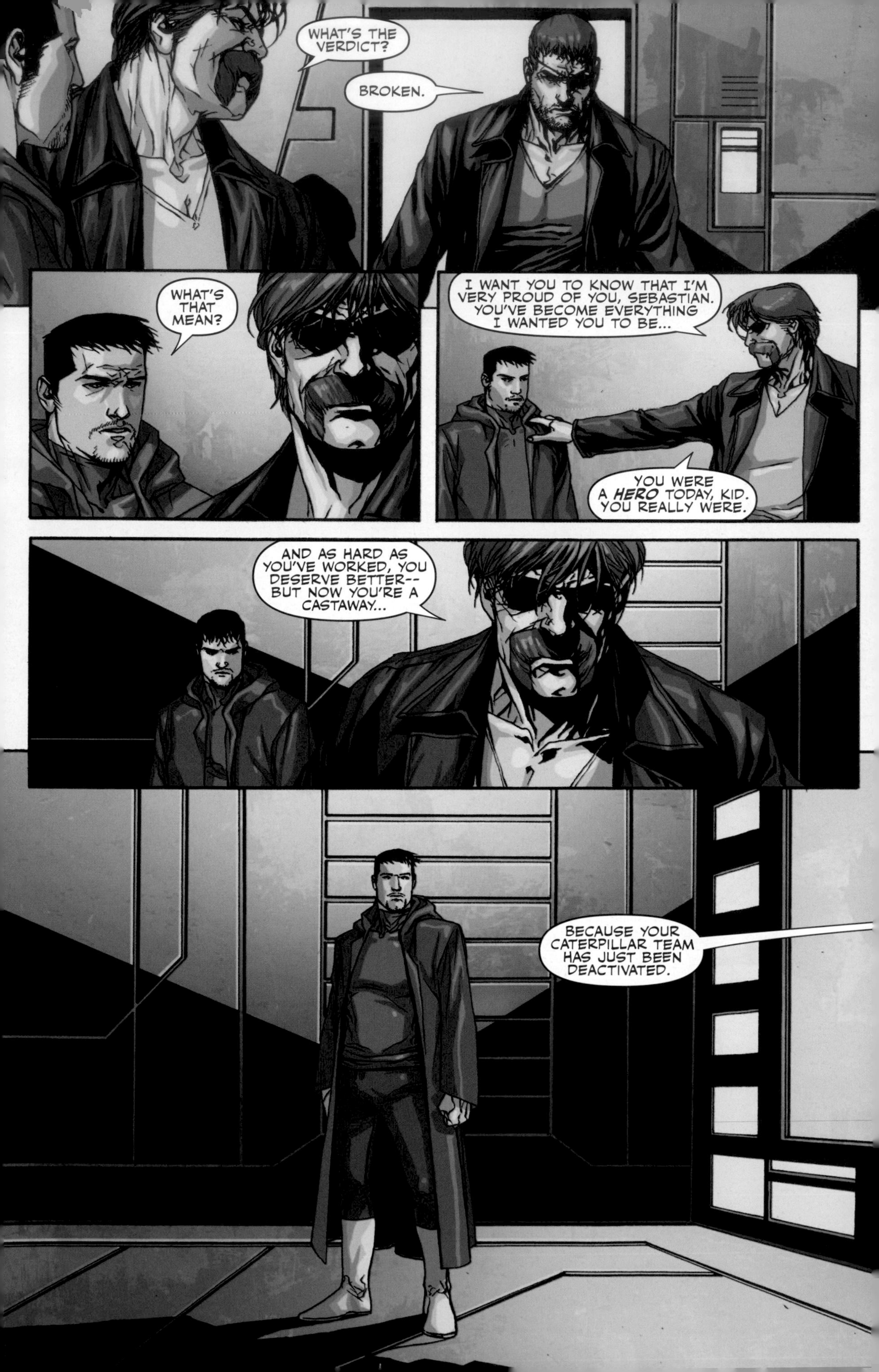
WHAT'S THE VERDICT?
BROKEN.
WHAT'S THAT MEAN?
I WANT YOU TO KNOW THAT I'M VERY PROUD OF YOU, SEBASTIAN. YOU'VE BECOME EVERYTHING I WANTED YOU TO BE...
YOU WERE A *HERO* TODAY, KID. YOU REALLY WERE.
AND AS HARD AS YOU'VE WORKED, YOU DESERVE BETTER-- BUT NOW YOU'RE A CASTAWAY...
BECAUSE YOUR CATERPILLAR TEAM HAS JUST BEEN DEACTIVATED.

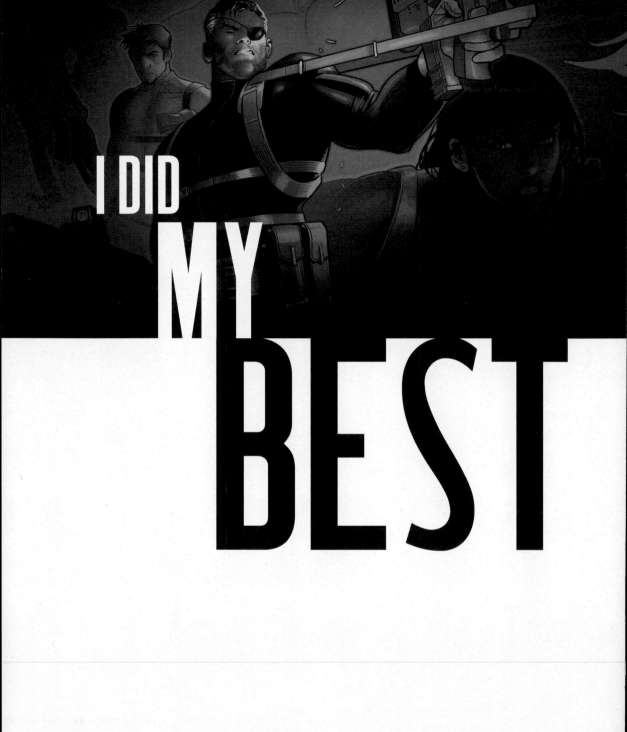

I DID
MY
BEST

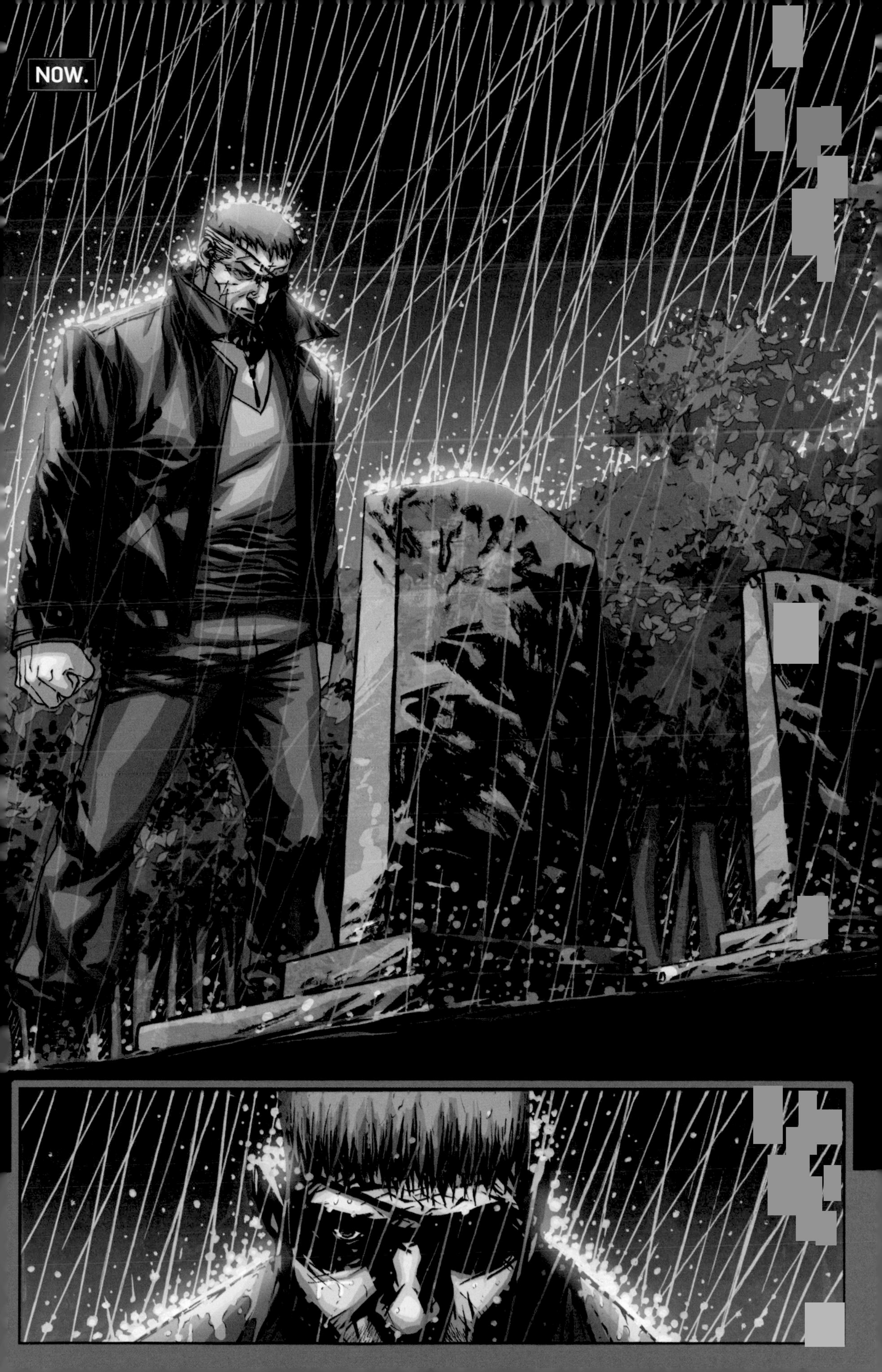
NOW.

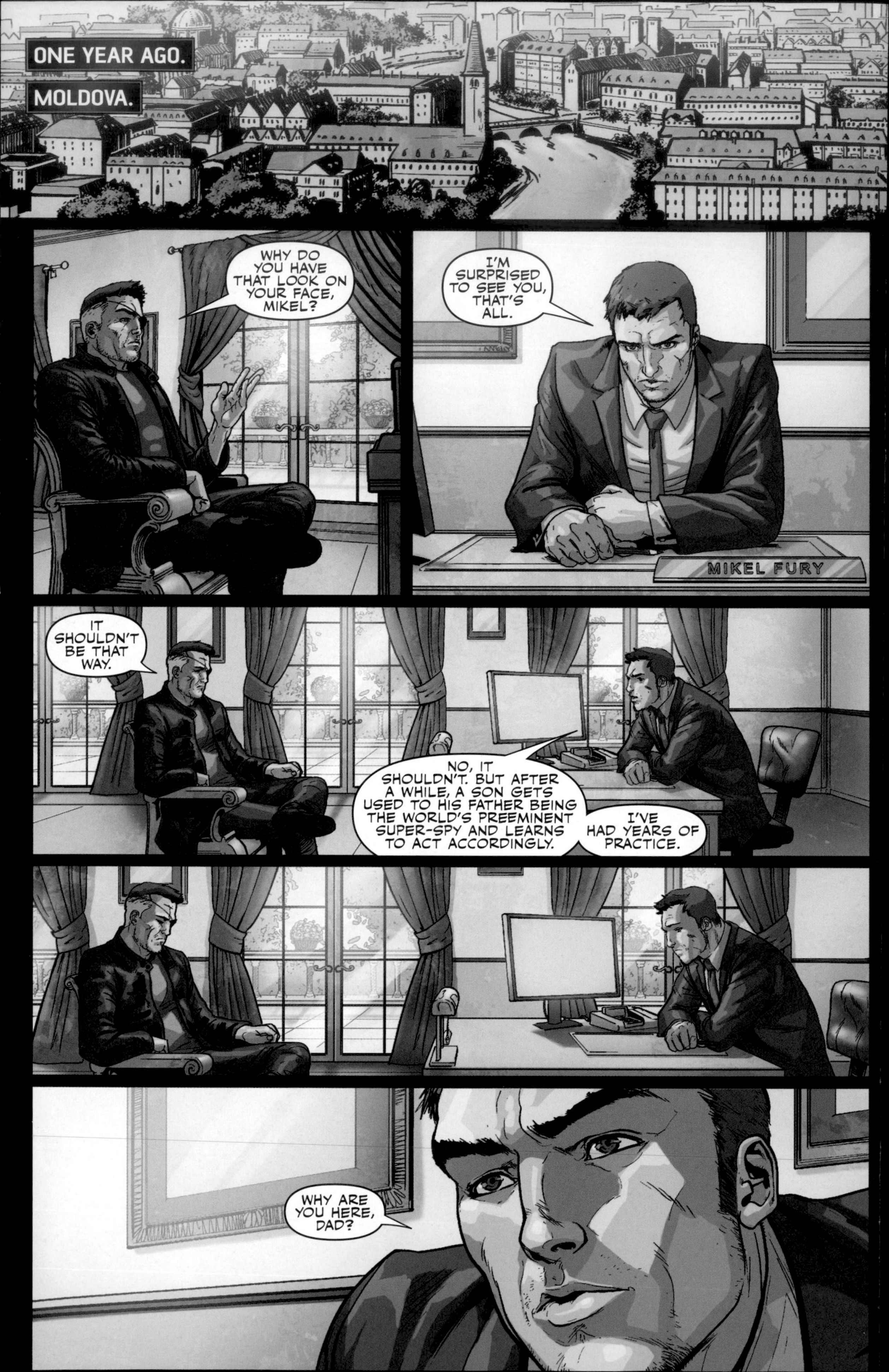
ONE YEAR AGO.
MOLDOVA.
WHY DO YOU HAVE THAT LOOK ON YOUR FACE, MIKEL?
I'M SURPRISED TO SEE YOU, THAT'S ALL.
MIKEL FURY
IT SHOULDN'T BE THAT WAY.
NO, IT SHOULDN'T. BUT AFTER A WHILE, A SON GETS USED TO HIS FATHER BEING THE WORLD'S PREEMINENT SUPER-SPY AND LEARNS TO ACT ACCORDINGLY.
I'VE HAD YEARS OF PRACTICE.
WHY ARE YOU HERE, DAD?

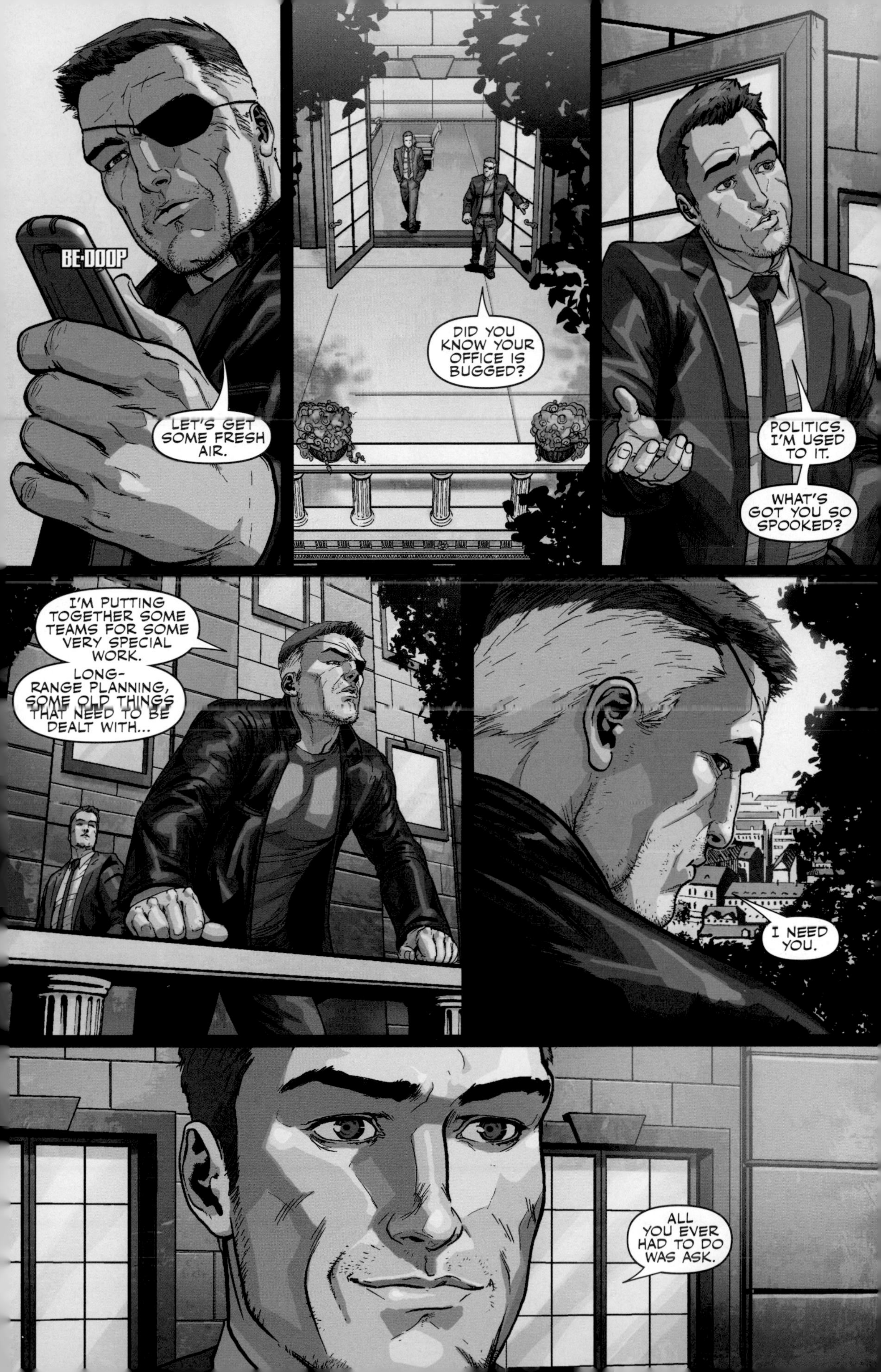
BE-DOOP
LET'S GET SOME FRESH AIR.
DID YOU KNOW YOUR OFFICE IS BUGGED?
POLITICS. I'M USED TO IT.
WHAT'S GOT YOU SO SPOOKED?
I'M PUTTING TOGETHER SOME TEAMS FOR SOME VERY SPECIAL WORK.
LONG-RANGE PLANNING, SOME OLD THINGS THAT NEED TO BE DEALT WITH...
I NEED YOU.
ALL YOU EVER HAD TO DO WAS ASK.

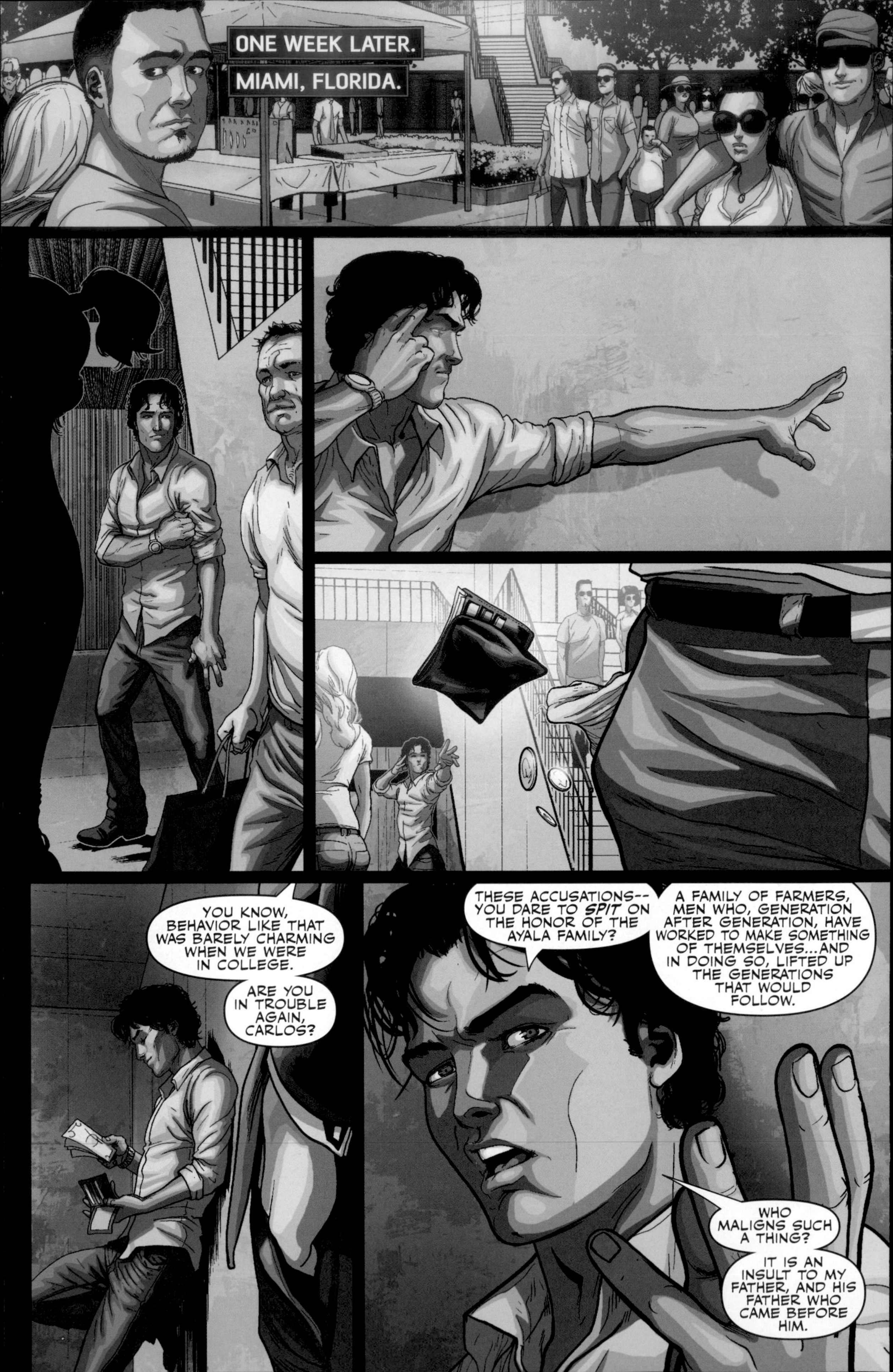
ONE WEEK LATER.
MIAMI, FLORIDA.
YOU KNOW, BEHAVIOR LIKE THAT WAS BARELY CHARMING WHEN WE WERE IN COLLEGE.
ARE YOU IN TROUBLE AGAIN, CARLOS?
THESE ACCUSATIONS-- YOU DARE TO SPIT ON THE HONOR OF THE AYALA FAMILY?
A FAMILY OF FARMERS, MEN WHO, GENERATION AFTER GENERATION, HAVE WORKED TO MAKE SOMETHING OF THEMSELVES...AND IN DOING SO, LIFTED UP THE GENERATIONS THAT WOULD FOLLOW.
WHO MALIGNS SUCH A THING?
IT IS AN INSULT TO MY FATHER, AND HIS FATHER WHO CAME BEFORE HIM.

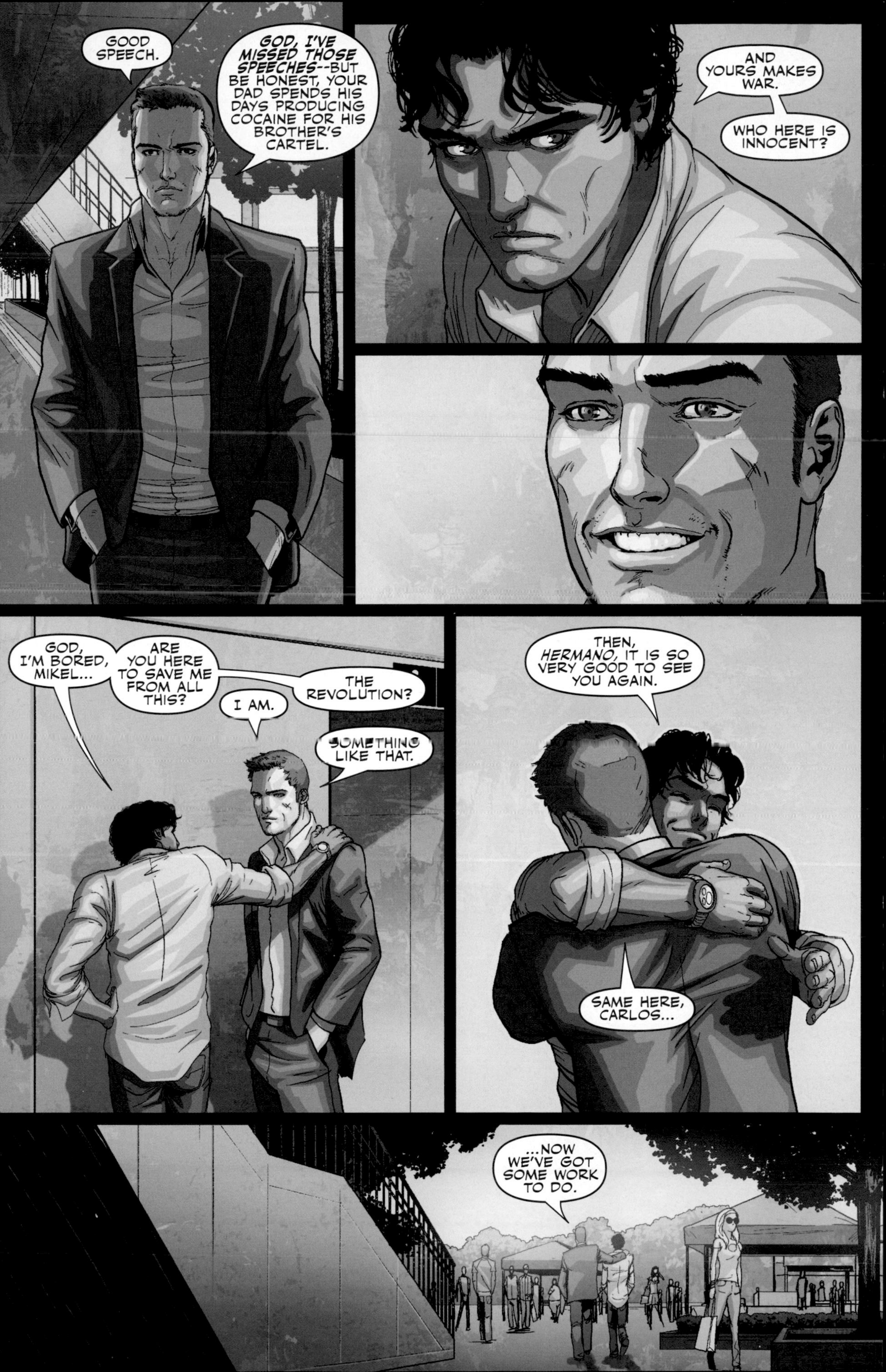
GOOD SPEECH.
*GOD, I'VE MISSED THOSE SPEECHES*--BUT BE HONEST, YOUR DAD SPENDS HIS DAYS PRODUCING COCAINE FOR HIS BROTHER'S CARTEL.
AND YOURS MAKES WAR.
WHO HERE IS INNOCENT?
GOD, I'M BORED, MIKEL...
ARE YOU HERE TO SAVE ME FROM ALL THIS?
THE REVOLUTION?
I AM.
SOMETHING LIKE THAT.
THEN, *HERMANO*, IT IS SO VERY GOOD TO SEE YOU AGAIN.
SAME HERE, CARLOS...
...NOW WE'VE GOT SOME WORK TO DO.

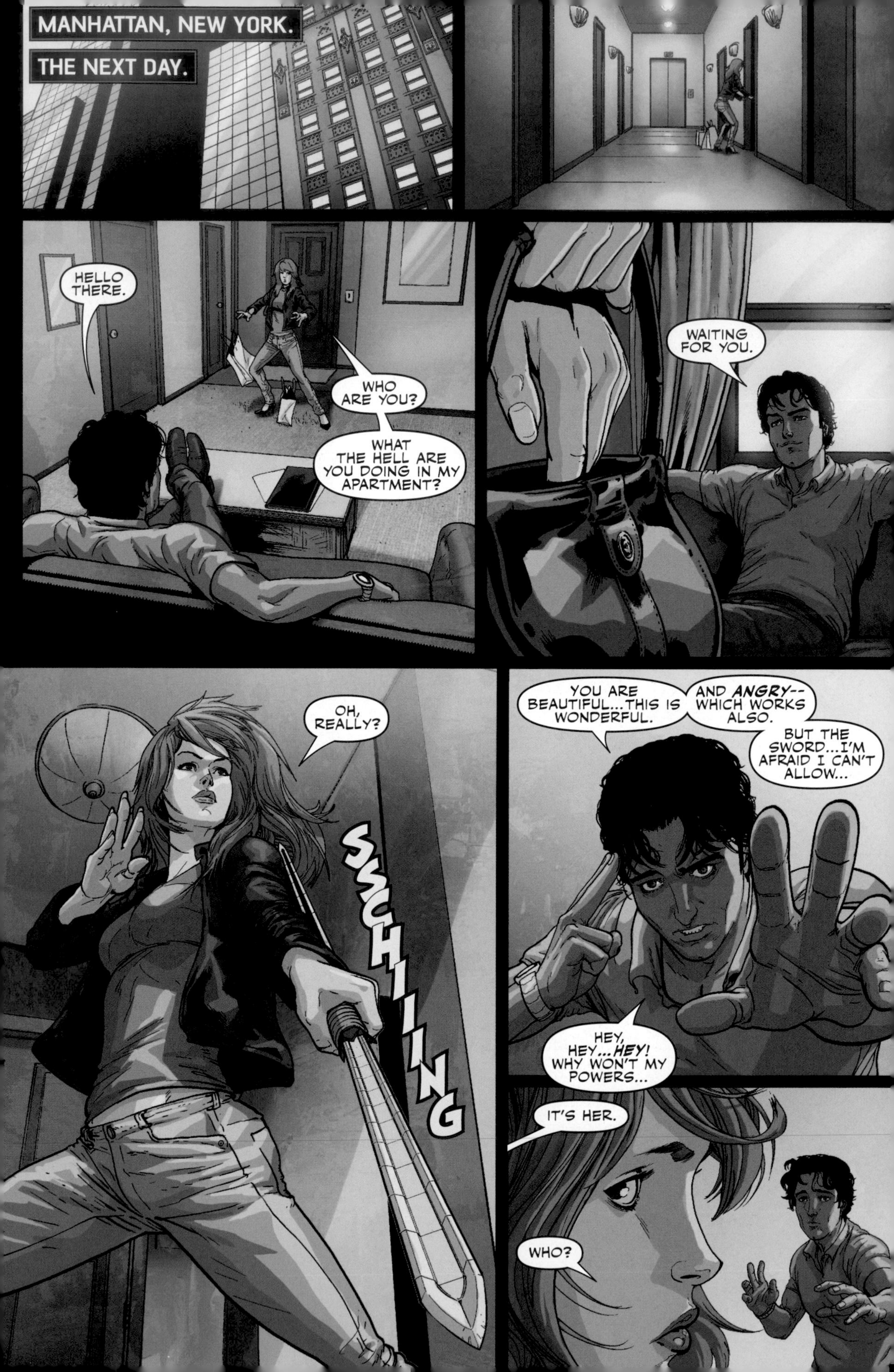
MANHATTAN, NEW YORK.
THE NEXT DAY.
HELLO THERE.
WHO ARE YOU?
WHAT THE HELL ARE YOU DOING IN MY APARTMENT?
WAITING FOR YOU.
OH, REALLY?
SSCHIIIING
YOU ARE BEAUTIFUL...THIS IS WONDERFUL.
AND ANGRY-- WHICH WORKS ALSO.
BUT THE SWORD...I'M AFRAID I CAN'T ALLOW...
HEY, HEY...HEY! WHY WON'T MY POWERS...
IT'S HER.
WHO?

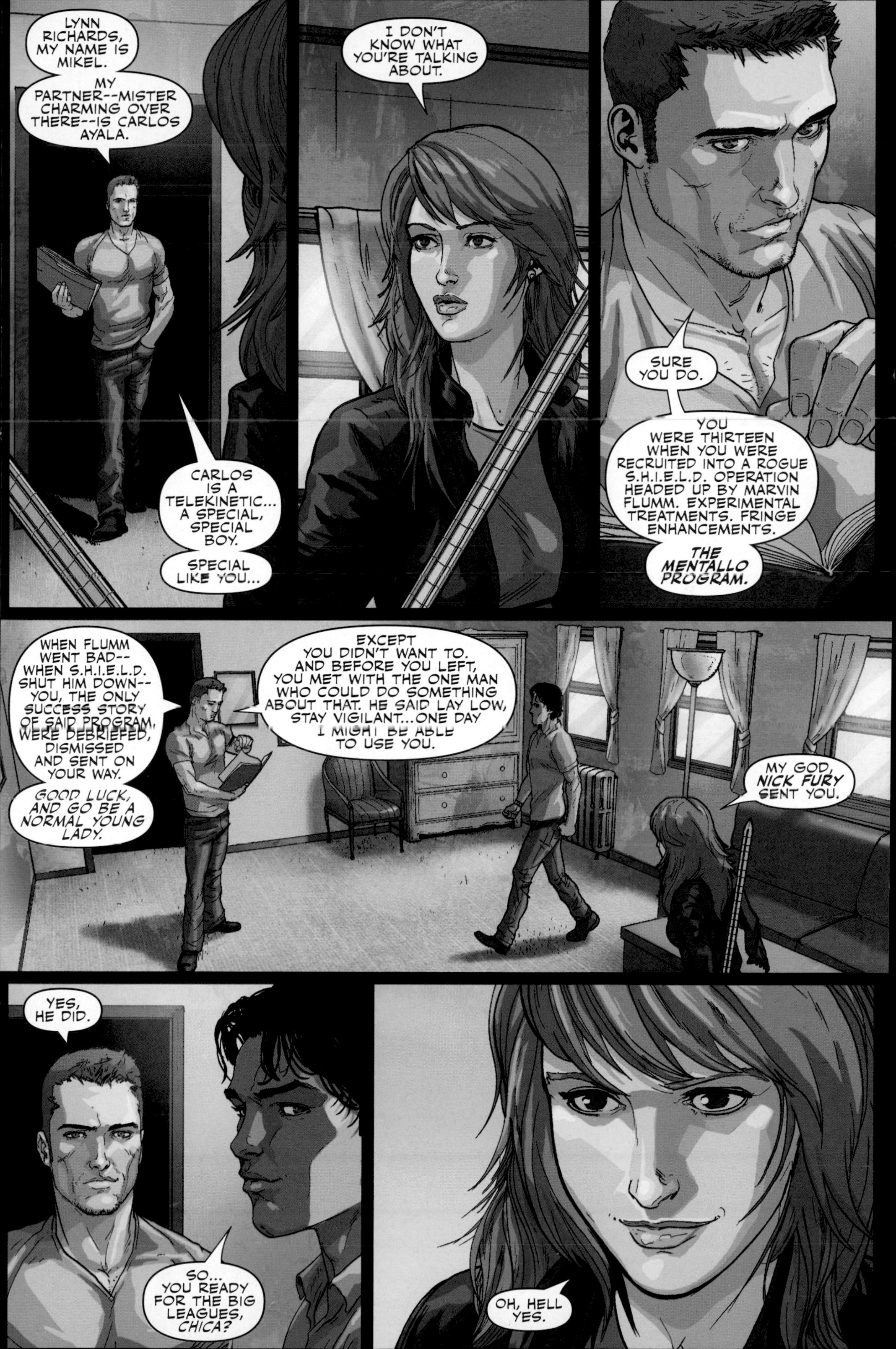
LYNN RICHARDS, MY NAME IS MIKEL.
MY PARTNER--MISTER CHARMING OVER THERE--IS CARLOS AYALA.
CARLOS IS A TELEKINETIC... A SPECIAL, SPECIAL BOY.
SPECIAL LIKE YOU...
I DON'T KNOW WHAT YOU'RE TALKING ABOUT.
SURE YOU DO.
YOU WERE THIRTEEN WHEN YOU WERE RECRUITED INTO A ROGUE S.H.I.E.L.D. OPERATION HEADED UP BY MARVIN FLUMM. EXPERIMENTAL TREATMENTS. FRINGE ENHANCEMENTS.
THE MENTALLO PROGRAM.
WHEN FLUMM WENT BAD--WHEN S.H.I.E.L.D. SHUT HIM DOWN--YOU, THE ONLY SUCCESS STORY OF SAID PROGRAM, WERE DEBRIEFED, DISMISSED AND SENT ON YOUR WAY.
GOOD LUCK, AND GO BE A NORMAL YOUNG LADY.
EXCEPT YOU DIDN'T WANT TO. AND BEFORE YOU LEFT, YOU MET WITH THE ONE MAN WHO COULD DO SOMETHING ABOUT THAT. HE SAID LAY LOW, STAY VIGILANT...ONE DAY I MIGHT BE ABLE TO USE YOU.
MY GOD, NICK FURY SENT YOU.
YES, HE DID.
SO... YOU READY FOR THE BIG LEAGUES, CHICA?
OH, HELL YES.

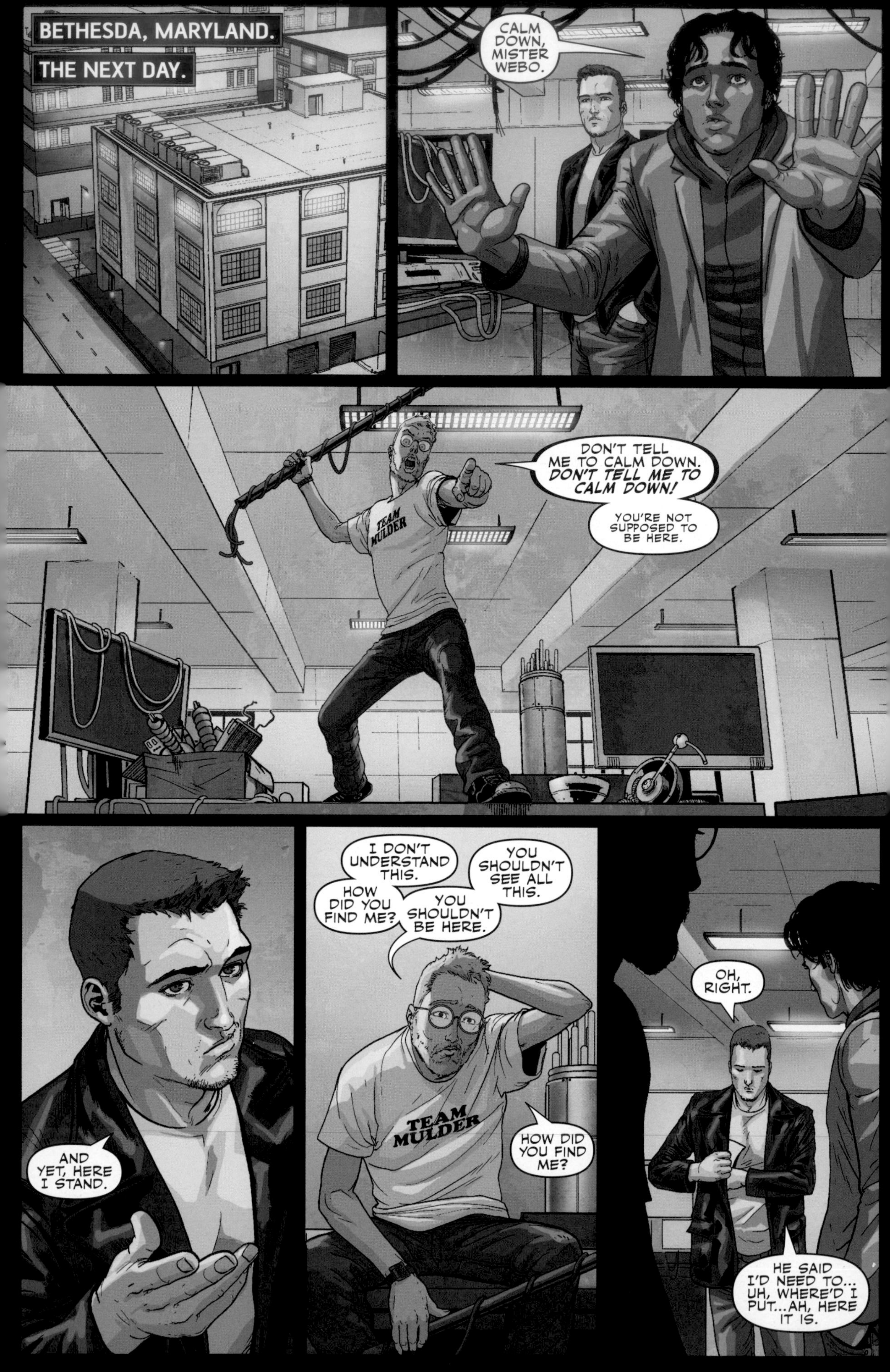
BETHESDA, MARYLAND.
THE NEXT DAY.
CALM DOWN, MISTER WEBO.
DON'T TELL ME TO CALM DOWN. DON'T TELL ME TO CALM DOWN!
YOU'RE NOT SUPPOSED TO BE HERE.
TEAM MULDER
AND YET, HERE I STAND.
I DON'T UNDERSTAND THIS.
HOW DID YOU FIND ME?
YOU SHOULDN'T SEE ALL THIS.
YOU SHOULDN'T BE HERE.
TEAM MULDER
HOW DID YOU FIND ME?
OH, RIGHT.
HE SAID I'D NEED TO... UH, WHERE'D I PUT...AH, HERE IT IS.

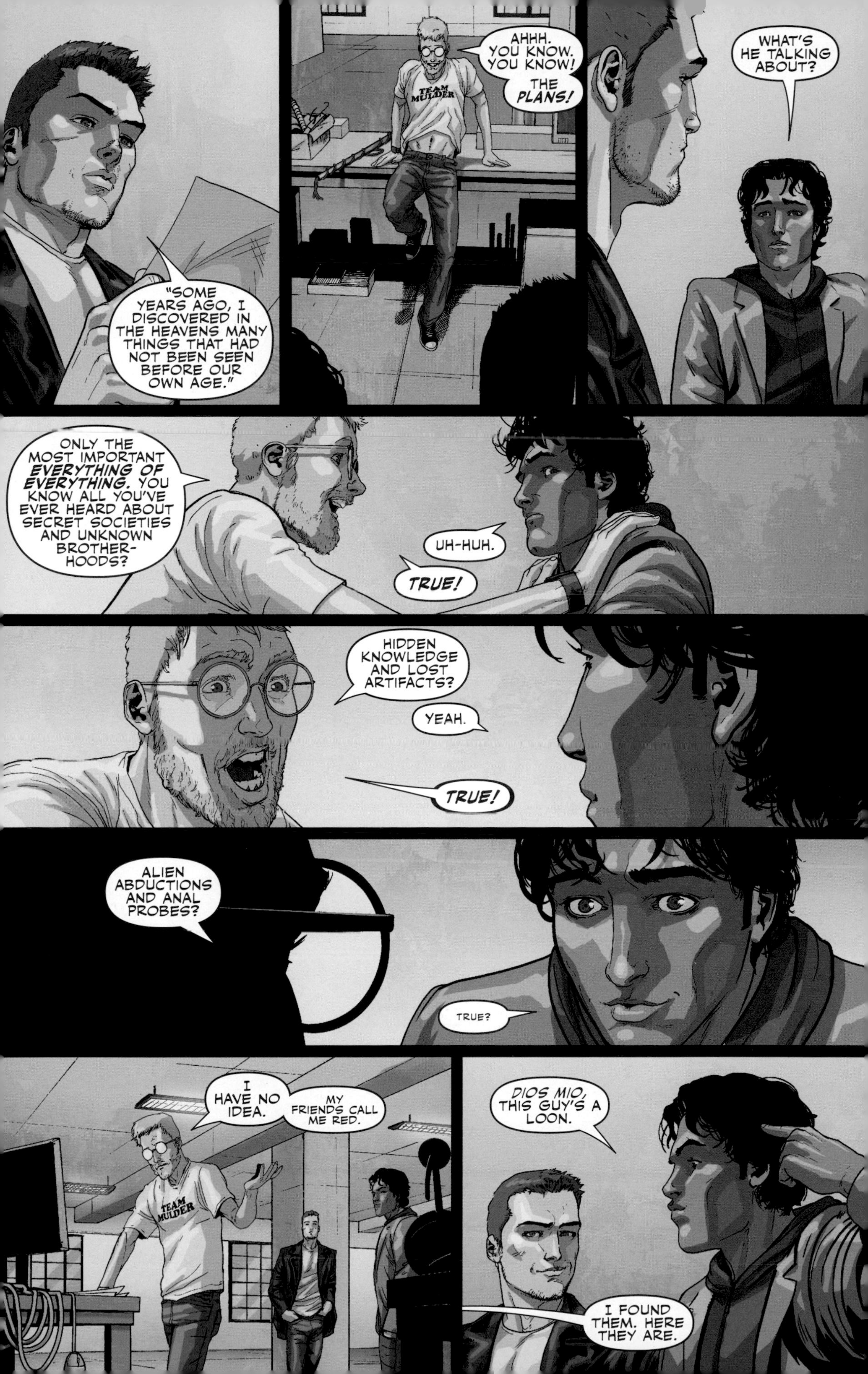
"SOME YEARS AGO, I DISCOVERED IN THE HEAVENS MANY THINGS THAT HAD NOT BEEN SEEN BEFORE OUR OWN AGE."
AHHH. YOU KNOW. YOU KNOW!
THE *PLANS!*
WHAT'S HE TALKING ABOUT?
ONLY THE MOST IMPORTANT *EVERYTHING OF EVERYTHING.* YOU KNOW ALL YOU'VE EVER HEARD ABOUT SECRET SOCIETIES AND UNKNOWN BROTHER-HOODS?
UH-HUH.
*TRUE!*
HIDDEN KNOWLEDGE AND LOST ARTIFACTS?
YEAH.
*TRUE!*
ALIEN ABDUCTIONS AND ANAL PROBES?
TRUE?
I HAVE NO IDEA.
MY FRIENDS CALL ME RED.
*DIOS MIO,* THIS GUY'S A LOON.
I FOUND THEM. HERE THEY ARE.

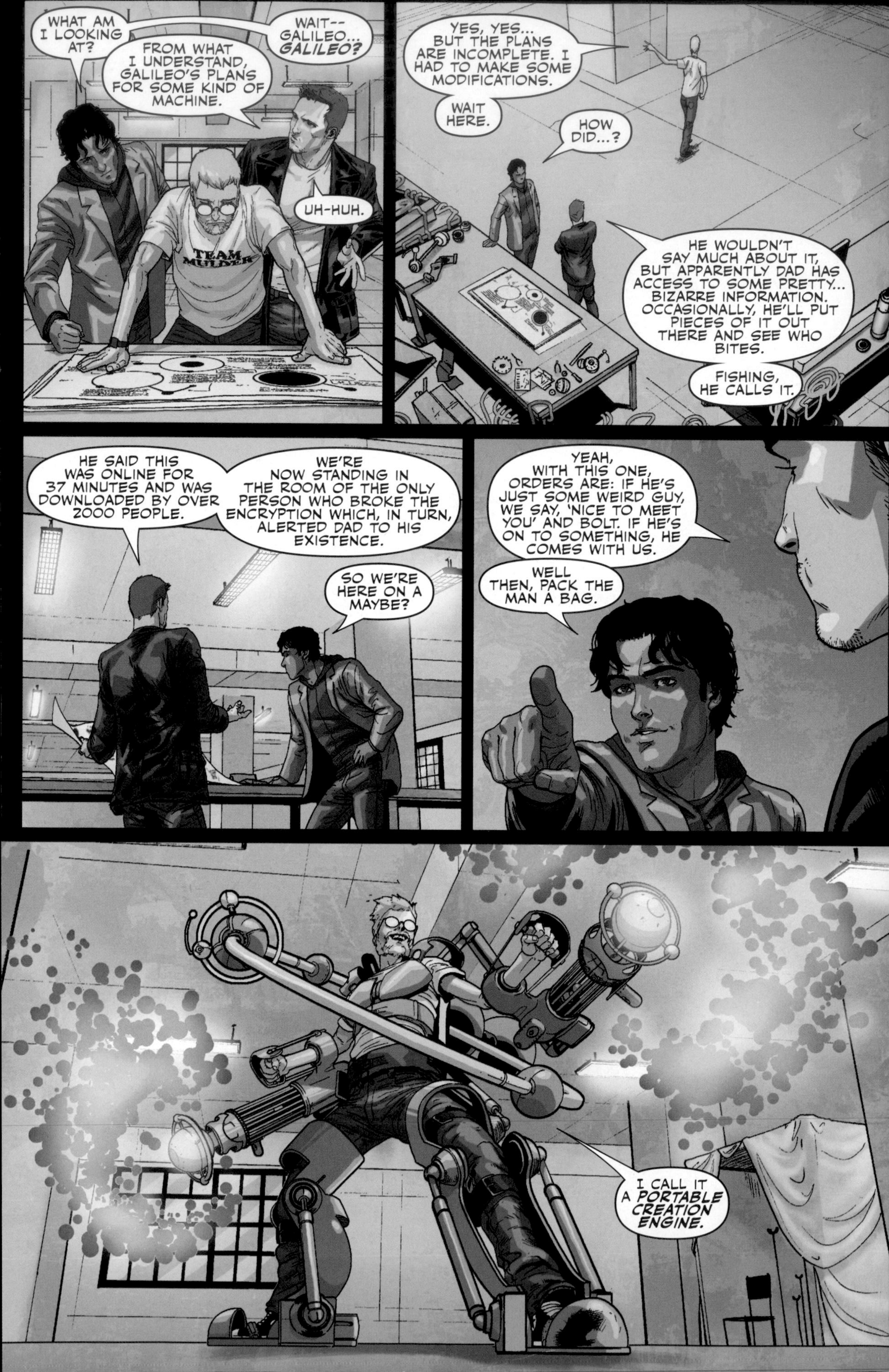
WHAT AM I LOOKING AT?
FROM WHAT I UNDERSTAND, GALILEO'S PLANS FOR SOME KIND OF MACHINE.
WAIT-- GALILEO... GALILEO?
UH-HUH.
YES, YES... BUT THE PLANS ARE INCOMPLETE. I HAD TO MAKE SOME MODIFICATIONS.
WAIT HERE.
HOW DID...?
HE WOULDN'T SAY MUCH ABOUT IT, BUT APPARENTLY DAD HAS ACCESS TO SOME PRETTY... BIZARRE INFORMATION. OCCASIONALLY, HE'LL PUT PIECES OF IT OUT THERE AND SEE WHO BITES.
FISHING, HE CALLS IT.
HE SAID THIS WAS ONLINE FOR 37 MINUTES AND WAS DOWNLOADED BY OVER 2000 PEOPLE.
WE'RE NOW STANDING IN THE ROOM OF THE ONLY PERSON WHO BROKE THE ENCRYPTION WHICH, IN TURN, ALERTED DAD TO HIS EXISTENCE.
SO WE'RE HERE ON A MAYBE?
YEAH, WITH THIS ONE, ORDERS ARE: IF HE'S JUST SOME WEIRD GUY, WE SAY, 'NICE TO MEET YOU' AND BOLT. IF HE'S ON TO SOMETHING, HE COMES WITH US.
WELL THEN, PACK THE MAN A BAG.
I CALL IT A *PORTABLE CREATION ENGINE.*

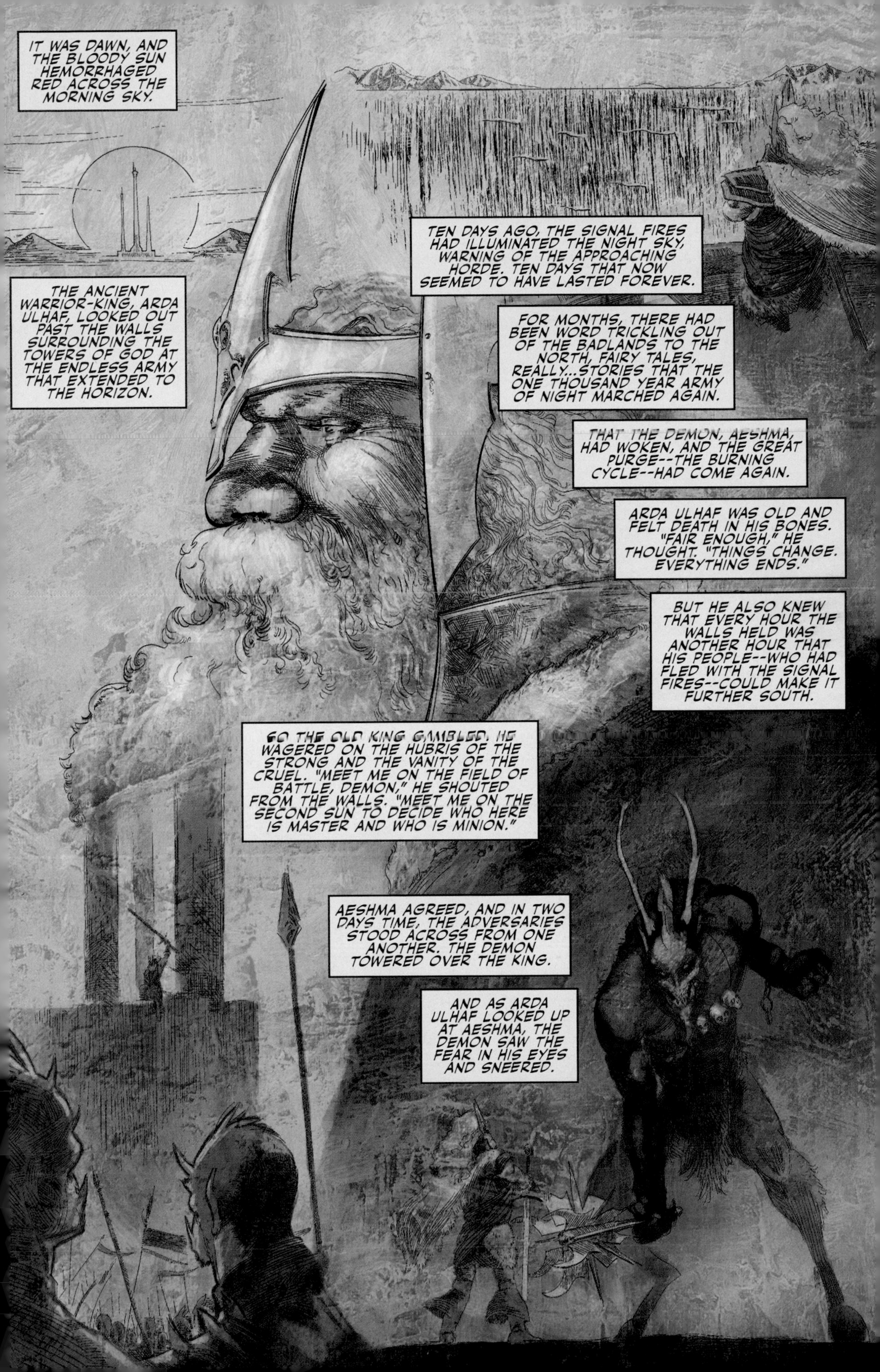
IT WAS DAWN, AND THE BLOODY SUN HEMORRHAGED RED ACROSS THE MORNING SKY.
THE ANCIENT WARRIOR-KING, ARDA ULHAF, LOOKED OUT PAST THE WALLS SURROUNDING THE TOWERS OF GOD AT THE ENDLESS ARMY THAT EXTENDED TO THE HORIZON.
TEN DAYS AGO, THE SIGNAL FIRES HAD ILLUMINATED THE NIGHT SKY, WARNING OF THE APPROACHING HORDE. TEN DAYS THAT NOW SEEMED TO HAVE LASTED FOREVER.
FOR MONTHS, THERE HAD BEEN WORD TRICKLING OUT OF THE BADLANDS TO THE NORTH, FAIRY TALES, REALLY...STORIES THAT THE ONE THOUSAND YEAR ARMY OF NIGHT MARCHED AGAIN.
THAT THE DEMON, AESHMA, HAD WOKEN, AND THE GREAT PURGE--THE BURNING CYCLE--HAD COME AGAIN.
ARDA ULHAF WAS OLD AND FELT DEATH IN HIS BONES. "FAIR ENOUGH," HE THOUGHT. "THINGS CHANGE. EVERYTHING ENDS."
BUT HE ALSO KNEW THAT EVERY HOUR THE WALLS HELD WAS ANOTHER HOUR THAT HIS PEOPLE--WHO HAD FLED WITH THE SIGNAL FIRES--COULD MAKE IT FURTHER SOUTH.
SO THE OLD KING GAMBLED. HE WAGERED ON THE HUBRIS OF THE STRONG AND THE VANITY OF THE CRUEL. "MEET ME ON THE FIELD OF BATTLE, DEMON," HE SHOUTED FROM THE WALLS. "MEET ME ON THE SECOND SUN TO DECIDE WHO HERE IS MASTER AND WHO IS MINION."
AESHMA AGREED, AND IN TWO DAYS TIME, THE ADVERSARIES STOOD ACROSS FROM ONE ANOTHER. THE DEMON TOWERED OVER THE KING.
AND AS ARDA ULHAF LOOKED UP AT AESHMA, THE DEMON SAW THE FEAR IN HIS EYES AND SNEERED.

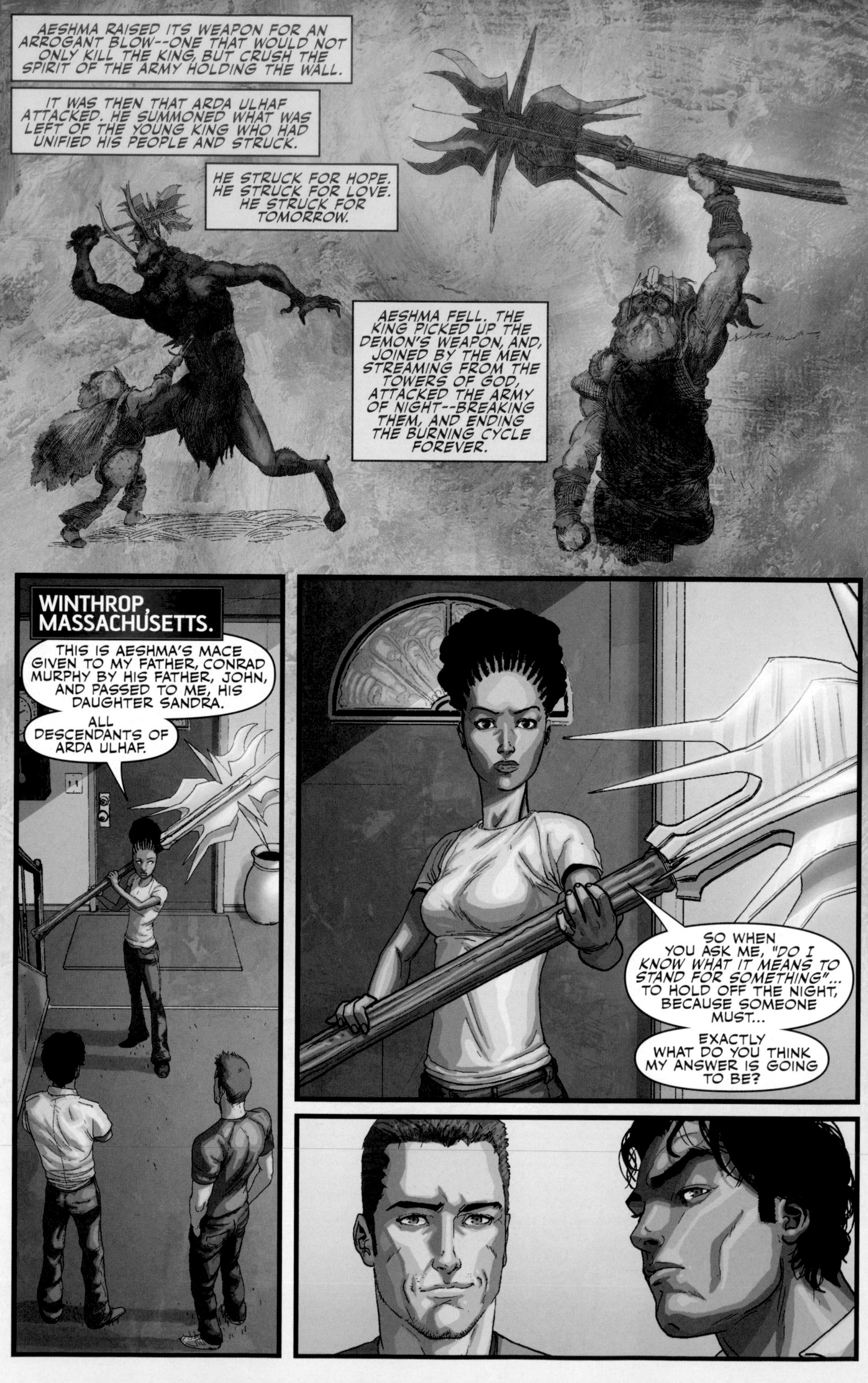
AESHMA RAISED ITS WEAPON FOR AN ARROGANT BLOW--ONE THAT WOULD NOT ONLY KILL THE KING, BUT CRUSH THE SPIRIT OF THE ARMY HOLDING THE WALL.
IT WAS THEN THAT ARDA ULHAF ATTACKED. HE SUMMONED WHAT WAS LEFT OF THE YOUNG KING WHO HAD UNIFIED HIS PEOPLE AND STRUCK.
HE STRUCK FOR HOPE. HE STRUCK FOR LOVE. HE STRUCK FOR TOMORROW.
AESHMA FELL. THE KING PICKED UP THE DEMON'S WEAPON, AND, JOINED BY THE MEN STREAMING FROM THE TOWERS OF GOD, ATTACKED THE ARMY OF NIGHT--BREAKING THEM, AND ENDING THE BURNING CYCLE FOREVER.
WINTHROP, MASSACHUSETTS.
THIS IS AESHMA'S MACE GIVEN TO MY FATHER, CONRAD MURPHY BY HIS FATHER, JOHN, AND PASSED TO ME, HIS DAUGHTER SANDRA.
ALL DESCENDANTS OF ARDA ULHAF.
SO WHEN YOU ASK ME, "DO I KNOW WHAT IT MEANS TO STAND FOR SOMETHING"... TO HOLD OFF THE NIGHT, BECAUSE SOMEONE MUST...
EXACTLY WHAT DO YOU THINK MY ANSWER IS GOING TO BE?

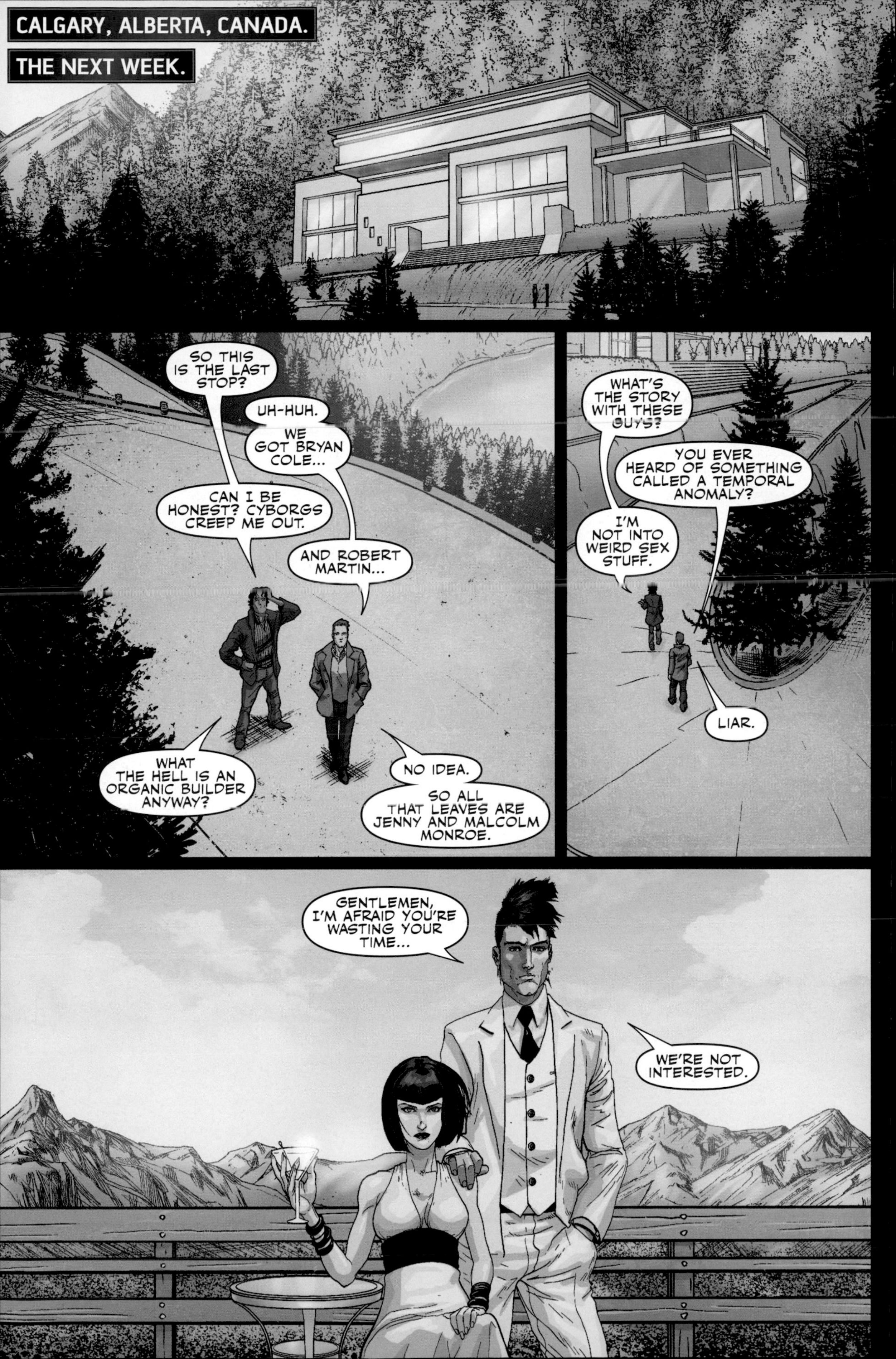
CALGARY, ALBERTA, CANADA.
THE NEXT WEEK.
SO THIS IS THE LAST STOP?
UH-HUH.
WE GOT BRYAN COLE...
CAN I BE HONEST? CYBORGS CREEP ME OUT.
AND ROBERT MARTIN...
WHAT THE HELL IS AN ORGANIC BUILDER ANYWAY?
NO IDEA.
SO ALL THAT LEAVES ARE JENNY AND MALCOLM MONROE.
WHAT'S THE STORY WITH THESE GUYS?
YOU EVER HEARD OF SOMETHING CALLED A TEMPORAL ANOMALY?
I'M NOT INTO WEIRD SEX STUFF.
LIAR.
GENTLEMEN, I'M AFRAID YOU'RE WASTING YOUR TIME...
WE'RE NOT INTERESTED.

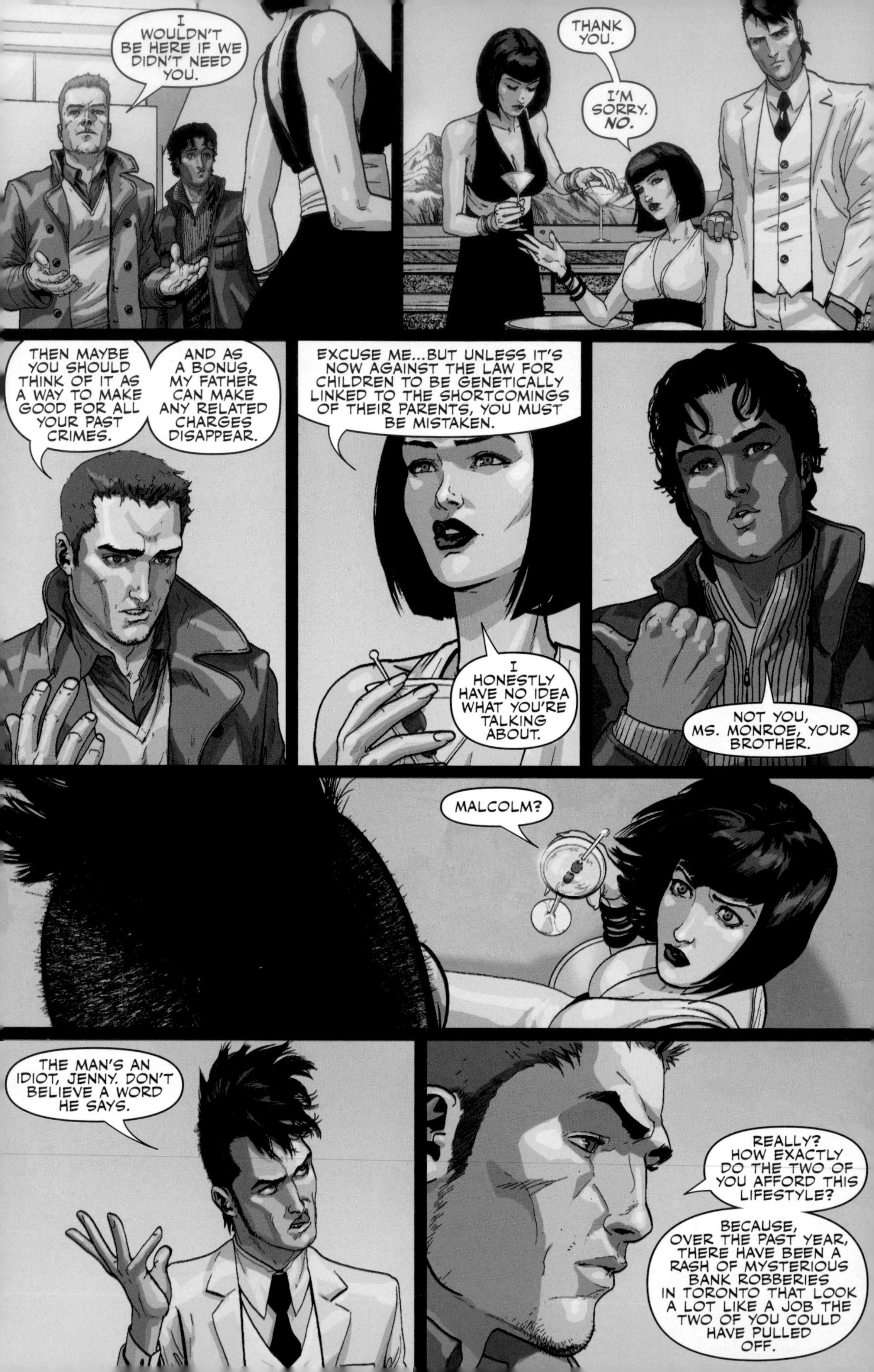

I WOULDN'T BE HERE IF WE DIDN'T NEED YOU.
THANK YOU.
I'M SORRY. NO.
THEN MAYBE YOU SHOULD THINK OF IT AS A WAY TO MAKE GOOD FOR ALL YOUR PAST CRIMES.
AND AS A BONUS, MY FATHER CAN MAKE ANY RELATED CHARGES DISAPPEAR.
EXCUSE ME...BUT UNLESS IT'S NOW AGAINST THE LAW FOR CHILDREN TO BE GENETICALLY LINKED TO THE SHORTCOMINGS OF THEIR PARENTS, YOU MUST BE MISTAKEN.
I HONESTLY HAVE NO IDEA WHAT YOU'RE TALKING ABOUT.
NOT YOU, MS. MONROE, YOUR BROTHER.
MALCOLM?
THE MAN'S AN IDIOT, JENNY. DON'T BELIEVE A WORD HE SAYS.
REALLY? HOW EXACTLY DO THE TWO OF YOU AFFORD THIS LIFESTYLE?
BECAUSE, OVER THE PAST YEAR, THERE HAVE BEEN A RASH OF MYSTERIOUS BANK ROBBERIES IN TORONTO THAT LOOK A LOT LIKE A JOB THE TWO OF YOU COULD HAVE PULLED OFF.

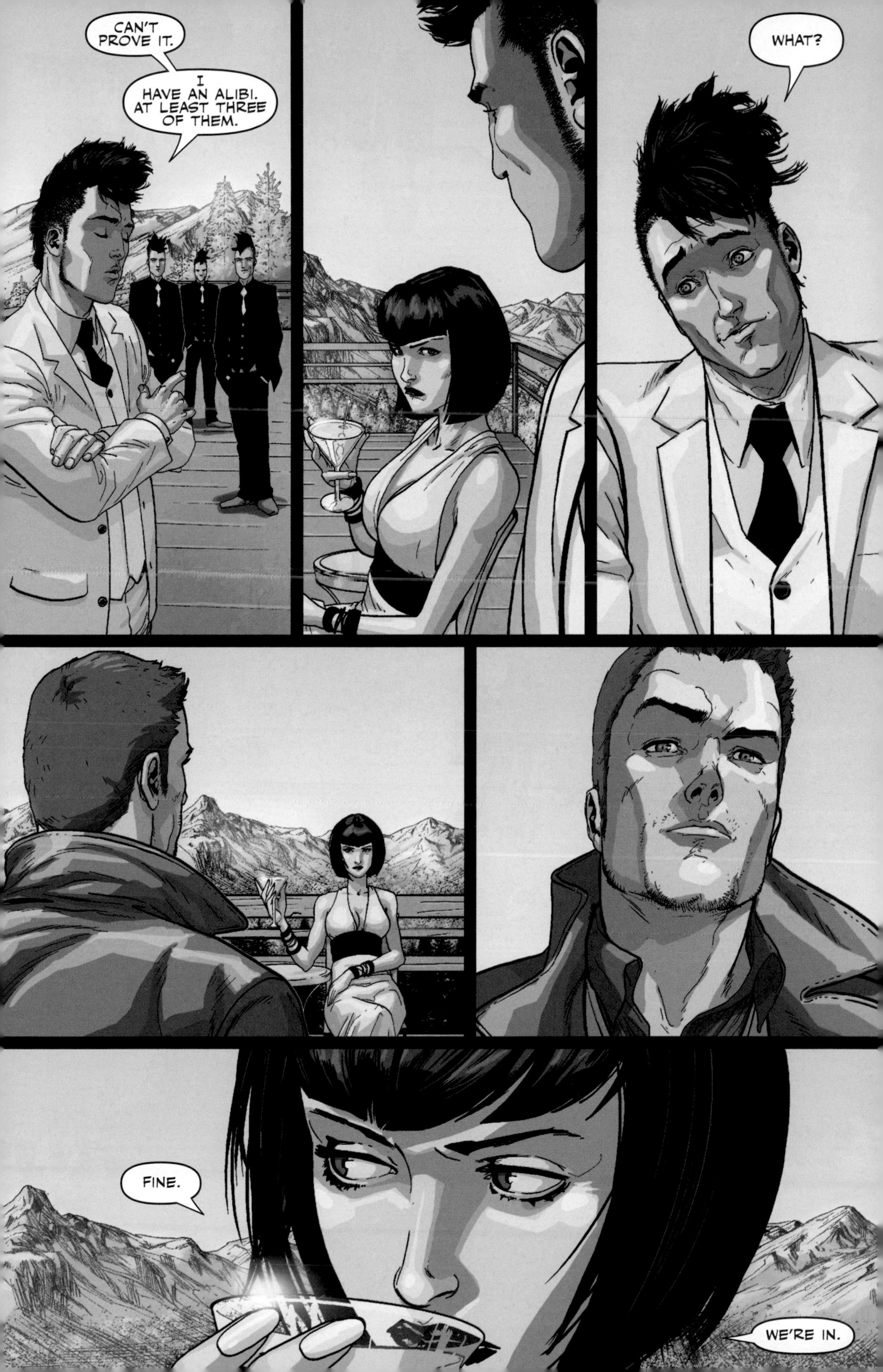
CAN'T PROVE IT.
I HAVE AN ALIBI. AT LEAST THREE OF THEM.
WHAT?
FINE.
WE'RE IN.

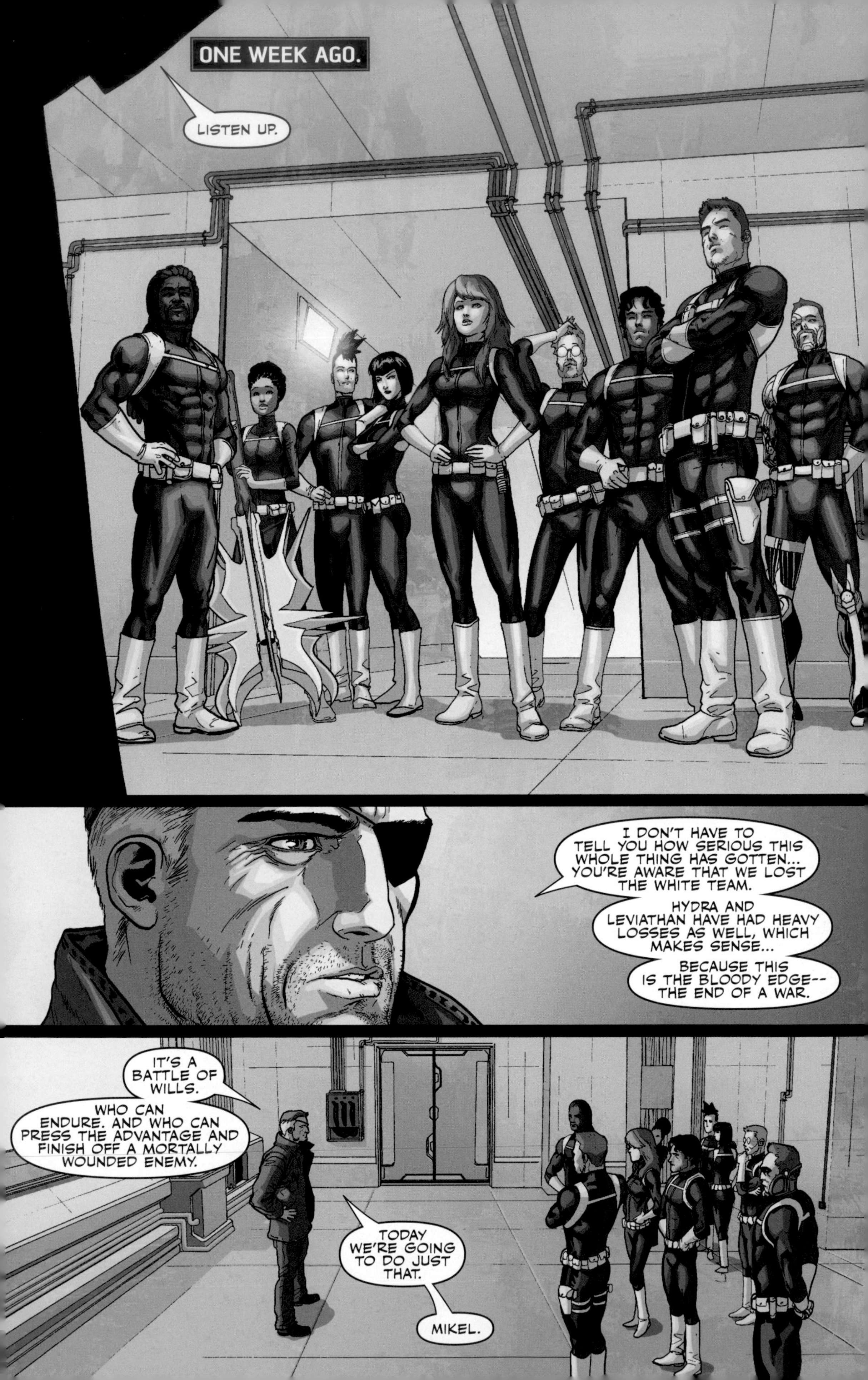
ONE WEEK AGO.
LISTEN UP.
I DON'T HAVE TO TELL YOU HOW SERIOUS THIS WHOLE THING HAS GOTTEN... YOU'RE AWARE THAT WE LOST THE WHITE TEAM.
HYDRA AND LEVIATHAN HAVE HAD HEAVY LOSSES AS WELL, WHICH MAKES SENSE...
BECAUSE THIS IS THE BLOODY EDGE-- THE END OF A WAR.
IT'S A BATTLE OF WILLS.
WHO CAN ENDURE. AND WHO CAN PRESS THE ADVANTAGE AND FINISH OFF A MORTALLY WOUNDED ENEMY.
TODAY WE'RE GOING TO DO JUST THAT.
MIKEL.

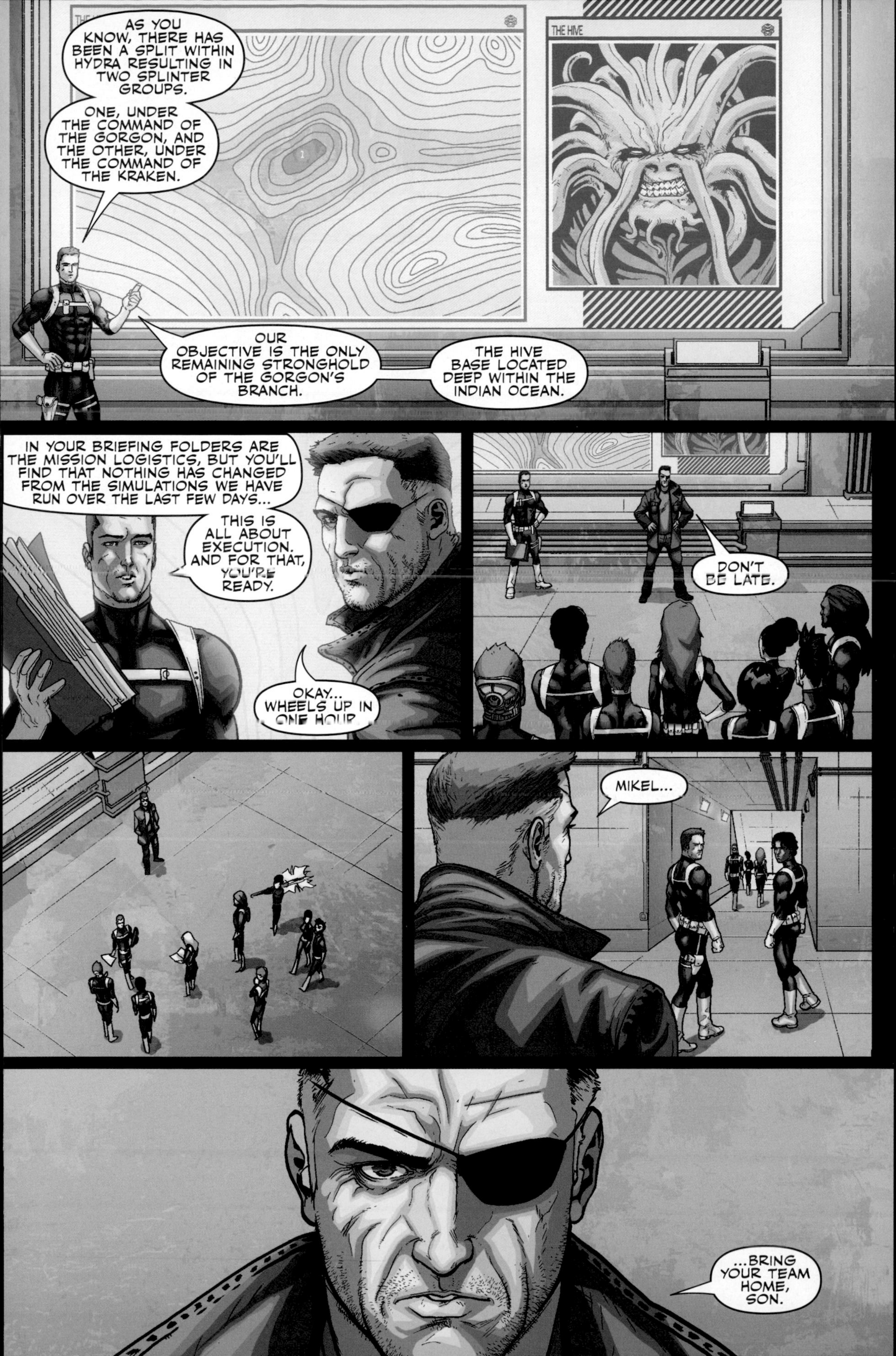
THE HIVE
AS YOU KNOW, THERE HAS BEEN A SPLIT WITHIN HYDRA RESULTING IN TWO SPLINTER GROUPS.
ONE, UNDER THE COMMAND OF THE GORGON, AND THE OTHER, UNDER THE COMMAND OF THE KRAKEN.
OUR OBJECTIVE IS THE ONLY REMAINING STRONGHOLD OF THE GORGON'S BRANCH.
THE HIVE BASE LOCATED DEEP WITHIN THE INDIAN OCEAN.
IN YOUR BRIEFING FOLDERS ARE THE MISSION LOGISTICS, BUT YOU'LL FIND THAT NOTHING HAS CHANGED FROM THE SIMULATIONS WE HAVE RUN OVER THE LAST FEW DAYS...
THIS IS ALL ABOUT EXECUTION. AND FOR THAT, YOU'RE READY.
OKAY... WHEELS UP IN ONE HOUR.
DON'T BE LATE.
MIKEL...
...BRING YOUR TEAM HOME, SON.

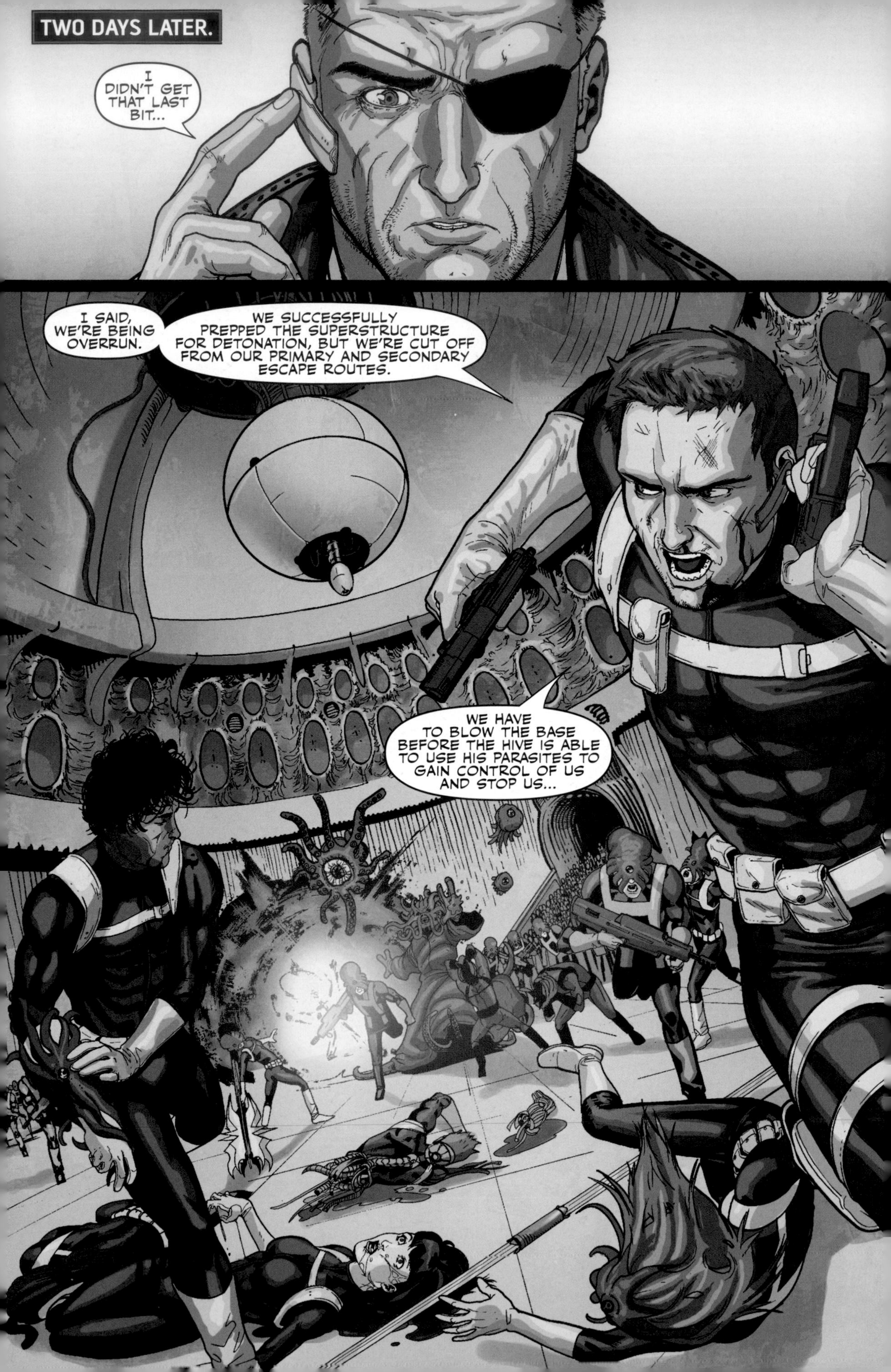
TWO DAYS LATER.
I DIDN'T GET THAT LAST BIT...
I SAID, WE'RE BEING OVERRUN.
WE SUCCESSFULLY PREPPED THE SUPERSTRUCTURE FOR DETONATION, BUT WE'RE CUT OFF FROM OUR PRIMARY AND SECONDARY ESCAPE ROUTES.
WE HAVE TO BLOW THE BASE BEFORE THE HIVE IS ABLE TO USE HIS PARASITES TO GAIN CONTROL OF US AND STOP US...

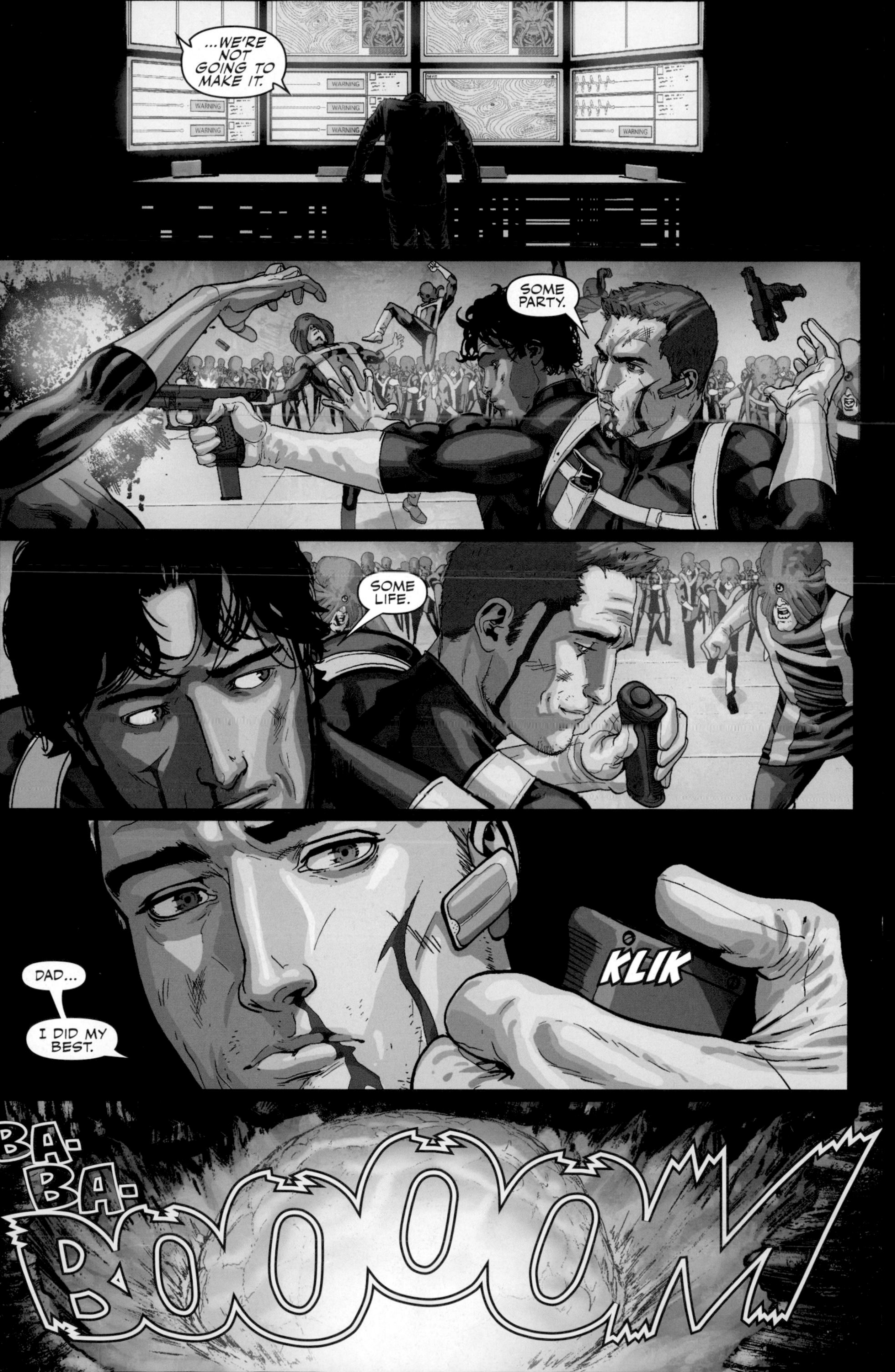

...WE'RE NOT GOING TO MAKE IT.
WARNING
SOME PARTY.
SOME LIFE.
DAD...
I DID MY BEST.
KLIK
BA-BA-BOOOOOM

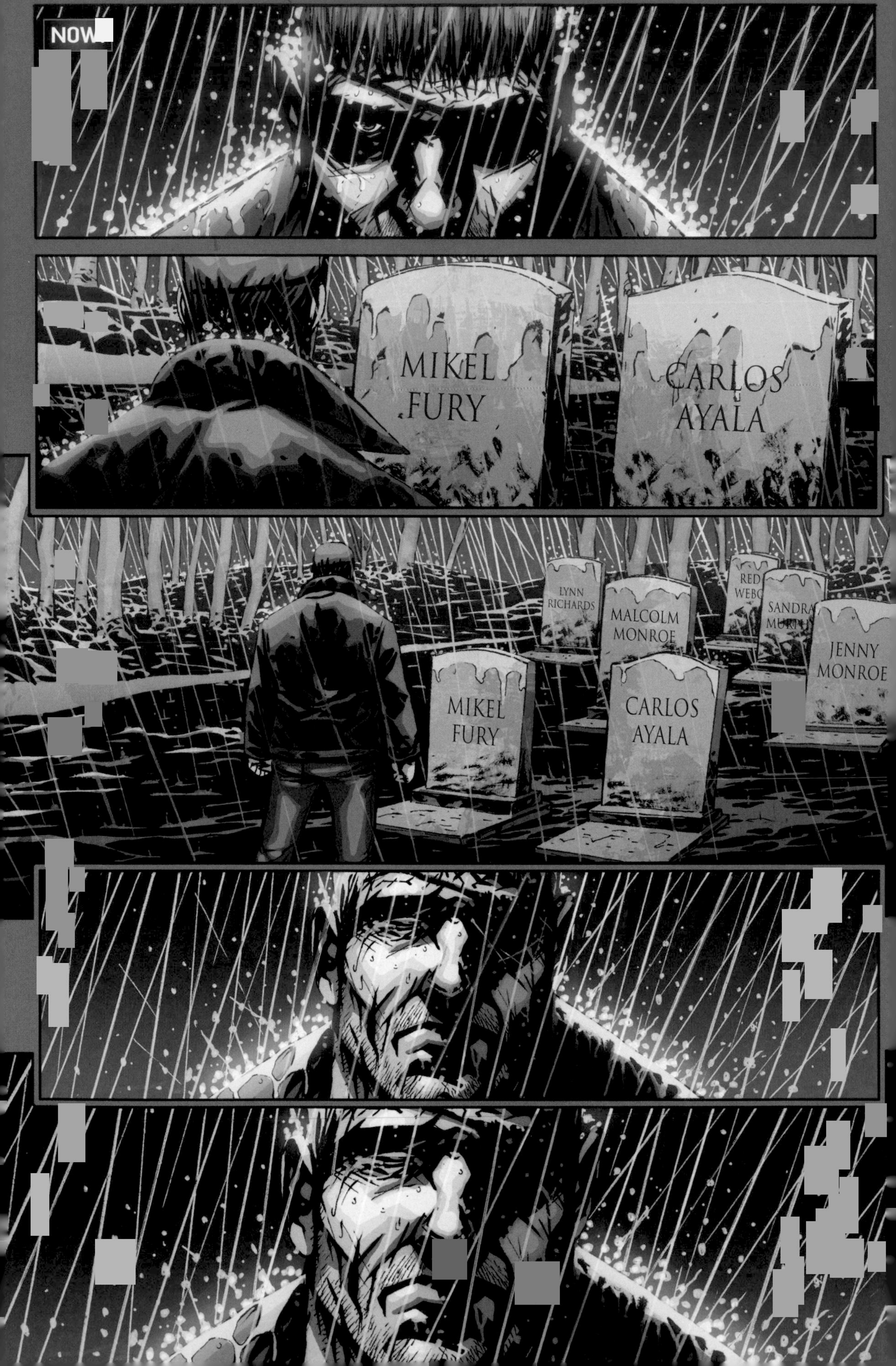
NOW
MIKEL FURY
CARLOS AYALA
LYNN RICHARDS
MALCOLM MONROE
MIKEL FURY
CARLOS AYALA
JENNY MONROE

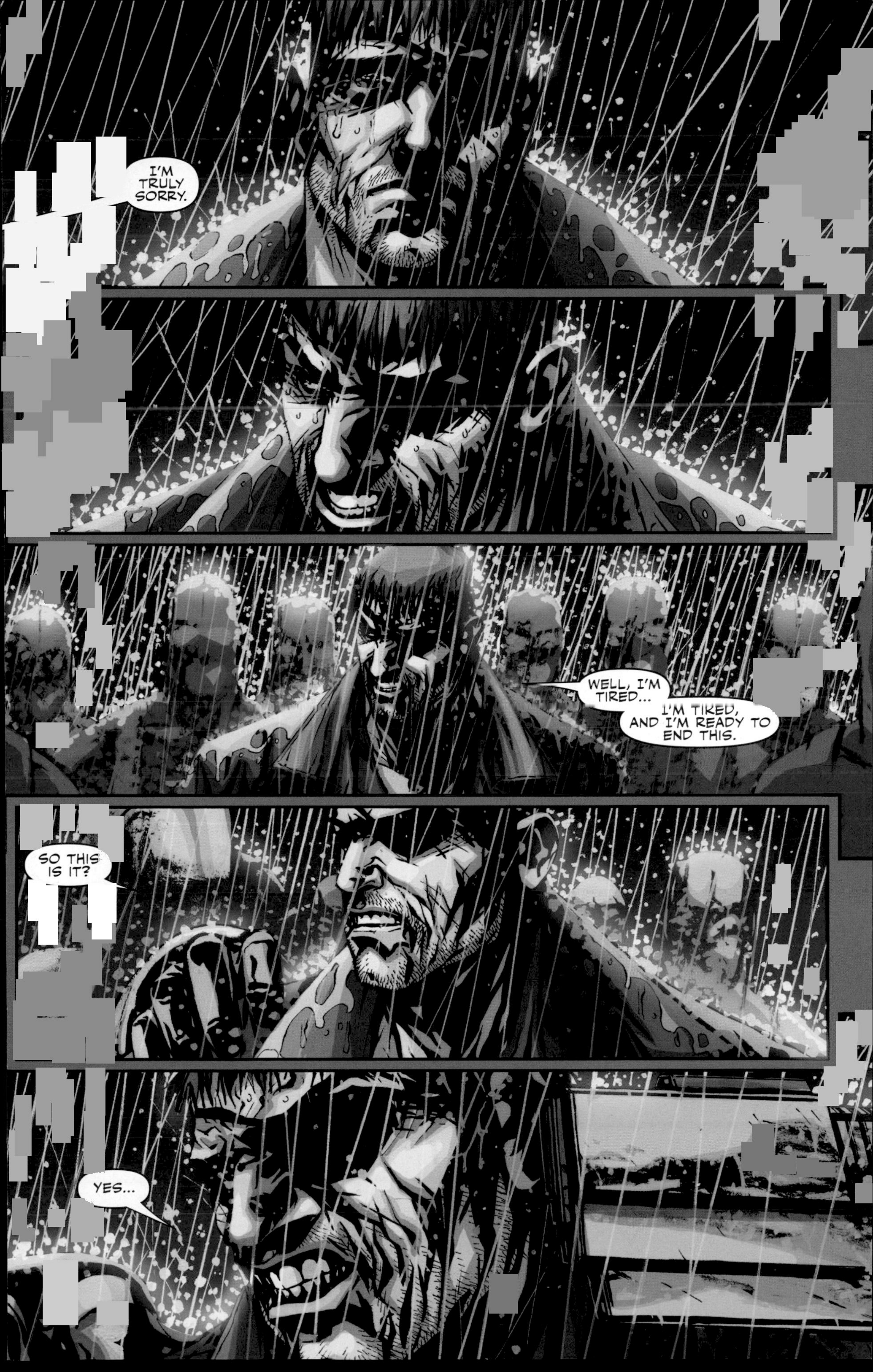
I'M TRULY SORRY.
WELL, I'M TIRED...
I'M TIRED, AND I'M READY TO END THIS.
SO THIS IS IT?
YES...

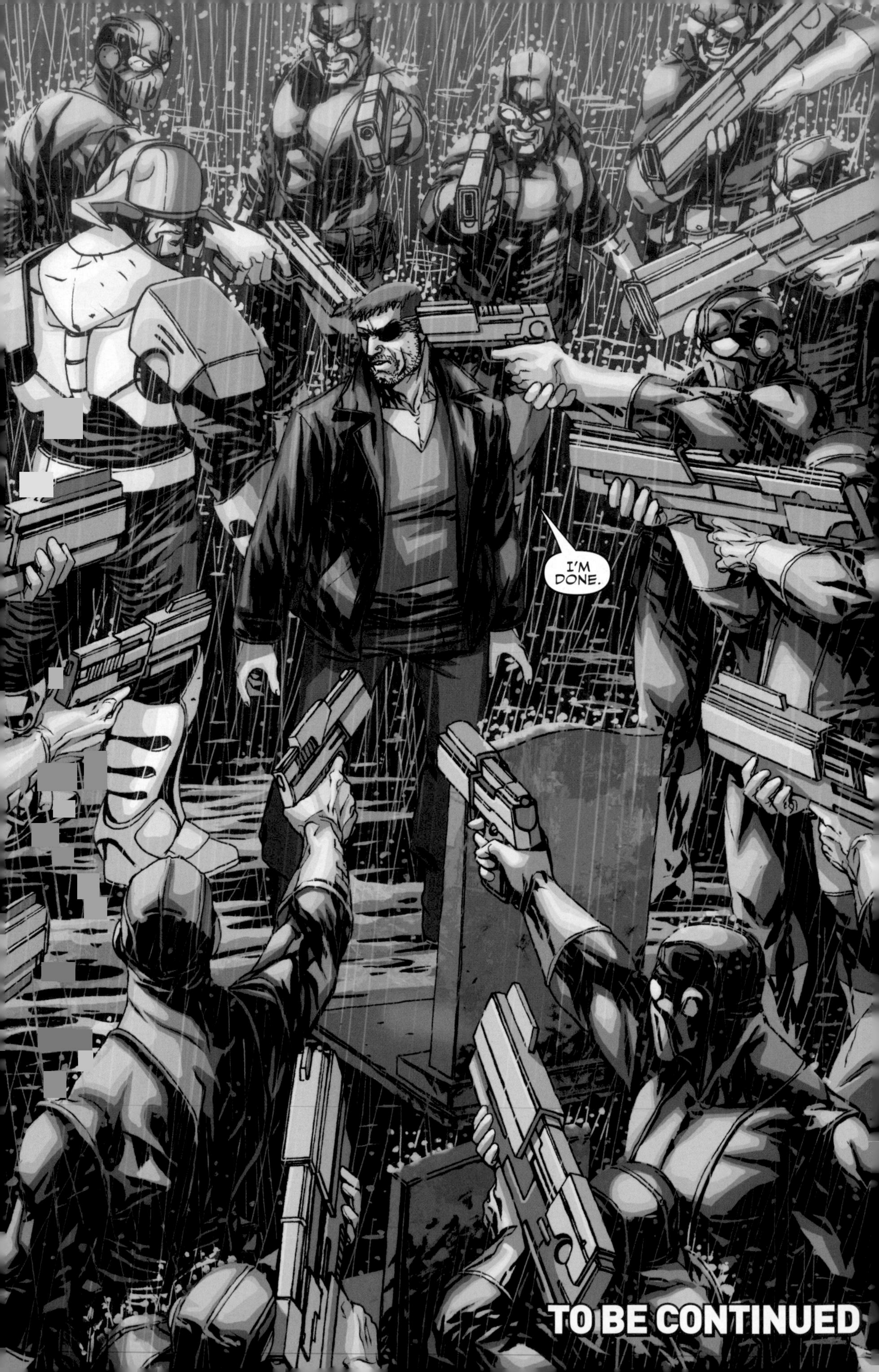
I'M DONE.
TO BE CONTINUED

# COVER GALLERY
## JIM CHEUNG
### AND
## PAUL RENAUD

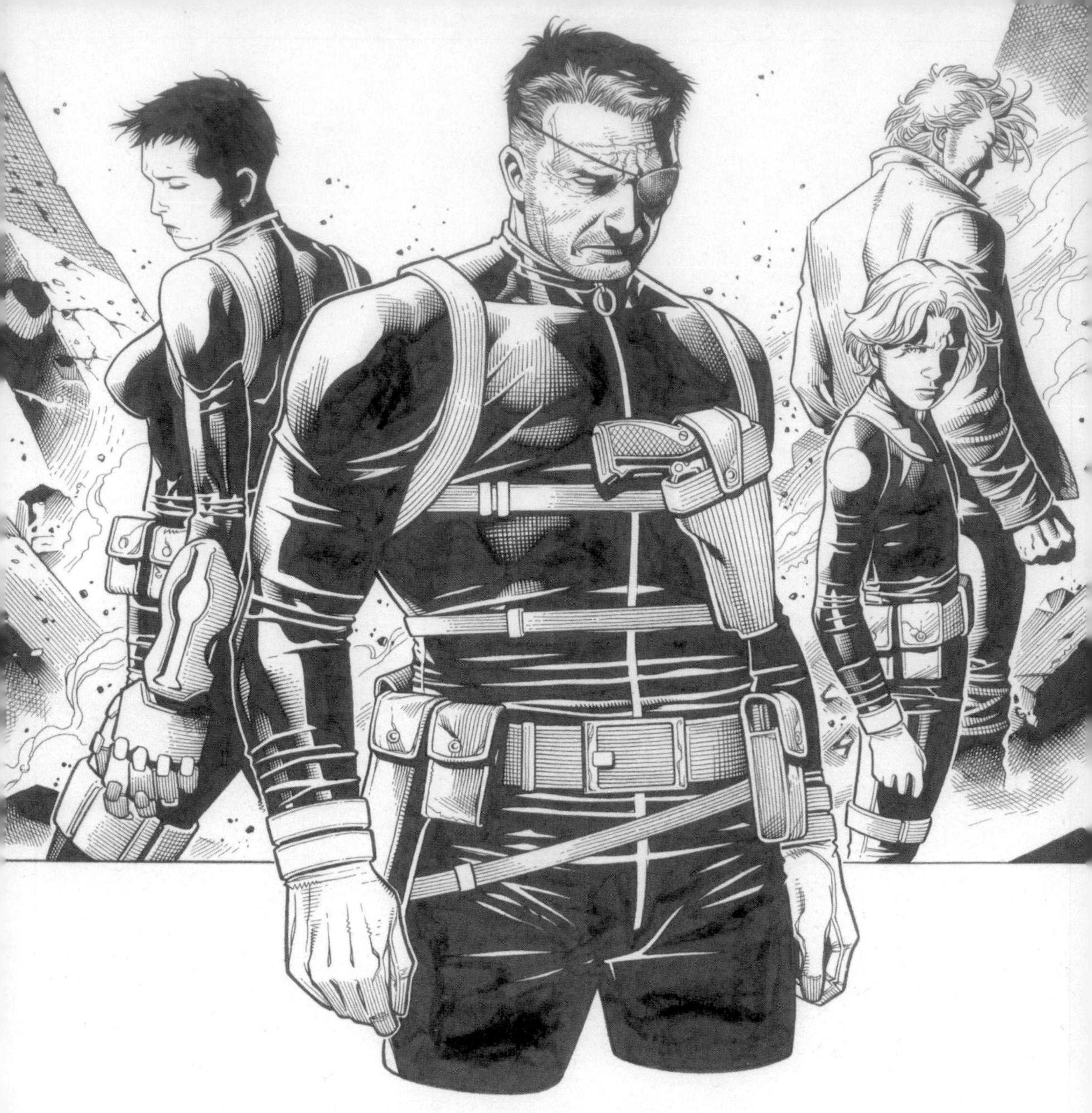

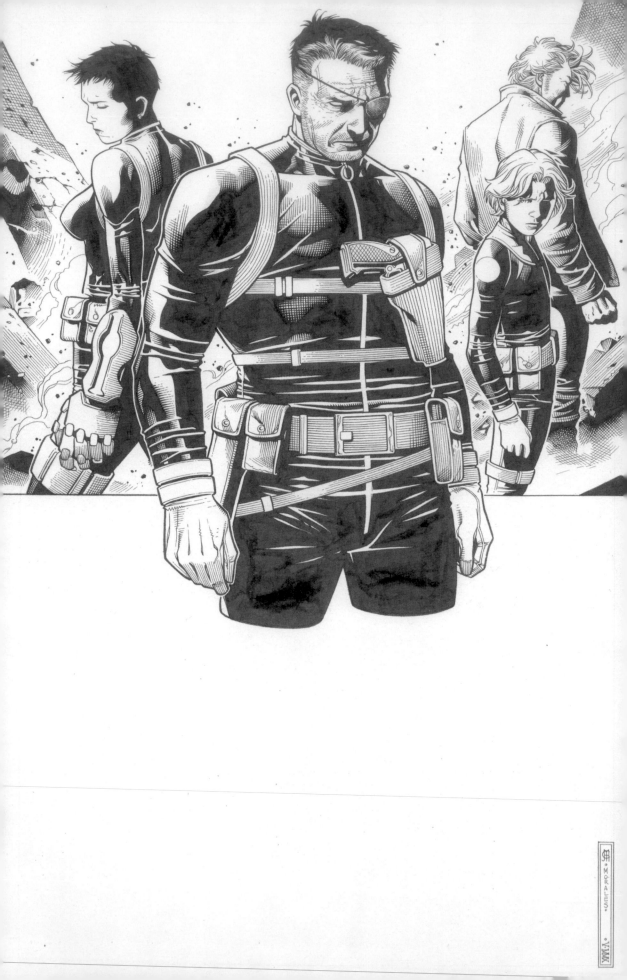

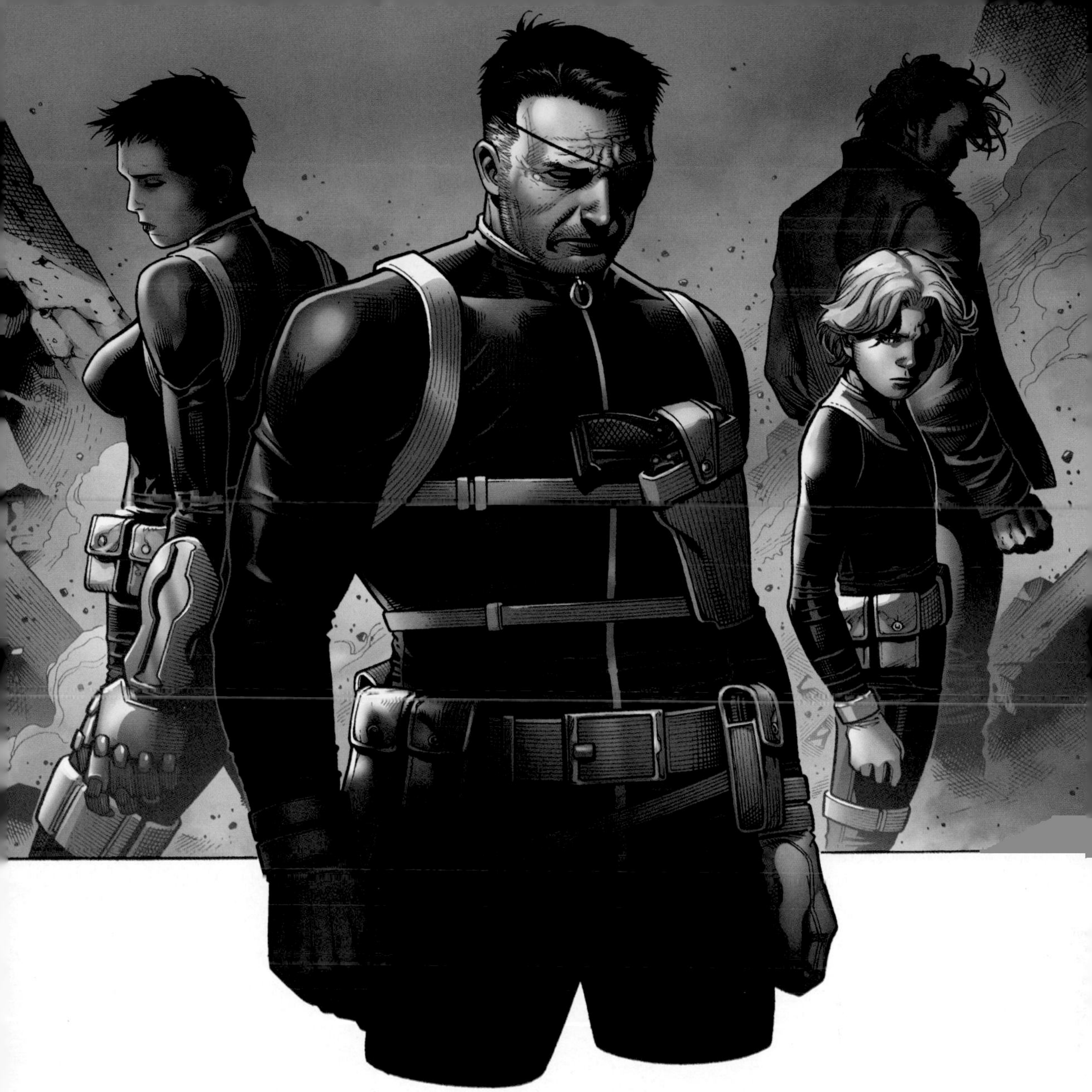

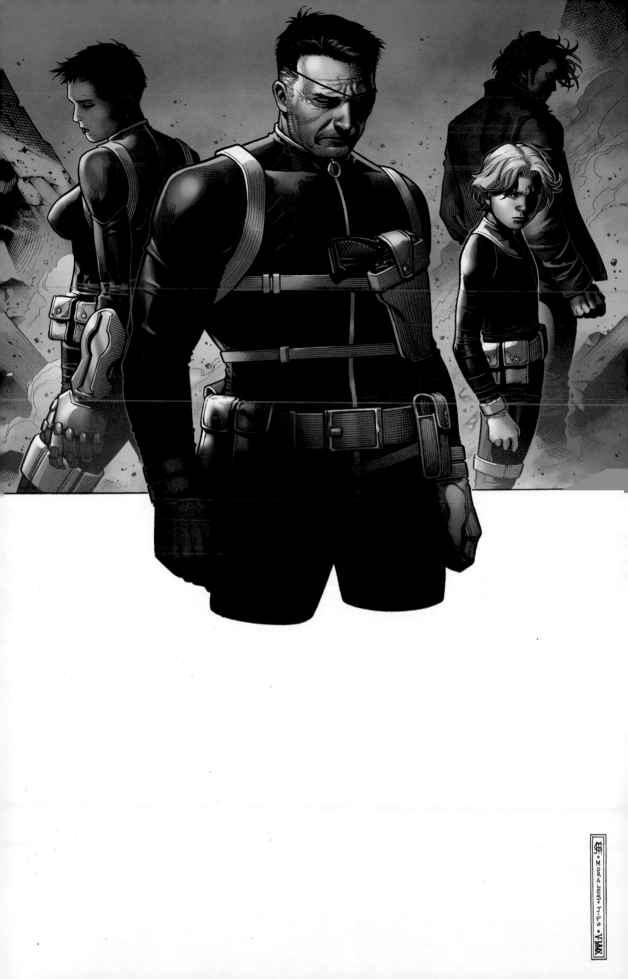

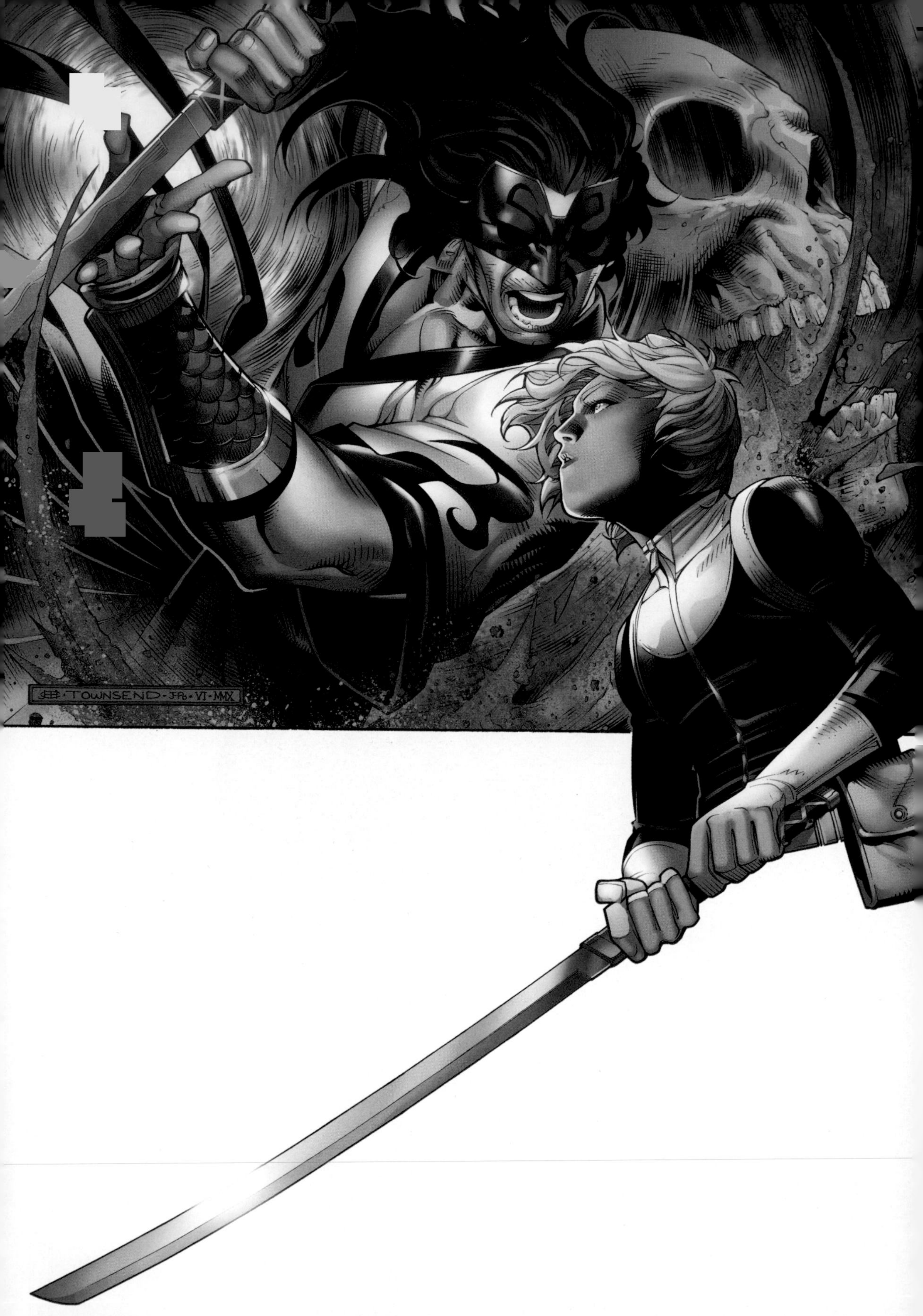
TOWNSEND · VI · MMX

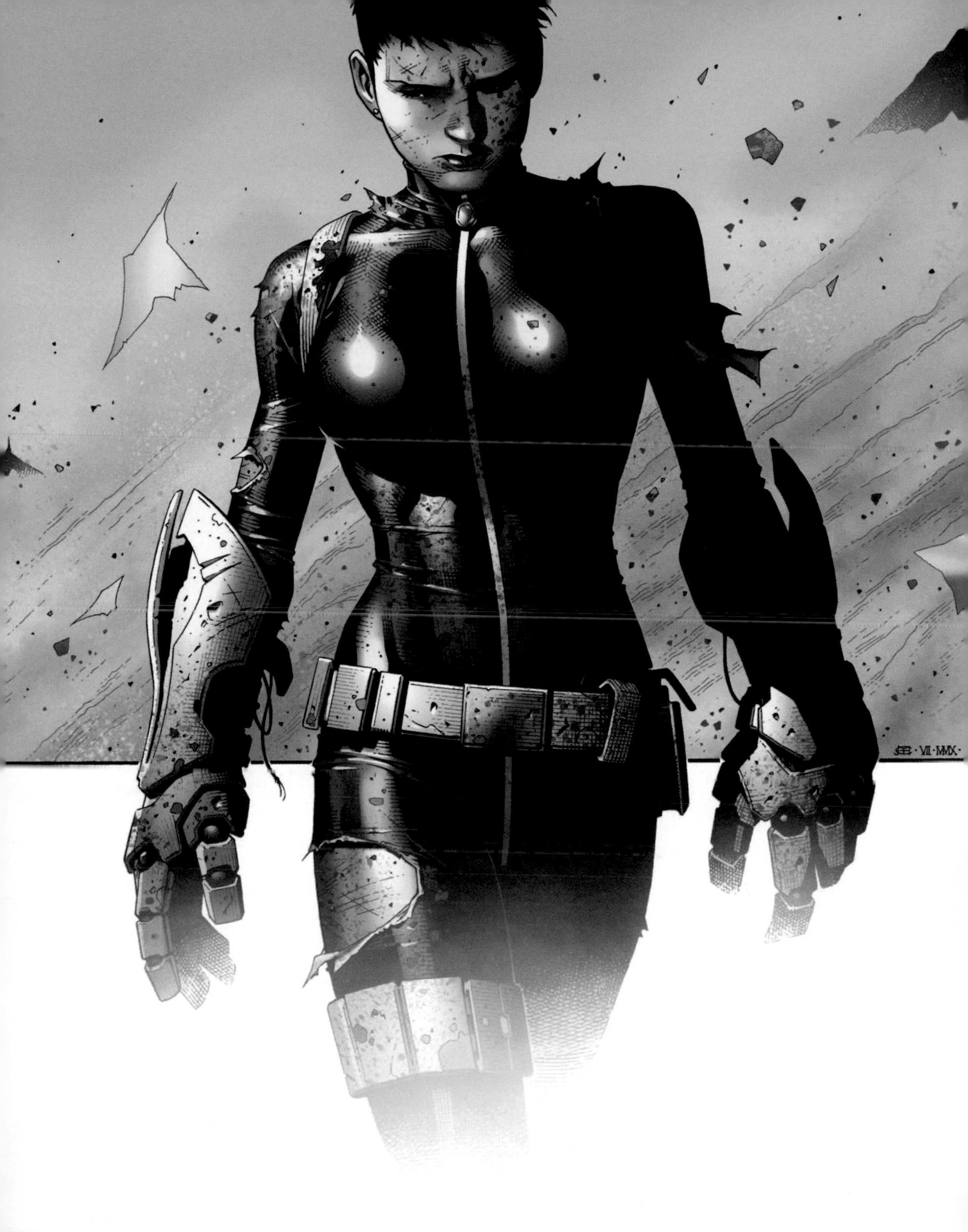
VII·MMX

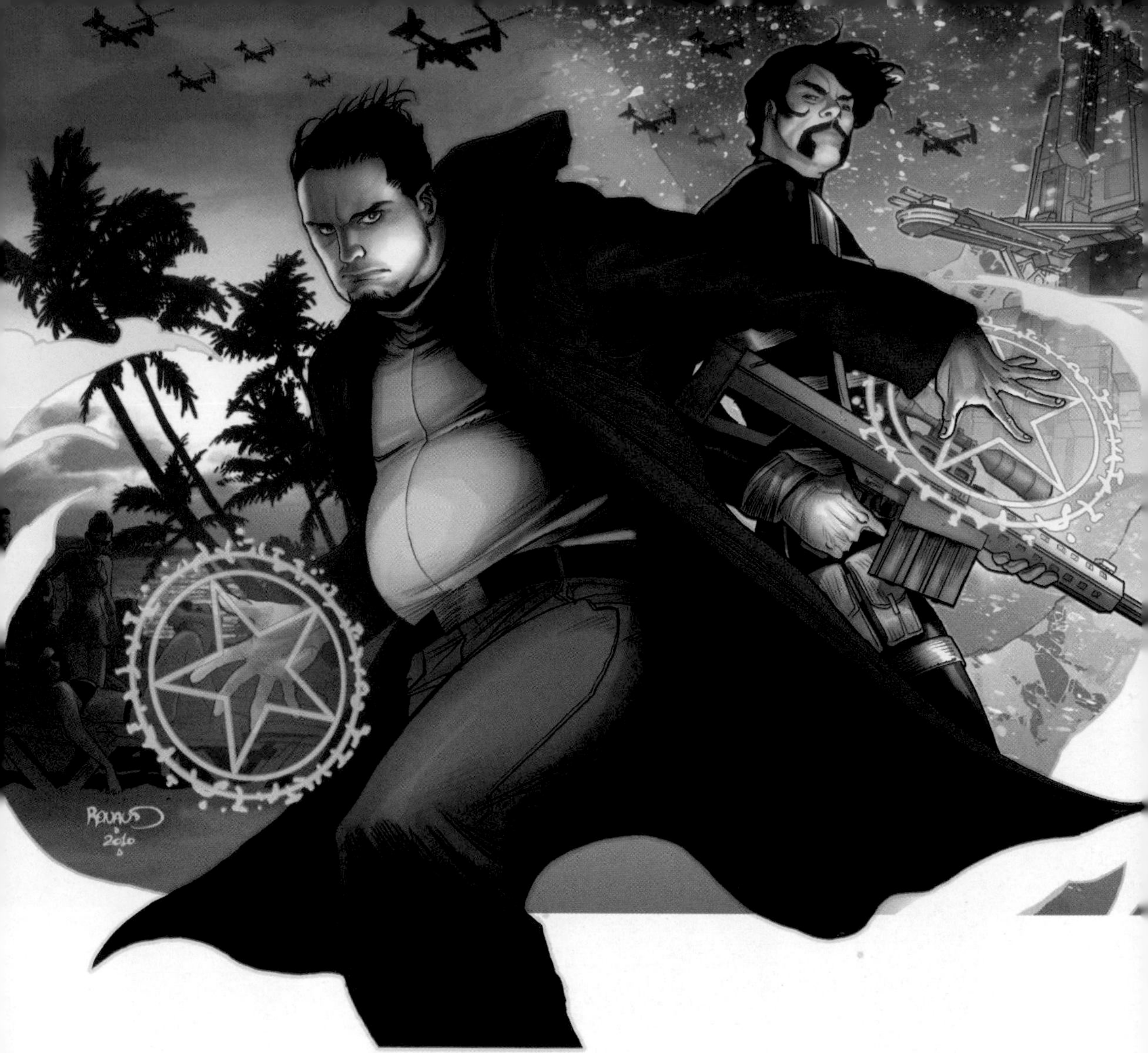

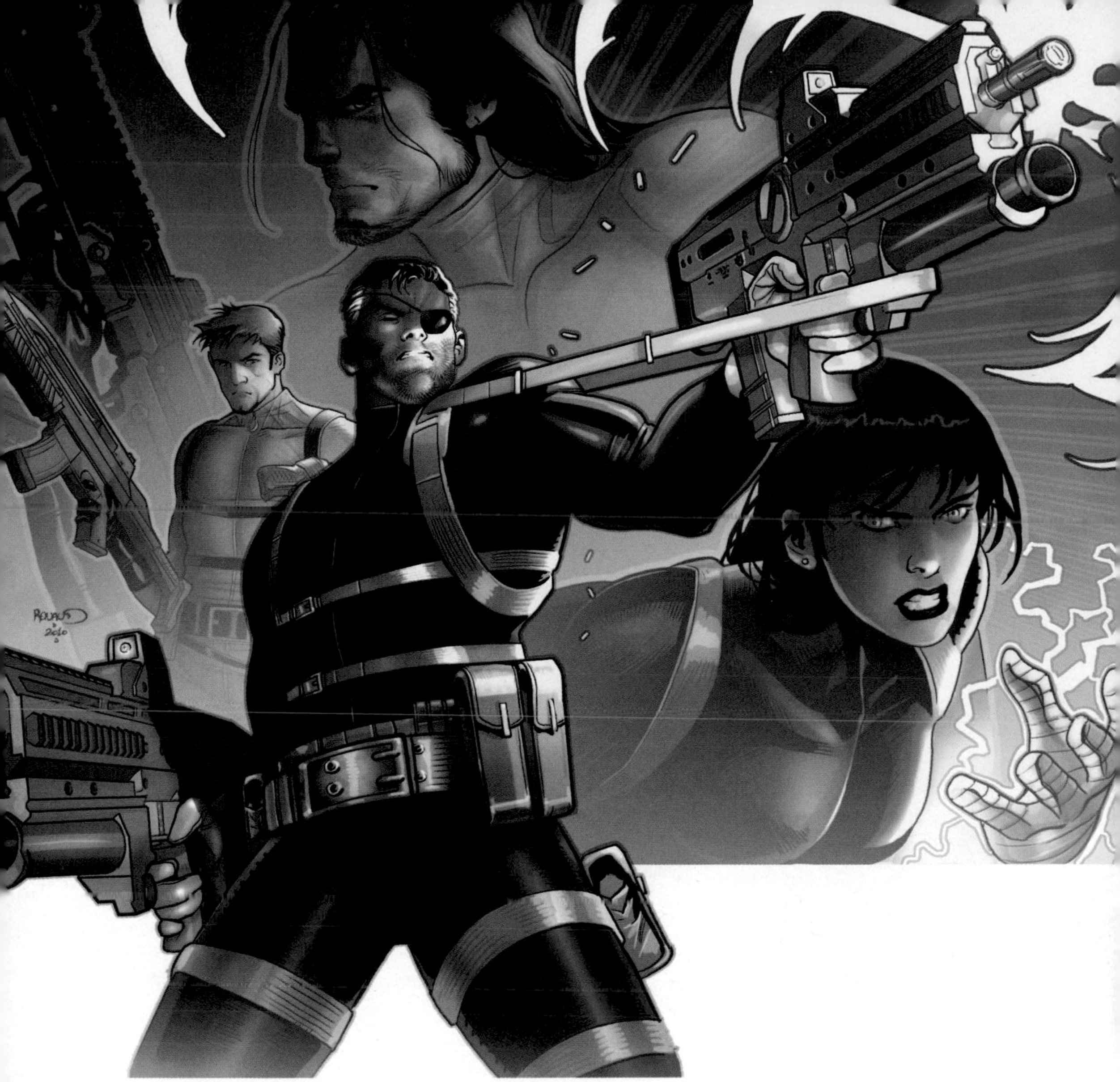

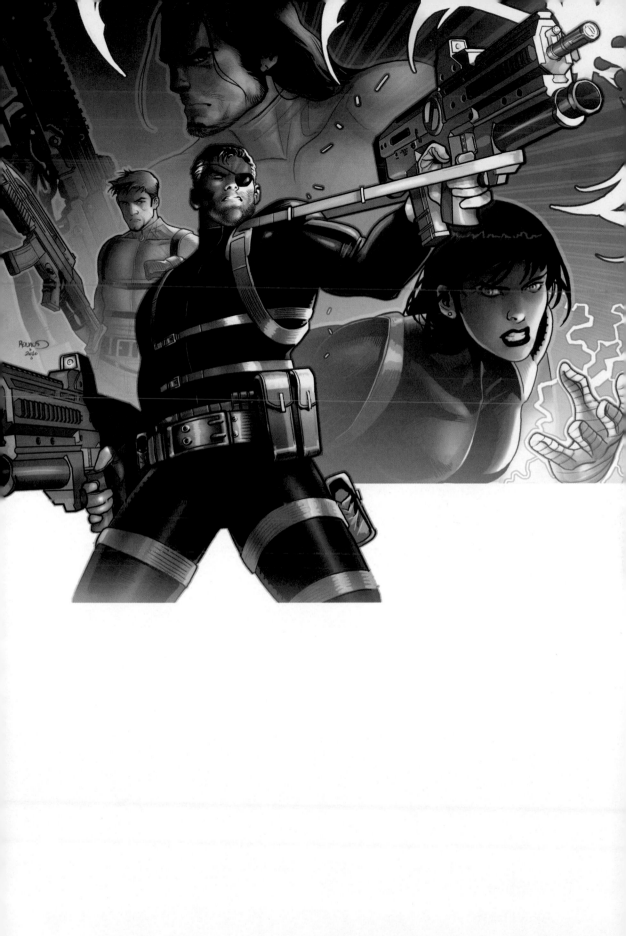